Real
Llanelli

For Elena Dôn and Onwy Siân

Real
Llanelli

jon gower

SEREN

Seren is the book imprint of
Poetry Wales Press Ltd
Nolton Street, Bridgend, Wales
www.serenbooks.com

© Jon Gower, 2009
Preface © Peter Finch, 2009

The right of Jon Gower to be identified
as the Author of this Work has been asserted
in accordance with the Copyright, Designs
and Patents Act, 1988.

ISBN 978-1-85411-506-5

A CIP record for this title is available from
the British Library

The publisher works with the financial assistance
of the Welsh Books Council

Printed by Thomson Litho

Also in the Real Wales series
Editor: Peter Finch

Real Aberystwyth – Niall Griffiths
Real Cardiff – Peter Finch
Real Cardiff Two – Peter Finch
Real Cardiff Three – Peter Finch
Real Liverpool – Niall Griffiths
Real Merthyr – Mario Basini
Real Newport – Ann Drysdale
Real Swansea – Nigel Jenkins
Real Wales – Peter Finch
Real Wrexham – Grahame Davies

CONTENTS

EAST

THE POEMS

INTRODUCTION

Llanelli – at the head of the Loughor estuary, half way between Swansea and Carmarthen, capital of the Gower, post-industrial power house of the golden west. But somehow the town just doesn't feel like this. If you come from the north or the east then you have decided to. Visitors rarely pass through. Llanelli is not on the main trade routes. You'll miss it, heading west for the coast or east for Cardiff. Almost everyone does. Yet the world knows of this place. Llanelli, high up there with Machynlleth and Pwllheli on the non-Welsh speakers' list of the impossible to pronounce. Red rugby running in the streets. Tinopolis. Sospan Fach. Lily Allen's father, the actor Keith Allen, came from here. So did newsreader Huw Edwards, porn-star Sophie Dee, rugby's Jonathan Davies, erstwhile Conservative leader Michael Howard, and amazingly the former guitarist for Rare Earth, our loved and lost Assembly noise-maker Rod Richards. More fame in this place than anywhere in a country of comparable size. Flanders and Swann's Donald lived in unassuming Coleshill Terrace. And if Llanelli had an airport then it would undoubtedly be named after the town's most famous sportsman, Ray Gravell. Punches above its weight sitting there in the sun, now you can see, now the smog of industry has completely gone.

That Llanelli was once the largest town in the world where more than half the population spoke Welsh is often forgotten, although its place as the home of both Felinfoel and Buckley's beer is not. Soon it will be famous for the new National Hunt racecourse at Ffos Las near Trimsaran. First new racecourse in Wales for a hundred years.

Walking the town you get the feel of Pontypridd without the hills and with wider-streets. Terraced housing stock like the Rhondda. Victorian grace with wrought iron balconies like the older parts of Swansea. Everyone talks to you. Wouldn't happen in Cardiff or Swansea. The centre is full of chip shops and charity shops and closed shops. Buildings standing empty waiting for something to happen. *Natural Look Wigs Has Moved to the Uplands Swansea.* The YMCA Senior Citizens Day Centre runs a Vertical Tanning Room. *The Beauty Spot has moved to Swiss Valley.* The deco-styled Llanelly Cinema is now a Weatherspoons. The Terry Griffiths Matchroom snooker hall stood closed when I passed although a sign on the front said it was open. Nineteenth century chapels stand powerless in their lost grandeur. Two town halls and a whole park, quiet and dignified, dedicated to Llanelli's Victoria Cross winner Ivor Rees of Felinfoel.

Opposite the parish church stands Llanelly House, an eighteenth century Georgian town house in the next state of repair to falling down. Built in 1714 by the MP Thomas Stepney this was allegedly the place John Wesley stayed in his many visits to this one-time hotbed of Christian revival. The house was championed by Laurence Llewelyn Bowen in the 2003 BBC-TV series *Restoration* in which it eventually lost out to Manchester's Victorian Baths. It has taken the Heritage Lottery eight years to find the resource to save the place from actually collapsing. Work is due to start in 2011. Meanwhile the lead downpipes continue to leak and the boards across doors to bend and creak. Welsh decay in all its glory. The Polish-Welsh Mutual Association next door watches from behind its vertical blinds.

Across the pedestrianised road the clock face in the tower of Saint Elli's church has a hole in it. Gravestones crack, cave and tumble but the preaching cross stands more or less intact. This place is about as ancient as you can get. Evidence of spire as well as tower. Church registers starting in 1683. Dedicated in 1066. Evidence of religious cell on site from the age of the saints and of a pagan site before that. God at the crossroads. Elli giving his name to the town that developed here. Llan Elli. God moved on now. I looked for drunks and cans and graffiti but there were none. Pretty reassuring, that.

The old market has been scraped flat and the place where the famous pottery once stood now has a giant ASDA and an even bigger ASDA car park. A blue plaque on a redbrick wall, work of Llanelli Community Heritage, sponsored by Carol & Robert Pugh, marks the spot. The plaques enterprisingly dot the town. On the Parish Hall one celebrates Emmeline Pankhurst's suffragette address given here in 1912.

The eastern outskirts, still flat, still estuary, are filled with the sort of out-of-town shopping parks with which all places of any size are today addled. New roads bind them, bend north of the future-uncertain Corus steelworks built on one-time marshland at Trostre. Llanelli ran on heavy industry, came to fame because of it. That world has gone. The gorse, returned in strength and in golden-honey bloom as I drive through it, recalls the Pembrokeshire coast. A near enough place. This is all the same country.

To the south where Llanelli looks to the future, the Machynys Peninsula is now Llanelli Waterside, much in the style of most new waterfront developments, renamed to make them sell. Nicklaus Village offers golf-club priced housing to incomers. Pentre Doc Y Gogledd does bracing holiday rentals.

The Wetlands Centre to the south-east is one of Wales' great underrated gems. Despite appalling signboarding, amateur maps and an information centre that resembles a primary school this Ramsar[1] site is as good as anything you can get in the American swamps or the African veldt. Pools, creeks, lagoons and lakes lace a 450 acre site created on low-grade saltmarsh at Penclacwydd on the Burry Inlet. They are linked by walkways, ridges, bridges, bird hides, seats, and cycle tracks – all as discreet and environmentally friendly as you could wish them. The centre is home to a diverse population of duck and geese, vole and dragonfly without equal. Duck in plumage coloured by Dulux glide the waters. Rare species such as long-billed dowitchers and green-winged teal occasionally dot the pools. The flocks from Greenland and the far north overwinter here among the reeds. They fly in from Asia and Africa in their thousands to an avian hub in the style of Schiphol or JFK. The air is thick with birds created in such diversity that you wonder why, in towns, all we ever see are starling, magpie and sparrow.

Jon Gower is a native. Knows these places. Speaks their tongues, has their lanes engrained on his shoes. He's also a writer, broadcaster, arts correspondent and natural historian of such skill to make *Real Llanelli* a high spot in the *Real* series. Llanelli runs in his veins. Take a look.

Peter Finch

---

1. The treaty for the preservation of Wetland habitats of international significance was signed at Ramsar, Iran in 1971.

WEST

STRADEY PARK

This has been the heartbeat of the town for many a long year. And a temple for rugby union and a Mecca for fans, both diehard and casual. One commentator went as far as calling it a cathedral,[1] but that's going a bit too far, like calling Swansea a great city (sorry, but the old arch-rivalry is in the blood). It's a stand-off, with a bit of name-calling. We call them Jacks, they call us Turks.[2] Which is not as bad as Merthyr folk referring to Aberdare snakes. Apparently they do.

On a good day, Stradey Park is where the game transcends. Where the rugby is as expansive as an albatross wing, the ball passing from fly half to centre to the edge of touch, where the winger seems to be taking flight, as if the wind itself wants him to score. And pulverising rugby, too, where the forwards move on with the arrogance of a Panzer division, seemingly intent on mashing the opponents, on crushing the very calcium of their bones into the winter mud.

But that's on a good day. Fans here have had their share of dark days too, when passes fumble and tackles fail. When any cup, Heineken or EDF, even the briefest sip of victory are entirely out of reach, when the league table is slippery as lard, when you go home after a match needing counselling. Black dog days of feeling alone in a lagoon of worry. Yes, that bad. It might have been worse had the team strip not changed to a defiant red. At different times it has been blue, black, black and red quarters and once primrose and rose. 'Go Yellow and Pinks' doesn't have the same ring to it. Mind you, some of the French sides are almost psychedelic in their choice of kit and

it works for them.

For many Llanelli fans these are moving times, as the Stradey Park era ends and the Parc Y Scarlets chapter opens. So many people have had their ashes scattered at Stradey Park, on the genuinely hallowed turf, that the club's chaplain, the Reverend Eldon Phillips, held a special service to commemorate the dead and took some symbolic soil to the new stadium. One fan flew 9,000 miles for the service, namely retired steelworker Anthony Davies, originally from Dafen but now living in Australia. He was brought up in the town and regularly taken to the see the rugby with his father Sid. Sid's ashes were scattered on the pitch twenty years ago.[3]

For a temple or, let's allow it, cathedral, Stradey Park has always seemed a bit jerry-built. No Parthenon this. Walking the cinder paths round to the North Stand for the last ever game on this revered pitch – pieces of it were due to be sold for ten grand apiece – I was reminded that this wasn't a place where plaudits were won for the luxury of the stadium seating.

It had not been a glorious season. But that was never the point, especially for the poor dabs that would stand in a Carmarthenshire monsoon as it emptied on the Tanner Bank. Hard town. Tough fans. Some winters they must have thought that the Met Office was in a conspiracy against them. Standing there in all weathers, from pelting sleet to whipping wind. Keeping warm by digesting burgers, no onions. Keeping the faith. What tattered shreds of it were left to them.

There have been some games here, 2,578 to be precise. To carry on in this vein, the Scarlets and Llanelli RFC secured 2,028 wins and to save you reaching for the calculator – stop right there – that's a success rate of more than 78 per cent. But it's how they reached that figure that counts. It's a showreel of fabulous rugby moments. Phil Bennett sidestepping the All Blacks and Ieuan Evans puncturing the Wallabies defence. Scott Quinnell gaining those hard yards like an enraged bull elephant, breaking determined tackles as if they were being made by finger puppets. Scarlets mauling Munster, taming the Leicester Tigers, pipping Perpignan, crushing Cardiff and stinging Wasps. All the clichés. Scarlet Fever.

There have been some marvellous players down the years, a tonnage of props, a delight of back rows and individual names that evoke pure mastery of the game. There were wingers such as the aforementioned Ieuan Evans, possessed of supernatural gifts, like Jonah Lomu only much, much smaller. Evans played like a man

running through Hell in a gasoline suit. Give him the ball and then light the blue touch paper. See him go. Billy Whizz.

And further back in time there were comparable marvels: Harry Bowen, who can be mentioned in the same breath as Joel Stransky, Jannie de Beer and Rob Andrew, a deft master of the drop kick. His three points against the Maoris in 1888 helped jet propel the team to legendary status. Llanelli fans have beheld a galaxy of superstars, considered men of stellar reputations, such as the tinplate worker Albert Jenkins, who was not alone in playing games straight after a long shift at the steelworks. Crowds could be halved when he didn't play. He was capped for Wales 14 times and captained Llanelli for three seasons, playing for 13 years between 1919 and 1932. And there have been inspirational coaches, too, not least the mercurial Carwyn James, who even took the team to Moscow in 1957, where he showed that he could speak Russian as well as calculate games and tactics with a chess player's brilliance. The Spassky of scrummaging. The Fischer of forward play.

Rugby in Llanelli goes back to 1870, brought here by John D. Rogers who had been a pupil at Rugby school. Nonconformist chapels opposed the very idea of this new contact sport. Churchmen played it, such as S.B. Williams, a curate at St. Paul's. But the game was well on its way to becoming a religion for some and by 1902 twenty-seven Llanelli players had been capped for Wales.

Stradey Park saw some soaring performances over the years, but one was entirely unexpected. In the middle of a game against Briton Ferry Steel the pioneering aviator M. Salmet landed his Bleriot plane on the nearby cricket pitch.

If there was ever a time to be a Scarlets fan it was the 1970s, when they reached the final of the Welsh Cup on five occasions and claimed it on four, with gentle giant Delme Thomas at the helm as captain and Carwyn James doing the navigating. Carwyn was a chess player who could see an opponent's move coming.

The last ever opponents at Stradey Park were Bristol, in the EDF

Energy Cup. You sort of felt sorry for them, here for display purposes only. Surely they couldn't withstand the Celtic emotionalism, which threatened to be as solidly un-moving as a scrummaging machine? The game itself was lopsided. Morgan Stoddart ran in an early try for the Scarlets. Simon Easterby powered over seconds before half time. Former Bristol player Rob Higgitt scored yet another with Stephen Jones proving sure footed both for conversions and penalties. The final score line? Scarlets, 27, Bristol, nil. It seemed like the right sort of margin for such an historic night.

As a casual visitor over the years I'd forgotten one of the greatest pleasures is the heckling, the barracking and the general craic. An old guy next to me who had purple skin bellowed his pessimistic takes at every juncture. Every move Llanelli made was the wrong one. They didn't pass it to the right side. They weren't giving it guts. They didn't look as if they wanted to win. The criticism was laid on with a trowel. And he was a supporter! Standing next to me on the other side a very well turned out lady of indeterminate age asked, with no discernible irony, if they'd be selling Chardonnay at the new ground, as she was tired of cider. Behind her a voice from the crowd singled out the referee for some scorn and did so in such a way that most everyone was perplexed and satisfied at the same time. 'Have a word with yourself!' Surreal, that. Up there with 'Cadbury's have better centres.'

The game was overshadowed, quite rightly, by the sense of occasion, the weight of event. Before the game a dignified parade of former captains, starting with the oldest, 87 year old Handel Greville, did an Olympic style parade around the pitch. It might have been a calendar shoot for Arthritis UK, what with all the broken bones and injuries these heroes of the red shirts must have sustained over the years. But there they all were, a litany of living captains, a pride of gentlemen: Peter Evans, Ray Williams, Howard Davies, Onllwyn Brace, Aubrey Gale, Marlston Morgan, John Leleu, Stuart Gallagher, Clive John, Barrie Llewellyn, Delme Thomas, Phil Bennett, Derek

Quinnell, Phil May, Phil Davies, Rupert Moon, Ieuan Evans, Robin McBryde, Wayne Proctor, Scott Quinnell, Leigh Davies and Simon Easterby. Men of flair, guts and distinction. And a bit of creaking.

Gareth Jenkins, a man who has given almost four decades to the club, first as player, then as inspired and inspirational coach and now as head of regional development, was given a gong, or something similar. Firecrackers of applause broke out from all four stands and terraces. Toward the west, under an apricot sky, people in the North Stand could see an orange rim of light around the symbolic saucepans on the rugby posts which serve to underline the links between this club and a hard working tinplate town. And as if there were need for any more reminders the song 'Sosban Fach' rang out from the red ranks.[4]

It's a song which itself enshrines two of the team's greatest days in two screamingly rhetorical questions. Who beat the All Blacks and Who Beat the Wallabies? And for a regional side to beat two thirds of the southern hemisphere big boys was no mean feat. They almost beat South Africa once, but as yet that hasn't made it into verse, or a verse.

But there was one hero whose absence was felt keenly: Ray Gravell, Ray o'r Mynydd, the most generous hearted mountain of a man and mountain man there ever was. Whose funeral was held on this pitch. With ten thousand people in attendance. No chapel in the land could hold that many. Grav was honoured in the presence of First Minister Rhodri Morgan. With tears falling like Llanelli rain. With Dafydd Iwan and Gwyneth Glyn singing. And his proud wife and daughters looking on.

GRAV

When I saw the film *Braveheart*, in which Mel Gibson gave Scottish history the Hollywood treatment, creating in the figure of William Wallace a hero for a new Scotland, I tried to imagine what the Welsh version might look like. The central figure would have to be Owain Glyndŵr, sword held high in hand and central casting would be invincibly convinced who should play the marauding rebel: it would have to be Ray Gravell. When he died at the age of 56 a man who was the very definition of modern Welshness was taken from us.

Some people carry a candle of national pride, which burns quietly within. Ray's was a blowlamp, an oxy-acetylene respect for and enjoyment of both place and people. As the W.R.U. put it, here was 'a man who epitomized the passion, flair and dignity of his beloved Welsh nation.' And as the heart-felt tributes paid to him attest so amply, it was a nation that was happy to return the love.

Ray was a great Welsh hero, with the very spirit of the country coursing through his veins. It isn't hyperbole to say he was the epitome of Welsh character and a great character to boot, carrying a drape of rugby laurels on his broad shoulders – the double Grand Slam, the cupboard's worth of Welsh caps, the pride of a British Lion – earned by a ferociously hard tackling centre who, in First Minister Rhodri Morgan's words, 'would tackle a Sherman tank if it was playing for the other side.' And Stradey Park meant everything to him.

The Grav statistics are impressive. From his first senior game in 1969 he amassed 23 caps and was a player in all four Tests on the 1980 Lions' tour of South Africa – not to mention two Grand Slam campaigns in 1976 and 1978 – but that obvious talent didn't generate a swollen ego. Here was a man of genuine humility which coupled easily with a trademark humour: as he said, 'get your first tackle in early, even if it's late.' It is a further measure of the man that he numbered among his friends many of those he had gamely crunch-tackled and made miserable in the mud.

Though his father's suicide troubled him throughout his life and probably accounted for Ray's constant need for reassurance, he once told me he played rugby for his father, which explains a lot. There were, of course, other influences, not least the coaching genius of Carwyn James. A few years ago Ray told the *Guardian*, 'I do not think I was that good a player, but Carwyn made me think that I was a world beater. I was 21 when Llanelli beat New Zealand in 1972, the youngest player in the side. I was terrified before the game, but listening to the captain Delme Thomas and Carwyn speaking before we went on to the field made me forget my nerves. Even all this time later, I can remember exactly what they said, the goose pimples their words provided and how tall they made me feel.'[5]

His rugby style seemed, on the face of it, more like a lack of style. It was, rather, a mode of determination, which forced commentators to coin the term 'crash forward.' It wasn't necessarily pretty, that ball-protecting charge which attracted opposing defenders like wasps to a honey pot. It was an attacking run that brought to mind images of a charging rhino, the angry bull, the bulldozer approach. But it worked, gaining yards as hard as anthracite, pressing for the line. Ray seldom admitted fear, but did tell people that when he was offered £25,000 in the mid Seventies to join a rugby league side, he turned down the offer because he 'was afraid to leave Wales.'[6] This small, mountainous country was a part of his make-up as certainly as chromosomes.

After he retired in 1985 he proved to have an aptitude as an actor, and I can still picture the bemusement with which he announced that he was going to appear in a film alongside Jeremy Irons when they both made *Damage* for the veteran French director Louis Malle. He starred in the 1985 BBC film *Bonner*, made for S4C, and appeared alongside Peter O'Toole in the big screen adaptation of Dylan Thomas' *Rebecca's Daughters*.

He developed a broadcasting career in tandem with the acting, and effused as the pitchside commentator for S4C rugby programmes. His ready gifts in front of a microphone were appreciated by audiences of both Radio Cymru and Radio Wales, where his trademark assertion that 'West is best' was often made alongside co-presenters such as Frank Hennessy and Roy Noble.

And there was one part of west Wales he treasured above all others. He described himself as a man from the mountain, Mynydd-y-Garreg, the pockmarked and quarried hill that overlooks the ancient town of Cydweli, where the industrial land of south Wales meets the green undulations of rural Carmarthenshire. And we knew he could handle a big sword, too, in his case the paradoxical symbol of peace he carried with pride in his role as the Eisteddfod's Herald.

When the Archdruid Dafydd Rowlands explained to the historian Hywel Teifi Edwards that he was going to ask Ray to be the Gorsedd's sword bearer, Hywel questioned the wisdom of letting Ray loose in the pavilion, asking what would happen if he saw a Swansea Jack?

But, of course Ray loved the Jacks, too, and Pontypool – he loved that factory of grizzly forwards also – just as surely as he treasured every square mile of this country and its culture that had both fashioned and sustained him. Indeed, he had incredibly fond things to say about an Ospreys supporter he met after having his leg amputated following complications deriving from diabetes, which was diagnosed in 2000.

The two rugby fans were being fitted for prosthetic limbs at Morriston Hospital. The Ospreys supporter was going to have his new leg made in Swansea colours. Little wonder, then, that Ray's leg was a Scarlet one – after all this was a rugby club where he had been a player, a captain and latterly President. And of course one of the first things he did after being diagnosed with diabetes was to learn about the disease and fundraise for charities connected with it.

Generosity of spirit. Dignity as a man. Winning combination.

On BBC Radio Wales his rugby colleague Gerald Davies described 'the desperately empty morning' that dawned after hearing the news of Ray's passing. I remember a time Ray and I stood at the grave of Llywelyn, the Last Prince of Wales, in Abaty Cwm Hir. We both had tears in our eyes but there were words ringing in our ears, too, those of the poet Gruffydd Ab Yr Ynad Coch, who wrote an elegy about this last Welsh prince:

> Poni welwch-chwi hynt y gwynt a'r glaw
> Poni welwch-chwi'r deri'n ymdaraw?
>
> Do you not see the path of the wind and the rain?
> Do you not see the oak trees in turmoil?

Ray Gravell was as solid as an oak, and similarly rooted in his beloved country. Wales embraced him – this man with generous open arms, this broadcaster who was as loquacious as mountain streams, this rugby player who was passionate as any man who has donned a Welsh rugby shirt, and a husband and father who adored his family with all the boundless love of his great Welsh heart. Llanelli beat Bristol that night for him.

He wasn't there for the last game at Stradey Park, but his spirit was. I could feel the breath of his singing.

How To Pronounce Llanelli Without Causing a Flu Epidemic: The Idiot's Guide

It's dead simple, you just need to get the hang of
The voiceless alveolar lateral fricative. It'll help with the double ls;
The other letters are simple:
A as in Apple
N as in Nebuchadnezzar
E as in egg
And I as the 'y' in industry.
As I said, straightforward.

Which just leaves that voiceless alveolar lateral fricative,
Like a wild card in a pub quiz.
So, its manner of articulation is fricative

It's all about constricting the air flow through a narrow channel at the place of articulation, causing turbulence, a mouth gale.
Its place of articulation is alveolar, so place the tip of the tongue against the Alveolar ridge, it's the hard bit of the palatte above your lower teeth.
Its phonetic type is voiceless, which I know is confusing but bear with me,
And soon you'll be saying the name like a native:
It is an oral consonant, which means air is allowed to escape through the mouth
(Ah! that's a relief)
It is a lateral consonant, so the airstream flows over the sides of the tongue
Rather than the middle
(Sorry if this is all entirely known to you)
The airstream mechanism is pulmonic egressive, the air coming out of the lungs and through the vocal tract, rather than from the glottis or the mouth.

Llanelli!

Little wonder the rock musician Lou Reed thought Welsh was a tongue disease.

Llanelli!

My home.

Now then, if you're an English speaker you can do it by saying 'h' and 'l' simultaneously.

But not if you've got some communicable disease, with airborne bugs.

That way lies pandemic.

SANDY

It's remarkable how often the serendipitous meeting is the best. While I was wandering along the stretch of land between North Dock and Sandy Bridge one autumn afternoon I met a cyclist, Howell Morgan. He'd admit to being your older sort of cyclist but one who turns out to have one heck of a life story.

In his younger days Howell was quite famous as an athlete. He was a schoolboy champion in shot put, throwing the discus and the 200-yard sprint. He won schoolboy caps in rugby in 1954, was junior sportsman of the year in both 1953 and 1954 and joined the Welsh secondary schools rugby team which toured South Africa in 1956, playing in Johannesburg, Cape Town, Port Elizabeth and Springs in the Transvaal.

When Howell came out of school he thought himself a man of the world, a notion bolstered by all that travel. He went to work in the Llanelli steelworks, which later became Duport.[7] 'It was volcanic,' he recalls. 'There were sparks all over the place. The first experience I had there was when they were tapping a furnace – the molten metal was pouring out into a ladle and when that was full the slag was forming on top and it was blowing holes in the slag and there were sparks everywhere – it frightened the life out of me and they tapped this huge ladle into ingots that were in a channel in the ground – the pit road they used to call it – and they used to put lids on them and the lids would be popping off and enough sparks showering around to make you run a mile. The steel workers were used to them – the sparks were bouncing right off them.'

Howell had understandably been attracted by the innocuous advertisment for a job that was described as 'preparatory work.' What he wasn't to know was that he had to prepare the ladles after they'd poured the molten metal into them. He had to go up a ladder with a dirty great hosepipe, pour water into the ladle and watch out as steam and fumes would pour out. He had to solidify the slag with the cold water, causing great clouds of steam and sulphuric fumes, and then had to chip the slag off the brickwork that was inside the ladles with a pickaxe and a crowbar. One time he remembers being bathed in sweat and another staying in too long so that he couldn't breathe, then rushing up the ladder, sticking his head over the top of the ladle only to see a red hot ingot coming toward him. Howell had to dive back into the ladle full of fumes and seriously thought he was going to die. He still thinks the comparison with dark

Satanic mills rather understates things.

Many of the men in the works had been employed there for a long time. Some got hurt. Others got killed. Howell recalls how Scarlets player Ossie Williams' mate fell into the pit road when they'd just tapped into the ingots and killed him instantly. Burned him to a frazzle. Ossie nearly dived in after him – even though people were being killed in the works right, left and centre. Ossie Williams was a legendary hard man who spawned many a myth. Working on the pit road one Saturday morning one of the ingots exploded and covered him in red hot sparks. Ossie just finished his shift and though his back was burned raw he went straight from work to play for the Scarlets. That hard. Titanium skin.

Howell thinks there were even more dangerous jobs, especially for workers called doublers. 'They used to get these rough steel sheets coming out of the presses and sling them along the floor and if the sheets caught you on your legs they chopped them off.'

But Howell stoically stayed in the job until the final straw. There was one incident where he had to come out of the ladle so quickly that he went over the side and so had to hang onto an anchor arm that stopped the ladle from tipping over. 'The gantry driver lowered the ladle down on my thumb and I had to shout at the gantry driver "pull it up" and I fell into the pit road and I thought this is it – I'm not staying here. The money was so good in a few months I'd earned enough for a motorbike, a BSA Gold Star.'

In 1959 he came out of the Forces after doing National Service and intended to train as a P.T. instructor. After he was demobbed he found himself a job in a clothes shop in Swansea and would travel back and forth on his BSA. But one day on his way there he was run over by a lorry. He damaged his legs, hips, arm, elbow and jaw and so severe were the injuries that someone threw a tarpaulin over him, believing him to be dead. But then someone saw him move and so began years of medical care. He was in hospital for months, people telling him his body was in a hell of a mess, that he was nothing more than a bag of broken bones. His leg was most seriously affected. After years of bone grafts he told the medics to cut it off.

After he recovered he worked in Fisher and Ludlows, making car doors, floors and panels for the automotive industry at a time when thousands worked there. The Sixties saw high employment rates in a range of industries. But that job morphed into another and time marched inexorably on.

Now, retired and with a body permanently affected by the awful crash which almost killed him, Howell believes that the cycle path has saved his life. He regularly bikes the 5 miles down to Loughor or the 5 miles to Pembrey Country Park and not only does it stop him going up the wall but it also keeps him supple and mobile. He's the sort of person you might meet on the path. If you take the time to stop and chat you might find yourself talking to a man of steel.

The places Howell worked are no more. The Duport steelworks are long gone – they scandalously sold the brand new electric arc furnace to Korea or South Africa – I can't remember which. I well remember the funeral staged in 1981 for the steel industry in the town, a poignant event that signalled Llanelli's move into the post-industrial era. The steelworks site has now been turned into a lake, surrounded by executive and not so executive housing and the National Eisteddfod was held here in 2000. The past has been gently erased. There are ducks dabbling now where once the ladles carried white hot metal. Black headed gulls preen their feathers where the pit road ran.

Sandy is a good place to ponder how industry shaped the town and people's view of it. By the early 1800s Llanelli was getting bad press. E.H. Malkin called it 'a small, irregular, dirty town, nor does the appearance of its inhabitants, chiefly miners and sailors, render it more inviting.'[8] This hardly improved on comments from a few years previously where a visitor called Henry Scrine dismissed 'the miserable village of Llanelly… famous for nothing but a deserted seat of the Stepneys.' The local Medical Officer was complaining, in 1849, about the slaughterhouses, tanneries, skinners' yards and pigsties. Cholera was rife. Drains were neglected. No-one came here on holiday. In fact workers for the Llanelli and Railway Dock Company called it Botany Bay, Old South Wales as a posting to the town was considered 'akin to transportation.'

Industry caused the population to skyrocket. In 1795 there were no more than five hundred inhabitants. By the first official census in 1801 there were almost three thousand. By the 1820s the Llanelly Bank was issuing its own pound notes even though the Cambrian tourist still referred to the town as 'a miserable, dirty place filled with miners and sailors.' But by now industry had claimed the terrain. Coal and tin were dominant but were not the only industries by a long chalk – there were several foundries, earthenware and tiles were manufactured, not to mention chemicals, steel, with steam sawmills, brickmaking plants and two breweries – all generating noise, effluent, jobs and money.

The population of both miners and metalworkers grew and grew. By 1841 it was into five figures, at 11,155. The first tinworks at Dafen followed by the Llanelli Tinplate Works helped cause another surge. By 1872 an astonishing 850,000 tons of coal was leaving the port and it was little wonder that there were over fifty master mariners and almost forty pilots. Countries represented by consular agents in the town included Sweden, Norway, the USA, Portugal and France and there were no fewer than 128 pubs to slake the thirsts of consuls and colliers alike. By 1880 there were seven tinplate works in the town and this second half of the century saw metal dominate as coal declined. And as the inhabitants grew in number so too did their houses. From 802 in 1831 to 1,552 in 1849, when there were also no fewer than 89 public houses. Other aspects of town life flourished too. As the *South Wales Press* boasted in 1895 the town had 'a Queen's shooting prize winner, a world class quoiter, a tip top football team, a brass band that beats creation and the finest choir in the world… Floreat Llanelli.'

And the accoutrements of the modern age came in steadily. A horse-drawn tramway in 1882, a telephone exchange in 1883, a General Post Office in 1885, a new glass and steel market hall in 1888, which cost £5,000. Electricity lit up the town in 1911 and an electric tramway followed in due course. But things were not all rosy. Llanelli's slum areas could have won prizes. An inquest in 1911 gives a glimpse of life as it was lived. The family of John Davies, an unemployed mason, slept four to a bed and stayed there as long as possible in winter to save on wood and fuel, with his baby daughter, Blanche suffocating there one night. The impossible price of poverty. By 1901 the population was still rising but at a much lower pace and by now there were many empty houses in the town, the result of an exodus to America, especially of tinplate and steel workers.

Standing near the Sandpiper Inn, as gulls squawk on the artificial lakes it's hard to imagine the noise and smoke here once, the sound of marching boots in the morning, the reveille of hooters. Yet this town was fashioned from hard work. It's appropriate we should remember this. I do, looking at my lilywhite hands, which have never made much more durable than a sentence, grafting over nothing more testing than a keyboard.

The Lost Industries of Llanelli

(Recite *sotto voce*. Imagine some Shostakovich music playing over flickering black and white film footage of chimney stacks crashing down and wrecking balls pounding walls into dust. Take a very deep breath.)

Dunkin's Arsenic Works, New Vanadium Alloys,
Llanelly Colour Works, Pembrey White Lead,
Llanelly Steel Works, Sandy Bridge,
Stradey Galvanizing Company, Nobel's Explosives,
Wellfield, Gorse, Alloy Syndicate,
South Wales Steel & Tin Plate Works,
Llanelly Galvanizing Works, Town Foundry,
Cambrian Tinplate, Metals Extraction,
Dafen Tinplate, Llanelly Copper,
Pwll Bricks, Cae Bricks, Penygaer,
Yspitty Iron and Tin Plate, Burry Port Foundry, finished,
H.H. Product Finishing, finished,
Cambrian (non-ferrous ore), Sandy Mount,
Wern, Lord Cawdor's Lead, Pembrey Dynamite,
Nevill's Dock De-Tinning, Tyissa, Cille Colliery Patent Fuel,
Advanced Metal Coatings, Francis Old Foundry,
Vitreflex, Burry Port Lead, Reliance, Taybrite,
George Davies, Llanelly Railway Foundry,
South Wales Varnish, Stanley, Stradey,
Towyn Bricks, Sandy I and Sandy II,
Wallis Tin Stamping, Duport, South Wales Gold,
Llanelly Steel, Pencoed Lead, Wern Brass,
South Wales Steel, Rosser's Arsenic,
Morfa Tin Plate, Burry Port Zinc Oxide,
Bynea Steel, Sandy Gate Works (red lead),
Morewoods, Spitty Bank Copper, Morfa Patent,
Towyn Bricks, Carreg Llwyd Bricks, New Lodge,
The tinplate works of Ashburnham,
Morfa, Old Castle, Old Lodge,
Western, Pemberton, South Wales, British Piano Actions,
Richard Thomas Mills, Lewis Foundry,
Burry, Burry Extension, Stradey Iron,
Cambrian, Trostre, Craig's Paint Works,
Dafen, Pencoed, Tudor Refinery,

St David's Tin, Cambrian Copper,
Morlais and Llangennech,
Glanmor and Dynevor,
Dock Foundry, Lanmore Foundry, Lewis Foundry, floundered,
Furnace Bricks, South Wales Pottery,
Penygaer, Trebeddrod Brickyard.

Breathe in. Contemplate the past.[9]

STRADEY CASTLE

The woods around this impressive pile attracted me as a schoolboy,
full of summer birds and their songs, with garden warblers, blackcaps
and less familiar species such as lesser spotted woodpeckers and
occasional pied flycatchers. These had flown in from Africa and in
their white and black plumage looked for all the world as if they were
sporting tuxedos. In the streams that dissect the woodland floor the
dipper hunted for food. This is the only songbird that swims under
water and you could see them in clear water, down on the pebbly
bottom looking for caddis fly larvae. And in the middle of this natural
splendour stood the castle, lending an aristocratic air to the
Carmarthenshire landscape.

The Stradey estate came to be owned by the Vaughan family of
Derwydd in about 1610.[10] Deeds of the period refer to 'Straddy',
'Parke Estrade' and 'Park Ystradey.'[11] John Mansel, the son of Sir
Francis Mansel of Muddlesombe, married Mary, daughter of Sir
Henry Vaughan of Derwydd
and came to live at Stradey,
although it remained the
property of the Vaughan family
until 1673, when it was sold to
the Mansel family. The Mansel
family continued here for a
century and a half, failing with
the death without issue of
Mary Anne Mansel (d. 1808)
the widow of E.W.R. Shewen.
In what might be described
nowadays as granny farming
she bequeathed the estate to

Thomas Lewis (d. 1829) of Llandeilo, Carmarthenshire, who had both helped out the family when money was scarce and managed the estate. When Mary Mansel lived here the mansion, on the banks of the river Dulais, boasted thirty-three rooms. Despite major improvements made to the building in the period 1820-1830, David Lewis decided in about 1844 to build a new mansion on higher ground, displaying pride in the past and confidence in the future. Lewis was a dashing entrepreneur, a graduate of Eton and Brasenose College, Oxford, who sank mines and exported coal as far away as Valparaiso in Chile.

The current occupant, Sir David Mansel Lewis catalogues the changes in the history of his family home:[12] 'The original house was at the bottom of the field and was presumably quite near the sea in those days, which was why it was built there. It must have been in prime position because, before the building of the railway and Sandy Road, the sea must have come up to the point where Sandy Road is now; in fact the house itself must have been very damp. They spent a lot of money on it but they eventually had to abandon it and they used a certain amount of material in this new house which my great-grandfather built between, I think, 1845 and 1850.'[13]

Stradey Castle was completed as a bold mansion in the neo-Tudor style, suggesting baronial antiquity, replete with tall chimneys, gangs of gargoyles, pointed gables, rounded off by an imposing castellation, all designed by Shrewsbury architect Edward Haycock. The old Stradey mansion was completely demolished in 1855. The home then was no bigger than the average country rectory, so when the new artistic squire, Charles Mansel Lewis, decided he wanted something altogether more dramatic he employed a firm of builders from London to carry out the remodelling. It cost some £30,000, which was a huge amount of money in those days.

Charles was by instinct and disposition an artist and had displayed a gift for painting early on. When he was a student at Eton he sent a letter home to his father, dated July 1863, which read: 'Dearest Papa, You will be glad to hear that I have just got the Drawing Prize… my last sketch was a very powerful one…'

He progressed from this early promise to being a serious and respected artist, who exhibited at the Royal Academy and later in his career depicted the workers on the Stradey estate in a way reminiscent of Millais, but with less realist a slant. He portrayed the workers in a gently romantic light: people such as Old Bet, a remarkable woman who would have been a gift to any artist owing to the fact that she wore traditional Welsh dress, tall black hat, shawl and all. On another occasion a poacher who was caught on the estate was given a curious 'penalty': he was forced to sit to have his portrait taken by Charles, who had built a studio for himself at the castle. But as is the case with so many painters Charles' artistic flair was comprehensively matched with an ability to conjure up debt. Adding flourishes to the castle's fabric added to the financial burden. Building a tower was a popular flambuoyance among Victorian gents. It was showmanship at its most emphatic. If you study the tower at Stradey Castle you'll notice that the windows get smaller as you get higher up, exaggerating the perspective.

The Mansel Lewis family remain at Stradey nowadays despite the crippling cost of the place's upkeep, especially of features such as the tower. Very few homes of the Welsh landed gentry are preserved as well. Many have been demolished or have been claimed by time and ivy.

The present owner, Sir David Courtnay Mansel Lewis grew up in the castle and was later joined by Lady Mary Rosemary Marie-Gabrielle-Montagu-Stuart-Wortley-Mackenzie, whom he met at a cocktail party in London, striking up a permanent relationship even though he at first thought her 'frightful.' At the time she had been a shop assistant in London, working in such stores as Peter Jones.

When she moved to Stradey Castle she was in her twenties and found the place dark and gloomy to begin with and then even gloomier, but now sees it as a super house, ideal for parties. They share the house with 'their two relatively saintly dogs, Tyssul and Cadog.' The house is still full of the furniture and paintings from the nineteenth century, and beneath it runs the typical array of servants quarters, laundries and substantial kitchen, reflecting the classical division of labour between 'upstairs' and 'downstairs.' The kitchen moved upstairs after the Second World War and the old kitchen is now used to house Sir David's Rolls Royce, under tarpaulin. There was in Sir David's early memories of the castle a nutty cook, who would give chase to maids with a cleaver. All a bit *Gormenghast* according to Sir David, ironically and tellingly referring to Mervyn Peake's trilogy of novels about life in a crazy house where characters such as Flay and Swelter hold sway.

When the new Stradey Castle was built a cornucopia of styles was available to architects but while medieval Gothic was *de rigeur* the choice for building churches, the Tudor and Jacobean styles were employed to trumpet the success of a more secular building's owner.

Stradey Castle is a chord of trumpet notes, deadened slightly by the surrounding oaks.

The key Tudor details of Stradey Castle are 'the exaggerated octagonal chimney stacks, pointed gables and the very distinctive hood moulding around the top of windows, a stone frame that, in the days before guttering would send water away from the windows, both practical and pretty. You see it in all the great Tudor buildings such as Lambeth Palace and Hampton Court.'[14]

As befits a building which commands stunning views over the watery expanses of the Burry estuary, out towards north Gower and the brontosaurus hump of Cefn Bryn, the windows make up a striking proportion of the frontage. They are divided up in the sixteenth century style with stone mullions and transoms – mullions being the upright elements and the transoms the pieces that run across.[15]

Pass through the front door – imagining an unctuous butler taking your coat without you noticing – and the staircase is as imposing as any, dominated by a painting of Alexander the Great's acrimonious visit to the wise man Diogenes. The staircase was made to measure in London with each pendant of the ceiling individually designed. Space under the staircase is put to good, pragmatic use, storing firewood. The ingenious upper landing served as a picture gallery, exhibiting the works of Hubert von Herkomer, who visited the place. The Victorian novelist George Meredith stayed here too and probably penned a novel or two while on his visit, such was his astonishing workrate.

Some of the design features of the ground floor rooms display the same sort of ingenuity as does the upper landing. Framed entrances are slightly different in size on facing walls, giving a sense of depth, a telescoping effect, making rooms seem bigger. On the outside, too, design came into play. Because the Victorians liked their structures to be functional the tower contained a vast water tank that fed all the up to date water closets which were installed. They're still in use today, bearing names on the porcelain such as 'The Deluge', 'Eclipta' and 'Valkyrie.'

Today Stradey Castle sits within an estate of some two thousand acres, including some 500 acres of forestry. Sir David's son, Patrick, a Llandeilo based solicitor, takes care of the running of it day to day, coupling it with his church duties: he was ordained as a priest two years ago. To their credit Sir David and Lady Mary and the rest of the family have kept the estate as a living monument to the past, both family home and museum, a grand carry-over from a bygone age.

PWLL

It's not the easiest place to come from: not when you have to explain to people what the name means. Hole, pool or pit. Makes you sound like a troglodyte, or a Pythonesque comedy miner: 'I was brought up in a pit.' And a Welsh pit at that, where you have to spit at people just to say the bloody name. Or at least that's what an English friend of mine said. They like to mock. It's all that's left to them after the Empire dwindled.

Pwll people were never synonymous with coal, even though the village had its share of mines – Pool, New Pool, Penllech, the Crown and Barclay. Rather, they were linked with cabbages. Cabbages? Villagers were known locally as *gwŷr y bonau*,[16] a biting reference to the belief that the successful, if miserly market gardeners of the village sold their cabbages but ate the stalks. The village name probably comes from a pool in the estuary, a place of deeper water where boats could land.

But the name Pwll stuck in the craw and from time to time debates would flare up about changing the name: Bronelli, Gwelfôr, Myrddin, Maenllwyd, Trehoward, Howardon and Gwelfro were all mooted at different times, though none have stuck.

Walk through the village now, along Pwll Road, the main road, or Elgin Road, known familiarly as Top Road, and there's usually both an absence of people and the presence of sleepiness. Not much goes on. Not much gives. But there was a time when this quiet village was an industrial hive. Land hereabouts was warrened with coal pits, not to mention two woollen mills, a sawmill and two brickworks – the Eastern and the Western – and an award winning pop factory.

Turn off the main drag opposite the Post Office, into Waun-yr-Eos and you'll be in the right vicinity. Where the Pwll Aerated Water Factory, better known as Rees and Richards, bubbled up its wares as far back as the 1890s, when the water came from a well on site.

In 1891 the census shows two factory owners, a messenger and a bottle washer. It grew from there. There were eighteen people employed there in the 1950s. At its peak it produced almost two thousand thirst quenching bottles every day – lemonade, limeade, dandelion and burdock, raspberryade, orangeade, orange crush, appleade, pearsnap, pineappleade, grapefruitade, cola, American cream soda, ginger beer, portello and shandy. Not to mention concentrated drinks, ginger wine and non-alcoholic sacramental wine. The red-letter day, though, came in 1938 when Rees and

Richards' lemonade won second prize at the Brewers Exhibition at the Royal Agricultural Hall in London. They had a certificate. But the company finally went pop in 1982.

The village made pop *and* crisps. Pwll had a short-lived crisp factory too, derived from a chippie where the Chinese takeaway stands today. Gone for a wok. The factory was more of a shed really, but it was home to the Pwll Potato Crisp Company. Catchy. Nine women were employed to put the crisps in bags along with wraps of salt in blue paper. Men worked the fryers. Interestingly the potatoes used to make Evans' crisps were a variety called Arran Banner, a spud with a genetic flaw, which meant that each one had a hole in it, and so too the resulting crisps. Evans crisps, as opposed to Walkers, were instantly distinctive, like Polo mints.

Pwll was culturally a very active place. The first village Eisteddfod, back in 1904, attracted over four thousand people. They ran special charter trains for the day. They still had eisteddfodau when I grew up. In the Sixties and Seventies standing on stage, to sing or declaim verse, stood many of us in good stead for later life, where performing in front of an audience held no fears for us. Over the years Pwll was a cultural beehive, producing David Brazzell, the Bryn Terfel of his day and one of the first names to appear in the catalogues of the early gramophone recording companies. The village also had a tradition of women poets, writing in Welsh. And the Edna Bonnell Company took its brand of spirited amateur theatricals all over Wales, always selling out. Not to mention jazz musician Wyn Lodwick, who managed to get pianist Dill Jones to come over from New York in 1978 to play at the community centre.

When I grew up here it was a Welsh-speaking village, or at least it seemed that way if you attended chapel up to three times on a Sunday, chatted engagedly with the old people and took part in the village eisteddfod and had friends who spoke the lingo. The villages around urban Llanelli such as Pwll, Trimsaran and particularly those in the Gwendraeth Valley are places where the language is still used both everyday and every way. In the last census, in 2001, almost 42 per cent of those who lived in the area covered by Llanelli Rural Council spoke the language. But over the years its music has fallen silent. Market day in Llanelli doesn't have the same sound. A language crinkles on dessicated old lips. Thank the Lord for local schools such as Ysgol Y Strade, which you pass just before you get to Pwll. They are helping to stem the flow and it's heartening that the last census showed a language on the turn, statistically. Yet even as the language arrests what had seemed like a catastrophic haemorrhage, the pretty and perfect dialect words spoken by the old people in Llanelli may still be lost, other than to lexicographers. These were words that marked us out as a local tribe, even if confluent with the Welsh spoken in Swansea. As a kid, a *crwt*, I'd play *cwato*, not *cuddio* when we went to hide. We'd eat *tato*, not *tatws*, when we ate a plate of spuds. We'd climb a *tyle*, or hill, not *allt* or *bryn*, such as Tyle Catherine, still the name for one of the steeper streets in the village. *Colfen* for tree, not *coeden*. That's what I climbed as a boy in Pwll and if I fell I'd seek some *maldod*, some comfort from mam, for whose embracing love there is no name, and never can be. That, my friend, is ineffable.

So this is my home village, though technically I come from Carmarthen. I was left on a hospital doorstep on Christmas Eve, 1959. This sounds like a fanciful Dickensian foundling start-to-life but it's true in the main. My mother, Mary Martha Onwy Mathias was a fifteen-year-old florist's assistant from Trevaughan who was raped by a local farmer. Back then having intercourse with someone under sixteen was statutory rape. I looked it up. Had to. Being the son of a rapist has its emotional complications. Just as surely as finding out, as an adult, that I once had another name, the one my natural mother gave me. Ian Mathias. I found that out in the Lilliputian setting of a Cardiff family centre, sitting on tiny plastic chairs meant for three year olds, which I winded with my bulk. Ian Mathias. Jon Gower. As far apart as Burke and Hare, and Cannon and Ball. The name I have suits me. Ian Mathias does not. What's in a name?

My natural mother – hard to call her mam really – was probably shown how to arrive at the hospital and turn her back on me – they rehearsed this last part as it was the most testing. I doubt that she left me on the steps, or in the porch, but that's the way things were done back then. Get in, leave baby, bugger off. The St. David's Diocesan Moral Welfare Committee arranged the adoption, though I'm not sure whose moral welfare they were concerned with. Maybe society in general. I don't think they were looking out for a fifteen year old.

So I was brought up by Des, a lifelong railwayman who had worked his way up from a tea boy to traffic supervisor, and Morwena, who worked in what would nowadays be referred to as the retail sector, but back then she was simply a shop assistant. Worked in a range of shops such as Puddys and Morris the Realm. Finally upscaled to Marks and Spencer and loved it. I worked there too, for a while.

Des was a drinker – Old English cider, guzzled straight from the flagon – and an inveterate smoker – Golden Virginia 'bacco, wrapped very tightly in a Rizla, Cardiganshire-style. Make one out of three strands if you had to. Smoking modus operandi? As you exhale fag smoke, tap out the ash into palm of your hand and then rub under your armpit. His work shirts had big grey patches under the arms, ashy reminders of this odd habit.

We first lived in a house opposite Bethlehem chapel, with my paternal grandfather Thomas John Gower and grandmother, Elizabeth, or Bess. It may be that Gwydion, the shape shifter in the Mabinogi was, by reputation, the best storyteller in the whole wide world but I tell you, Thomas John could give him a run for his money. As a lad he'd gone to Siberia on a boat out of Burry Port, all the way to Kamchatka, and *dadcu* could give you a rum account of the voyage and its consequences. Was a poacher, too. He had notebooks meticulously cataloguing the game he'd snared or shot when the keeper wasn't looking. She, on the other hand was real piece of work. Bess.

They had a bathroom in their part of the house but Bess wouldn't let us use it, so we had a zinc bath in front of the fire, praying to all the Celtic gods that no-one would call at the house when we were in it, as that would mean being carried shivering into the passage to wait until they took their leave. There wasn't a toilet in the house and Thomas John seemed always to be in the outside lav, with the door open, his pipe cleaner legs underlining how thin he was.

When they knocked down the nearby woollen mill Bess single-handedly stole the timber from the roof. A member of the demolition gang came knocking at the door asking if an old lady in black lived here. Bess used to dress like an Albanian peasant woman back then – black dress, black dust cap, cheery costume. It took six men to haul the timber back, and bear in mind Bess was in her eighties.

Bethlehem is one of two chapels in the village. It suited Bess that we lived opposite, as she liked nothing better than to spy on a funeral. It seemed to make her genuinely happy. Just as surely as putting on her reading glasses to read the obits in the *Western Mail*. One year I thought about getting her a scythe for her birthday, and a cowl.

One of the most interesting features of the chapel is a secular one. There used to be mooring rings set into the south facing wall of the graveyard. These marked the former reach of the sea before the embankments carrying the railway separated the village from the water. That was in the mid 1800s, when Isambard Kingdom Brunel drove the South Wales Railway through. Another railway, the Burry Port and Gwendraeth, also cut through the village later on and its route can still be followed along Ffordd y Wagen, which starts near the recreation ground.[17] But the sea laps and leaves in the names of many of the village's houses – Glan y Don, Sŵn y Don, Glan y Morfa, Min y Môr, Môr Awel, Ochr y Môr, Angorfa, Brig y Don, Gower View and Craig y Don.[18] And there's a row of cottages called Sailor's Row. And the remains of a tidewaiter, or custom man's cottage too, just behind the Talbot Inn. But the swimming club that used to swim in the estuary and was based in the slaughterhouse at Gower House is long disbanded.

As a family we went to the other Pwll chapel, Libanus, often three times on a Sunday and once midweek. When the foundation stone was laid in 1878 one of the speakers, the Rev.J. Ossian Davies, offered a religious rallying call that must have stoked up the spirit:

> May hundreds be prepared in this Pit, Pwll, for Heaven! And may no villager fall from this Pit to the bottomless 'Pit of perdition.' Satan left Paradise for the Pit, but I hope many will leave this Pit for Paradise. Ye hosts of the living God in this vicinity, march on! God's Holy Spirit will inspire you. God's gleaming shield will protect you! God's word for omnipotence will strike out for you. God's glorious Angels will serve for the fray. March On! Stand by Your Colours!

The way the village almost melded with the estuary helped shape me. An asthmatic youngster, I had to entertain myself when other boys played sport. So I beachcombed – snowmobile oil containers from Newfoundland, tea chests from India, an occasional stranded dolphin – and birdwatched. My dad caught sea bass, or mackerel. Cockles were picked by the bucket, too, and I remember washing them, ready for the boil. Still my favourite food. Villagers said you should wait three tides before eating them. It tested a boy's patience.

Solitude had its various pleasures: lying on a moss bank on a warm

May morning watching buzzards circle and mew overhead, discovering blurts of marsh marigolds, the yellowest things you ever did see. Or to hear the unfamiliar sound of a grasshopper warbler, skulking in a briar patch, reeling in a thin string of notes as if he's fishing for a tune. It was my equivalent to Laurie Lee's Gloucestershire. Idylls and halcyon days.

Pwll was almost a coarse fisherman's paradise. Almost. As part of the spectacular multi-million pound reclamation and landscaping project that created the Millennium Coastal Park a series of ponds were excavated – you can see them on the left hand side of the road as you drive west on the old Carmarthen road – and filled with fish. But the hydrologists got it pretty wrong. Although the lakes created as part of the Welsh Federation of Coarse Anglers' 'Centre of Excellence' were stocked with a rare array of fish – carp, roach, rudd, tench, skimmers, perch, crucian carp, golden tench and gudgeon – salt water came in with the tide and many of the fish died. But there are still enough to keep the herons happy, and with them, nowadays, little egrets, the starch white birds that were once a rarity in Wales but have now become a beautiful commonplace in watery habitats. Nearby Penclacwydd, is one of the best places to see them in the Principality.[19]

Being so near to the water, sea fishing quite naturally had its enthusiasts and adherants, none more so than a character called Clocsen, whose modus operandi was to drive nails through the soles of his wooden clogs and walk across the sands at low tide, spearing flounders and other flat fish as he went.

But the sea has its dangers as well as its harvests, and dead sailors have been washed up. At low tide, just south of the Talbot pub you can still see the 'death stone' which marks the spot where two daughters of Cilymaenllwyd house, Isabella and Anna Rees, drowned in 1855 along with their maid Jane Grier. There have been other drownings, too. Behind the Post Office, Pwll Diwaelod, the Bottomless Pool, claimed the lives of two young boys before it was filled in.

Pwll has had its share of great characters over the years, although one would be forced to admit that they're a declining species nowadays. My favourite was a man called Texas Dan, who had been to America and made every effort to let you know he had. On one occasion he found the body of a woman in the woods and raced back to the police station and asked the man behind the desk 'Are you the sheriff in these here parts? Because if you are you'd better rustle up a posse because there's a stiff up in the canyon.' There was the well-known herbalist John Williams, who operated from the Farriers pub until 1910. And there were other locals who could cure things, too.

If you had jaundice you could do worse than visit Martha Jane Davies. Her niece Ruthie Jones remembers the cure. 'She washed small snails in a colander at the outside tap and she'd put them on a tray and put them in the oven. There'd be a smell of roast beef. It was a cremation. After cooling she'd put something with them, crush them into a powder and bottle it.' You might take the powder mixed with home-made jam. Boiled mallow leaves could cure boils. Sores could be treated with fern juice. Hedgerow wisdom was a valuable thing, and so much is now lost.

One of the Big Moments in village history came when Amelia Earhart, the pioneering aviatrix landed her Fokker Friendship seaplane off the second slipway after almost running out of fuel on a flight from Newfoundland. Although she was towed into Burry Port, Pwll likes to claim its small role in her story. Earhart and her crew were lucky, as was Flight Lieutenant Wilczewski Baranski, from the 316 Polish squadron based at Pembrey, who crashed his Hurricane in Pwll in 1941 and walked away. Not everyone was so lucky. There was the unlucky crew of the B26 Marauder which crashed into the hillside north of the village in 1943.

To visit the village nowadays is to glimpse a case of what the Llansteffan-based artist Osi Rhys Osmond calls Cultural Alzheimer's: 'The Industrial Revolution occurred in our recent past, it is the only memory some have. It is also part of the short term memory of the nation and it is therefore likely to be the first to go.' As all evidence of Pwll's industrial business and busyness fades, it becomes a bit more like everywhere else. So it's worth looking for the traces of factory and mine. They were built not just from bricks and stone but also bound together with the sweat of a man's brow.

CILYMAENLLWYD

This substantial mansion overlooking the sandy reaches of the Burry estuary – at least sandy at low tide – has a long and fascinating history – and a house has stood on this site as far back as 1571. It has variously been known as Kilymaenllwyd, Killemaenllwyd and Killymaenllwyd, which according to Burke's *History of the Landed Gentry* means 'seat of grey rock' and was derived from a ridge on the sands below the house.[20]

There's an interesting grey rock set into the lawn in front of the house. It stands some 1.3 metres above the ground and is roughly square cut. There are incisions in the soft sandstone but these do not form a pattern, dispelling the belief that this was an inscription in Ogam.[21]

When I was growing up in Pwll there was a recurring story, which I presumed was apocryphal, that Wales' most dypsomaniacal poet, Dylan Thomas, used to stay regularly at Cilymaenllwyd and, moreover, that he was having an affair with a woman who lived there. It was a tale often told, or at least hinted at. So it came as some surprise to find out that Dylan was indeed familiar with Margaret Howard Stepney, know familiarly as Marged Fach, of Cilymaenllwyd.

Marged was one of a small army of patrons who kept Dylan on his feet, albeit unsteadily. Dylan's wife Caitlin wrote with bitterness about nights when the phone would ring and it would be Marged '…who was very rich and came from a family that claimed descent from the Tudors. Marged had inherited huge estates in Carmarthenshire from her mother and lived in a large house near Llanelli.'

The determined Marged would attend the poet's readings in London and Caitlin believed that she was doing her best to have an affair with him and claimed that she had already bedded down with John Davenport. By some accounts Marged became eccentric and hit the bottle hard, often in Dylan's company, when she would be lavish with gifts for him and anyone in their company.

This friendship has a literary outcome. In 1952 Dylan wrote her a letter which started 'My dear Marged, You told me, once, upon a time, to call on you when I was beaten down, and you would try to pick me up. Maybe I should not have remembered....

> You told me, once, to call on you
> When I was beaten down...
>
> Dear Marged,
>
> Once upon a time you told me
> I remember in my bones.
> That when the bad world had rolled me
> Over on the scolding stones.
> Shameless, lost, as the day I came
> I should with my beggar's cup
> Howl down the wind and call your name
> And you, you would raise me up...

And the poem continues very much in that vein. It's a sort of love letter as poem. But hold on to that word 'shameless.'

In a letter to Charles Fry, of the publishers Allen Wingate, on the 16 February 1953 Dylan wrote, 'early this year, my best friend in the world, a woman of my age, died of drink and drugs. And I've been ill too.' He referred to her as that 'Marged gin woman,' who died in London on 22 January. The inquest was told that she suffocated after a dose of sleeping pills; the verdict was misadventure.

Marged had meant to take over the Boat House from Margaret Taylor (the wife of the eminent historian A.J.P. Taylor and another patron of Dylan's excessive lifestyle) and pay its expenses for the Thomas family, but her financial advisers were making it difficult for her to spend her money in as profligate a way as she desired.

She had been with Thomas the night before she died. In a letter, written in the Boat House in Laugharne to John Alexander Rolph in March 1953 Dylan wrote, 'I do hope we'll have another evening soon without so many people & so much confusion. The thin, pale woman with us – Marged Howard Stepney – who drank sherry very quickly, died the next evening of an overdose of a sleeping drug.'

The impecunious Dylan had extra reason to mourn Marged's

passing. In a letter written the next day to John Malcolm Brinnin he referred to a promise that would never now be kept. 'Then a woman – you never met her – who promised me a real lot of money for oh so little in return died of an overdose of sleeping drug and left no will, and her son, the heir could hardly be expected to fulfil that kind of unwritten agreement.'

This wasn't the only tale of complicated love connected with Cilymaenllwyd. A lady called Bridget Price was married to one Thomas Jones, who died two years after their wedding, and she became a much sought after widow.[22] One of those she magnetized was Richard Savage, a friend of such literary luminaries as Samuel Johnson, Alexander Pope, Henry Fielding and the eighteenth century Carmarthenshire poet, John Dyer. Dyer was a friend of William Rees of Cilymaenllwyd, who probably introduced Savage to Jones. He fell completely in love and gave chase without reserve and mainly in verse. He penned an epitaph when her mother died (always a good ploy). He wrote three poems to the good widow herself, possibly with designs on her money as well as her heart. But she spurned him, a fact commemorated in a couplet composed one St. Valentine's Day in which he proclaims:

> Cambria farewell. My Chloe's charms no more
> Invite my steps along Llanelly's shore.

In January 1745, Savage was thrown into jail in Bristol for debt and died there.[23]

Some years ago, when I was researching the history of Pwll I was delighted to come across a beautiful letter about Cilymaenllwyd, written by a hundred year old woman, Mrs. E. Arengo Richardson, who lived in Switzerland. It was addressed to her grandson Roddy on his baptismal day. It evokes past times with elegance and enormous charm. I'll quote it in full:

> Two years ago when your big brother Gregory was baptized I was much younger and could move. Your granny was making your Christening Cake when she stayed with me. She asked me to help. So I stirred and mixed it up in the bowl. As I did so, I thought of little Gregory starting out on his life, and I wished and prayed for his happiness.
>
> Now I am much older and I cannot move any more. But I can still think and pray. So for your Christening I have mixed and stirred up lots of thoughts and ideas for you. I have put them into a letter which

you can read all your life. One day perhaps, when you are much older, you might re-read this letter and think what a strange world your ancient Great Grandmother must have lived in. But my thoughts and prayers will never change and I hope will be a strength and comfort to you all your life.

It is almost 100 years since I was born, a second baby in the family like you. There is no record whether I was a very good baby. A hundred years is a very long time isn't it?

I was born at home. We lived in a big house. It has not changed much since the days I was there. In front of the house there were green fields and beyond we could see the sea. As I grew older I loved to look at this, and listen to the birds, and sometimes I wished I could be a bird and be free to fly wherever I wanted.

My mother, your great, great Grandmother, was a very gentle lady. She was very beautiful and she loved to wear big, shady hats to keep the sun off her face. But I didn't see much of her, because I had a Nurse and a Nanny to look after me. After tea they would change my dress and stockings and take me to my mother in her drawing room – a very special sitting room where my father was not allowed to smoke. My mother would look at books with me and then I would be taken back up to our nursery in the top of the house. We didn't go for walks – I was put into a large pram and pushed out into the garden under the trees. I slept in a rocking cradle which my Mother pressed with her foot and then it would rock for a long time. At teatime we either had bread and butter, or bread and jam, but never bread, butter and jam.

There were stables behind the house for our horses, and big kitchens where Cook made meals for our big family and the people who worked in the house. Cook kept the meat on slate slabs in a large airy room away from the sun, and the butter was hung up in cages outside, in a windy corner of the house. Big sacks of flour, and sugar and things like that were delivered to the house. These were kept in a big storeroom. My mother and Cook would go to the Storeroom in the morning, and take out what was needed for the day. They opened the door with a big key which my mother kept on a chain round her waist.

Today is your baptism. For my baptism we went in a carriage with horses to another village where there was a big church.24 My father, whom I loved dearly, gave our village a small church so that my mother could walk to church every Sunday. He was a clever man, and drew the plans, and then gave the stones, the marble and the money so it could be built. When he was a very old man and he had finished with his life, we laid him to rest in the garden of his church.

Life today is so very different from the time when I was born. It was very quiet in those days, and life was so much slower. We had no telephone, no television or radio, only a gramophone. We had no electricity and in the evening we lit candles and oil lamps, so the house seemed very dark and rather scary. Perhaps it was quiet because there were no cars. When the first carriages without horses came on the roads, somebody had to walk in front waving a red flag to warn people that a dangerous vehicle was approaching.

A hundred years is a long time, isn't it? I've learnt a lot during those years.

I have learnt always to speak the truth.

I have learnt not to quarrel with anyone, or make an enemy.

I have learnt to think of others, to be considerate and not to speak rudely.

I have learnt to think things through.

I hope you will have a very happy life, dear, and if you stick to these things, and try always to be kind and helpful you have nothing to fear. I shall think of you often, growing up to become a big boy.

In her 101st year, Elizabeth Richardson died peacefully in her sleep in Switzerland.[25]

BURRY PORT

I used to love Burry Port when there was a gale blowing – literally a gale blowing. Some Septembers, at the tail end of the hurricane season, winds gusted at 100 mph, blustering and blowing in with ferocious energy from deep Atlantic. For a birdwatcher, these often brought in birds from deep ocean and occasionally from the other side of the ocean. So no matter that the winds threatened to turn humans into matchsticks, bending them over to snapping point, there were always birdwatchers on the coast, laden with 'scopes and binoculars, braving the eye of the storm to spot these exotic strays.

Burry Port was a great place to find these vagrants not only because its topography meant that it was one of the first places such birds could make landfall but also because the hot water pumped out from the turbines of the enormous Carmarthen Bay Power Station attracted fish from the estuary.[26] It was the seabird equivalent to putting out peanuts. You could often see shoals of little dead fish, which we collectively lumped together as 'whitebait' near the outlets, silvery unfortunates that had been seemingly steamed to death and then pumped out for a summary burial at sea.

Nineteen seventy-six was the standout, landmark year, an autumn of such ferocious wind that it blew the roof off of our newly built house in Pwll, my father only narrowly escaping with his life when he went outside for a rollie. It was hard to walk along the coast as one was buffeted and battered. But it was worth it when I got to the power station outlets, as there were many species I'd never seen before. Little gulls, their black and white wing patterns making them look like butterflies made of chalk and newsprint. Grey phalaropes, delicate wading birds with needle-thin bills, which swam in circles in shallow water and proved tame enough to get within a few wind-tossed feet of them. There must have been a half dozen of them. A Sabine's gull went upstream in mid channel of the Burry estuary. Red-letter day bird. Another to tick off in my *Collins Field Guide to the Birds of Europe* when I got home. At that point I could have died a happy teenager.

To visit Burry Port nowadays is to encounter a gentle mixture of picture postcard harbour and quiet. Where once stood the power station, Rio Tinto Zinc's plant, the foundry, and the substantial railway sidings there is now open ground. But even this has had its ornithological advantages. Black redstarts, which found a new habitat in the bombed and razed ground left after the London blitz have found the wastelands here to their liking. They're not that common, but they can occasionally brighten a winter's day such as this.

The village was a relative latecomer to the boom and bust of the industrial age. It had plenty of boom when it evolved to satisfy the need for a way to export coal hewn out of the Gwendraeth Valley. But

you'd have to listen long and hard to hear even the most distant echo of that busy age.

Originally Burry Port was a part of the parish of Pembrey,[27] which extended eastwards all the way to Sandy Bridge when villages such as Achddu and hamlets such as Tywyn Bach were very small dots on the map. It grew like topsy in the boom years with the success of early industry, which saw a rash of new housing and extensions to the harbourage. But it could be a place of bust, too. The village suffered a deep depression in 1877 when over 300 men became unemployed in the lead works, with many decamping for work in Glamorgan.[28]

It was the harbour that made the place, which came into being because of the shortcomings of nearby Pembrey harbour. In 1805 Captain John Wedge of Goodig was commissioned by the Committee for the Improvement of the Navigation of the Burry River to survey and report back about a route into a new harbour, and note where buoys should be placed to secure safe passage. He concentrated on a likely spot where the Derwydd stream flowed through some sandbanks into the sea. In September 1830 work commenced on building the harbour to a design by the appropriately named Sir Joseph Banks, who had already proved adept at such matters by his work developing Sheerness in Kent as a port. The east side was designed to connect with tramways to collieries such as New Lodge and Pwll and to another tramway, which ran from Mynydd Mawr to the Carmarthenshire Dock in Llanelli. Another tram road ran in from the north linking with Cwm Capel colliery while a new canal was excavated from Tŷ Gwyn Farm in Pinged.

The name Burry Port came into existence in 1835, replacing the name Tywyn Bach (Little Sea Shore or Little Dune) referring to just the docks area itself. The East Dock was completed by 1840 and the West Dock, or Pownd Clai, the Clay Pond, served as a scouring basin. The East Dock was limited in the size of shipping it could accommodate: it was unable to take any vessel over 500 tons, so it required the complete development of the West Dock, which opened in 1888 to welcome much bigger ships, weighing up to 3000 tons. Off-site developments, which happened in tandem with this growth, included the establishment of the Helwick lightship in 1846 and the erection of the Whitford Lighthouse in 1854.

The harbour catalysed commercial industry. The Mason and Elkington copperworks grew up alongside the dock,[29] with one of its stacks reaching 280 feet into the air, a height sufficient to make it the third tallest in Great Britain. The silver works were opened in 1853 and copper, silver and shipping were to be the bedrock of the local economy for many years. When enough silver was gathered it was formed into ingots which were sent to the Royal Mint in London under armed guard.

Meanwhile the South Wales Railway was also making inroads. The company embanked an area of marsh and salty creeks between the village and Pembrey and complemented this action by enclosing and draining what was then an area of common land, south of New Street and Station Road. A station, called Pembrey, was opened in 1852 and its name was extended in 1887 to include the name Burry Port. Advances in technology brought their own changes. The railways edged out canals as means of transport. The Burry Port and Gwendraeth Valley Railway Company came into being in 1866, following the towing path of the canal from Burry Port Docks all the way to Pontyberem. It was later extended to Cwm-mawr.

Mason and Elkington, and in particular the Elkington family, played a pivotal role in further expanding Burry Port. They invested substantially in coal mining at New Lodge, Pool colliery and Cwm Capel. Meanwhile the Pemberton family, still evident in the name of one of Burry Port's pubs, invested money in the docks. The place was a hive of activity. The Burry Port Lead Smelting Works opened in 1865 and Risley and Burgmann's White Lead Works in 1871 was followed by a foundry in 1874.[30] Work was hard and accidents frequent. Some were grisly, such as the accident that led to the death of fourteen-year-old Myrddin Morris, a cold-roll boy at the Burry Tinplate Works. His clothes were caught by the rolls so that the machine whirled him around so vigorously that 'fragments of the poor lad's remains were scattered around, and had to be collected and placed in a sack for conveyance to his home.'

And this increase in industry caused a sharp rise in the demand for housing. There's a square collection of streets just south of Station Road, built in the 1850s and 1860s, including Woodbrook, Silver and Burrows Terraces. It's an area known locally, or at least once known

as Y Bace because they were later to back on to the power station. I used to come here once a week to have heavily discounted piano lessons with my Auntie Lil. The fact that I still can't play a note says something about this tuition. Lil happened to be deaf but she was no Beethoven.

The opening of the station accelerated growth on New Street and quite obviously along Station Road and in the

1870s the area north of Gors Road grew quickly and was known as Goodwin's Town. A place that only had 20 houses in the early 1800s had a hundred by 1851 and 800 by 1876. This expansion caused a need for attendant cultural and religious institutions. Nonconformist chapels mushroomed, with no fewer than ten opening in the nineteenth century. The erection of St Mary's church in 1877 by the Elkington family served Anglican needs.

The Burry Port chapel I knew best was Carmel, tucked away at the end of what the Rhondda writer Gwyn Thomas would have called a riven gulch. Seen a lot of Westerns, he had. This was where my grandfather and grandmother went of a Sunday, and also where they were interred. They had been a quarrelling pair, with my grandmother reputedly breaking my grandfather's skull when she threw him over the bannisters of the pub they ran in Burry Port. They came from an age of uber-tough people and anthracite hard-heartedness and died within hours of each other. When my grandmother was laid to rest in the front room it was as if the air was animated; restlessness filled the room. As soon as my grandfather was brought back from Bryntirion Hospital where he died, a quiet settled in that front parlour. A few days later, at the very moment when their coffins were placed in the ground, it seemed as if all the birds had stopped singing. It might have been an extraordinary coincidence of synchronicity but I can still hardly credit that all the willow warblers, robins, wrens and black-birds in a heavily wooded valley in Wales on a sunlit May morning could have stopped singing at one and the same time. Other people who were present remember that instant, too. As Hamlet says to Horatio: 'There are more things on heaven and earth than are dreamt of in our philosophies.' Perhaps.

To mirror the growth of chapels more secular institutions flourished too. Inns and taverns opened at what was then the equivalent to warp speed, call it steam express speed, offering a source of safe refreshment in an era before clean water supplies. Don't drink the water, drink the ale. The Coasting Pilot was the oldest hostelry, which opened

its doors in 1824 and has them open still. By 1841 it had been joined by the Hope and Anchor, Porto Bello, Newfoundland Inn, Butcher's Arms and Farmers Arms. The Neptune joined the list of hostelries as did the Pemberton. My auntie Sarah ran that for a while and was known as Sarah'r Pem. I went to see her laid out, the first time I'd seen a cadaver. It wasn't frightening, but wasn't nice either. She looked dreadful. I'd have preferred to remember her with breath in her. By 1861 there were sixteen taverns in Burry Port in total. This could cause unexpected problems. In 1915 there was an explosive situation when workers from the munitions factory were found to be drinking too much during working hours. Orders to restrict the sale of alcohol had to be brought into force, defusing the situation.

Early in the twentieth century Burry Port was granted urban powers after Llanelli had been in dereliction of its duties in supplying water supply and adequate lighting. Indeed, a correspondent – albeit from Burry Port – to the *South Wales Press* lamented that, 'if Burry Port only had urban powers, it would become in a very short time, a second Naples. Llandrindod and other places of less size than Burry Port which have urban powers, would in my opinion, not be in it.' Now I've been to Naples and love that crime ravaged and gloriously sited city. I can only suggest that the letter writer was being overly fanciful. Mind you, as they say in Welsh, *gwyn y gwêl y frân ei chyw.*[31]

An early example of 'clean' industry coming to Burry Port was the foundation of the Lando Soap Company in 1933, which carried on the business of 'soap manufacturers, merchants, importers, exporters, and refiners of and dealers in oils and oleaginous and saponaceous substances.'

The largest employer in Burry Port today is Spencer Davies Engineering, employing thirty people and run by founder Spencer's son Owain, who is the sort of M.D. who'll go to meetings on a fast motorbike. His father flies a Cessna and both of them are members of the local lifeboat crew. They're businessmen embedded in the local community. I've been around S.D.E. and it seems they can build pretty much anything. They were building a mock-up Army tank when I was there. They're very good company, too and the workers there are amiable and full of good humour, although there have been recent redundancies with all their attendant pain. On the other side of the harbour you can see another local business, Parson's Pickles, who preserve

cockles among other things. I've visited this plant also, where the sharp tang of vinegar can take your breath away.

The docks are still substantial affairs and it's possible to imagine how busy they were in their heyday. In 1914 Burry Port was exporting over 7,000 tons of coal a month, not to mention 400 tons of tinplate. So 5,000 tons of mud were dredged from the East Dock, a new engine house was built, and new dock gate installed.

The dock walls of the West Dock support an unusually rich diversity of wild flowers, such as round-leaved cranesbill, bladder campion and Danish scurvygrass, not only because of the industrial history of the harbour but also because of the rocky substrate which resembles that of sea cliffs. This is the only place in the whole of Carmarthenshire where you can find the rare small-flowered catchfly, which is found growing along the top of the wall. It's possible that this little plant arrived in ballast from Portugal when coal was being exported there.

Other plants around the dock are precisely the kinds you'd expect to find on sea cliffs, such as the rock samphire, once used as a spring vegetable and in pickles, and the rare rock sea-lavender, once sold as everlasting blooms. There is floral evidence of the Roman invasion, too, what with Alexanders, an umbellifer used both as a spring vegetable and as a tonic, and fennel, which is now widely used in cooking, imparting a distinctive flavour to anything from fish stew to Italian sausage. In summer pyramidal orchids add blurts of purple colour; later the musk thistle will add its large nodding flowers to the harbour-scape while the golden flowers and attractive ferny foliage of the tansy, once a popular herbal remedy, adds to the sense of botanical profusion.

I walk on to the lighthouse, still the best nautical landmark for miles around. It's sited on the west side of the outer harbour by West Dock and reached via the breakwater. In 1842 Trinity House gave permission to the Burry Port Harbour Authority and Navigation Commissioners to create a flashing light which would be visible for fifteen miles. It was sited on top of a 24 ft white painted stone tower, which remains to this day.

I conclude my visit to Burry Port with the quietly pleasurable pastime of reading the name of the boats in the harbour as a gentle breeze soughs through their rigging. *Fisherman, Swˆn y Mor, Susan B, Barbican Maid, Niwl y Môr, Glas y Dorlan. Edwin, Alisam* (presumably a portmanteau word made of the names of both owners), *Josie Anna, Sailfish, Sea Otter, Sonic* and my favourite, *Plan B.* You should always have a Plan B.

PEMBREY COUNTRY PARK

The long, wind-sculpted stretch of beach known as Cefn Sidan, or silky back, can be both as elegant as silk and as dangerous. As danger-ous, that is, as a silk stocking turned into a garrote. It's been a fatal shore for many ships, yet for nature it's a place of bounty and abundance, although this could also be said for human looters in the past as they plundered wrecks.

To stand here on a winter's day one – on a stretch of coast once known as Tywyn Mawr, or the Large Sea Shore – one can feel like the last person on earth, the last man standing on the edge of the conti-nent. The wind is a whip and the sand scours your cheeks. Pity then the rarest bird ever seen here, a cream-coloured courser, blown here in the early 1970s. It normally lives in the Sahara.

Look directly offshore, right into the waves and surf. As your eyes become accustomed to the metronome pulse of the breakers you'll start to spot little black dots, like burnt corks, cresting the waves and then disappearing as the waves roll over and into themselves. These are common scoter, heavily built sea ducks, and Carmarthen Bay is one of the most important sites for them in Britain.[32] Aerial, boat and radar surveys suggest that there can be up to 25,000 birds gathered here, defiantly choosing to fish where the waves crest, crash and fold.

The male is the only all black duck – relieved by the merest hint of orange on the bill – and the sea, whatever its turbulence and fury, is its chosen habitat. When the ducks moult offshore the tideline at Cefn Sidan can sometimes be black with feathers. At this stage of their lives the birds are particularly vulnerable and two recent oil spills claimed many avian lives.

There are natural phenomena, too. Sailor-by-the-wind jellyfish can be washed up here by the million, probably by the billion. And unnatural phenomena, too. One day the

whole shore was a bright orange. Eyewitnesses aver that the tideline had been painted a shade of neon tangerine. A cargo of Hawaiian Tropic sun tan solution had been washed in. Along 8.4 miles of coastline noticeably untanned folk with their own trucks harvested lotion. From the very next weekend every car boot sale in south Wales had discount Tropic for sale. Probably still have some stock left. If you look. Check the sell-by date.

Of all the beaches in Wales this is the one which gets more cetacean bodies – animals such as porpoise and whales – washed up than any other. They even had a walrus once, back in 1986. An adult female minke whale weighing one and a half tons was grounded here in 1991. There have been many, many others, as many as three whales per decade. During the ration years after the war whale meat was officially distributed in the area should one be found on the tideline.

Other matter brought in by the tide has been more poignant, such as items from a wrecked Air India aircraft, which was blown up in mid Atlantic. Noises off. Terrible events elsewhere. Seemingly a long way from this beach on this bright day, with the wavelets corruscating as the sky overhead reveals the main of light. Here on land's edge sanderlings, diminutive little wading birds, are probing in the sand. They are right on the shoreline, one step away from being aquatic birds. The birds are needling the shimmering edge of the waves, their silvery bodies moving like little clockwork toys as they scurry back and fore to avoid the waves. There's something comical about the mechanical way they feed. Brave and timid at one and the same time.

And after the toss and hurl of storms birds of deep ocean, truly pelagic species, can be blown in, birds such as storm petrels, sometimes known as Mother Carey's chickens. This species is no bigger than a house sparrow, yet the wind-tossed birds feed way, way out there at sea. To see them, their little legs trailing weakly behind them as they flutter exhaustedly, it's hard to picture them in the middle of gales. Yet the wide ocean is their habitat, the salty emptiness their feeding ground. Brave little critters.

And there is supernatural flotsam, too. There was a sighting of a mermaid here once, 'just like the pictures in books, only lovelier, and her beautiful mass of golden hair gleamed in the sunshine.' As the man who had spotted her took to his heels she shouted after him, promising great riches if he returned and a terrible fate if he didn't.[33] Myself, I've never seen a mermaid here, but then again I've never been here while taking LSD.

Over the years the Pembrey Country Park has been vying with the amusement park rides of Oakwood in Pembrokeshire for the title of 'best Welsh attraction where you have to pay an admission fee.' The accolade has been vacillating back and fore between the two these past fifteen years. If the weather's good hundreds of thousands come to Cefn Sidan and the Park's many visitor attractions. And it can be as many as between 400,000 and 500,000 visitors a year.

The Park opened in 1980 following the defeat of controversial plans to move the M.O.D. artillery range from Shoeburyness at the mouth of the Thames to Pembrey by a spirited and passionate campaign to 'Save Our Sands.'

The country park utilizes what was once a heavily militarized area, the site of the Royal Ordnance factory, producing munitions for the Allied Forces during the Second World War. The dunes here were ideal for the dangerous business of making munitions, providing screens and minimizing damage in case of accident. In terms of context, makers of gunpowder and dynamite had been drawn here as early as 1881. The factory made TNT, ammonium nitrate and tetryl for the First World War and when it was run down at the end of hostilities the main building became a convalescent home and rehabilitation centre for the children of unemployed miners who produced 'carbon black,' which was used in the manufacture of printers' ink.

The Second World War caused a surge in demand for explosives and the factory was re-opened. At its peak, in 1942, 3000 people were working here, and the factory had its own laundry, its own reservoir and its own electricity station, more like a self-sufficient town, and was a hugely important employer in the area. It was the country's main producer of TNT, but was gradually run down after the war, despite a busy spate during the Korean War. During the fifties the factory was dedicated to breaking down obsolete bombs and shells, and the workforce ran down to some 400 by 1961. The factory was finally shut in 1965.

So creating the Country Park first involved some major reclamation, including some very valuable metals. Every machine and tool employed at the site had to be non-sparking so a great deal of bronze was used along with lead. Reclamation was precursor to demolition but because the magnificent structures at the factory were designed to be bombproof this was no small undertaking. Some of the second wave of bunkers used for decommissioning of armaments are here still. You'd need high explosives to blow them up, ironically.

Even when the factory was open a privileged few were allowed through the perimeter wire to get to the shore, where they could enjoy great bass fishing. Country Park ranger Dave Hughes' father used to bring him down in the summer when they'd be lucky if they saw more than half a dozen people in a whole day. Dave has worked here since the park opened and loves the combination of seclusion and beauty. Mind you, he's seen some things in his days.

One time there was a locally infamous section of the beach that was promoted by certain magazines as being suitable for nudists. Dave remembers, 'this gentleman who may have taken this quite literally. It was a warm day and I was on duty on the barrier at the entrance to the park because there were so many visitors trying to get in. A man drove up to the booth who was completely naked. All I could think of to say was, "Yes it is warm isn't it?"' Dave subsequently imagined what would have happened if he'd had to stop for petrol, or blown a tyre en route for Pembrey. He'd have had nothing with which to spare his blushes.

Some of the excitement nowadays is on a grand scale, such as Hercules transport aircraft landing on the beach by way of practicing landing in Afghanistan. The big planes prepare for short landings and equally tight take offs. The training has given a new lease of life to the range. Specialist troop-carrying Chinook helicopters bring in Marines along with tanks and personnel carriers, depositing them in the dunes, carrying out complete maneuvers. On one occasion the boorish television presenter of Top Gear, Jeremy Clarkson tried to race one of the Hercules in his Jag. When you need a rogue missile strike there never is one….

Dave Hughes grins as he recalls the reaction from the public to the noise from military manoeuvures. 'People come up to me to ask me to phone someone to stop the jets and ask them to stop immediately. As if my ringing Strike Command will have any effect. Anyway, as they say in the Falklands, that's the sound of freedom.'

The military does impinge on life in the Park. Between Monday and Friday there are restrictions on the Cydweli end and Tywyn Point is out of bounds between eight in the morning and four thirty in the afternoon. There's a safety ricochet area on the range itself the other side of the dunes.

Neil Perry has been the Countryside Facilities Manager for Carmarthenshire Council for two years, and worked at Pembrey for a further fourteen years. He points out that despite the transport planes, the Chinook and Apache helicopters and the spillover noise from the motor racing circuit it's still a place for passive recreational pursuits.[34] Luckily the forest is a buffer for a great deal of noise. Many people arrive at the park courtesy of the Sustrans cycle route and they've made a special entrance point for cyclists. It's a good green way to arrive here.

The Park has ten full time staff and they're open 364 days a year. They're closed only for Christmas Day. Curiously Boxing Day is one of their busiest periods. As Neil explains, 'we have the Walrus Dip – where a lot of daredevils brave the cold sea. Last year we had 250 actually dipping – and it was very cold. We had between four and five thousand people watching. It's quite a spectacle: we had a load of walruses in fancy dress and we had a marching band leading them into the sea and back out again. It was the fullest the car parks had been during the whole year, owing to the weather.' They also host a range of sports including land sailing and paracarting championships. Historically the area has hosted other sports. Neil's seen a photo of the beach in front of Pembrey busy with motorcycle races.

Over the years they've developed a range of attractions such as ski slopes and nature trails and that work continues. They're planning to introduce a new lifeguard service courtesy of the R.N.L.I., as well as two attractions: hill rolling, a.k.a. sphering or zorbing, in which willing victims are strapped into a rubber ball and rolled downhill, and one which allows visitors to swing from treetops in 2010. Bring bananas.

Neil's team of co-workers try to balance ecological harmony with visitor pressure. This is a place of incredible natural richness. The area hosts 34 butterflies out of the 60 British species. The flora flourishes with many orchid species – butterfly, early marsh, southern marsh, pyramidal, bee orchid and the rare lesser twayblade.

But some the plants are less attractive and less benign. Bane of the place is sea buckthorn – and a priority for control and eradication as far as the local authority and the Countryside Council for Wales are concerned. This tough, invasive and resilient species is the equivalent here to rhododendron in the Snowdonia National Park. It provides berries aplenty for hungry thrushes, but smothers all other plant species. As the Daleks croakingly put it – exterminate!

The shore is treacherous hereabouts. Since the late 1600s there are records of 182 vessels that have come up on the beach. In 1753, the *William and Mary* travelling from Newfoundland to Waterford carrying grain was lost, at a cost of eighteen lives. Six years later the *William* from Newfoundland sank with its cargo of seal skins and oils. In 1810, the *Union Cadiz* bound for London with its cargo of indigo, copper and cochineal voyaged for the last time and 14 lives were lost. *La Providence* en route from Bordeaux to Dunkirk carrying juniper berries, wine, brandy and coffee was grounded on Cefn Sidan, attracting crowds of 2000 people who 'exhibited the most disgraceful scenes… plundering all they could get out, breaking in the heads of casks and drinking to such a degree, both male and female, they became extremely intoxicated, one found dead from suffocation and two others missing.' In 1828 *La Jeune Emma* plying between Martinique and Le Havre, carrying rum, sugar and coffee ran aground with the loss of thirteen lives, among them Lieutenant Col. Coquelin and his daughter Adeline – niece to Josephine, consort of Napoleon Bonaparte. In 1833 15 lives were lost when the *Brothers* sank with its cargo of buffalo hides and cotton.

Excerpts from a letter written in December 1833 by J.H. Rees, a local magistrate, give an idea of the scale and severity of the illegal operations. Referring to the wreck of the *Brothers*, bound from Brazil to Liverpool, he says that 'as I followed the Sea-shore I observed numbers of Country People employed in cutting open the Bales of Cotton which were lying in quantities along the shore of nine miles in length, and carrying them away in Bags and Carts, etc. – and as I approched Kidwelly, I informed the People, chiefly of that Town, engaged in breaking up the wrecked vessel with Saws, Hammers, etc. and conveying the Timber, etc away in Carts – I warned the People, many of whom were Farmers of respectability of the consequences of the proceedings… Carts from twenty miles around have been sent to convey away the Bales of Cotton…I myself was assaulted in the execution of my duty. Unless people be checked in their Lawless proceedings, there is not knowing to what lengths opposition may be carried, as they come prepared with short hatchets, hammers, etc.'

Pounding waves continued to bring in plunder. In 1842 *Die Gute Hoffung* bound from Italy to Hamburg sank with cargo that included a marble statue valued then at £2000. 'The vagabond race who prowl the sea shore' were again in evidence and stole, among other things, the Captain's and his wife's clothes and belongings. In 1859 the *Stadfelt* travelling from Mexico to Hamburg, with wine, tobacco, cordial and arrowroot, was lost at the cost of seven lives. More misery followed in 1877 when the *Daisy* on its way from Africa to Bristol sank with four lives lost.

Wrecked ships attracted local souvenir hunters like moths to a candle. In 1859 when the *Sir Henry Pottinger* sailing from Peru to Liverpool mistook the light on Caldey for the Tusker light, four unfortunates from Pembrey were hauled before the court in Llanelli for 'purloining articles from the ship.' These weren't common or garden 'articles' either. The ship was laden with silver bars and copper ore, valued then at £ 25,265. Serious plunder. Booty indeed.

In 1846 a cargo of palm oil and coconuts was lost when the *Huskisson* out of West Africa ran aground. The deaths of many members of the regular crew meant that the ship was manned by slaves, many wearing ivory tusk rings on their arms and bodies. The slaves assisted in rescuing the cargo and were put up in the Neptune Hotel in Burry Port. Eventually reinforcing the militia barracks at Pwll, coupled with regular horseback patrols, made looting much more difficult.

Ranger Dave Hughes tells me about the visible signs of wrecks on the beach nowadays. The best and most visible wreck was made out of Northern European oak, growing in the mid to the late 1800s, proved when it was dendrochronologically examined. 'You can still see metal fixings, treenails and square sectioned copper nails. If you go further up the beach there are two small spindles of what we call short shore vessels. Then you come to the steel hull of the *Teviotdale* sailing from Cardiff to Bombay with coal. When she hit the storm they thought they were coming back to the Bristol channel and grounded in 1886. And unfortunately seventeen members of crew lost their lives, but when locals tried to loot the ship thirty of them were arrested, even as the bodies of the dead crewmen lay on the shoreline.

Dave continues, 'Only a few months ago we had a magnificent find. Three guys asked if they could come down and they said they'd bring the ship's bell down. Good gosh, I said. They popped down one weekend and they opened the boot and there it was – this bell with the name of the ship on it and when it was launched. The ringer was still in and one of them held it up on a piece of string, rang it and there was such a tone and volume to the ring that our golf attendant in the middle of the park heard it.' The men in question were maritime history's equivalent to Colombo and Sherlock Holmes. A member of a diving club in Cardiff told them about the bell; it was upside down in a lady's garden, painted blue and being used as a flowerpot.

One of the other wrecks, which is still visible, is the *Paul*, grounded in October 1925 bound for St Anne's Head, from Nova Scotia, carrying timber. When she arrived off Pembrokeshire she was due to await instructions about where she would eventually dock. But for the last nine days of her 27-day journey gale force winds tore her sails into shreds, one by one. Her rigging was destroyed in a storm out at sea but she drifted into Carmarthen Bay when it had calmed off, then she just settled on the sand. Tugs from Cardiff were unable to pull her off. She came in whole, masts and everything – apart from the sails and the rigging. Rumour has it that fine foreign timbers found their way into houses being built in Llansaint and Cydweli at just about this time!

Sadly wrecks are not confined to the past. A yacht called the *Resolva* from Morocco on its maiden voyage took the wrong turn and four members of the same family drowned. It had stopped in Gibraltar for supplies, was observed by Portuguese customs all the way up to Carmarthen Bay where it was washed up, complete with a cargo of hashish, no less than three quarters of a million pounds worth of Lebanese black.

PEMBREY

As you drive on the main road between Llanelli and Cydweli the tall church tower at Pembrey is striking, a commanding bulk which sports Irish stepped battlements and dates from the sixteenth century, having been added to the north of a low thirteenth century nave. It looks like a church that could withstand a determined siege just as well as any castle and is the village's dominant building, with a circular animal pound set beside it. Indeed, this village was known for over a hundred years as Llan, underlining the centrality of the church.

St. Illtyd's is one of the larger medieval churches and dates back

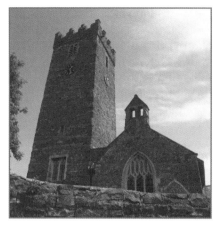

to the Age of the Saints.[35] The church was restored by James Wilson of Bath in 1856-7 and again in 1910-11. There was also a recent restoration in 2004 which brought back whitewashed renders, lightening the interior no end. Inside the porch is a list of vicars dating back to 1066. The churchyard has a grave belonging to a Middlesex man, George Bowser, with an inscription which claims him as the instigator of the main harbour developments hereabouts, at Pembrey and Burry Port. His role was pivotal. By 1813 an extension of Kymer's canal had reached Pembrey and an iron works was erected soon after. The Pembrey Harbour Company was established in 1825 and the dock itself excavated out of a rabbit warren, but the upkeep of the harbour proved difficult and costly owing to silting and work was started on Burry Port harbour not long after, in 1830. When they excavated the new docks the scouring of the sand laid open a bed of blue clay, in which were discovered numerous prints of deer and cattle. The new floating dock at Pembrey, called Burry Port, was described at the time as 'unquestionably the best shipping place in south Wales, having at the lowest neap tides 13 feet of water through the dock gates, and 24 feet at spring tides.'[36]

The main door of St. Illtyd's carries the inscription 'Haec Domus Dei Porta Coeli' and there are stained glass windows inside carrying the crest of arms of the families of Court Farm, situated on the mountain road, Heol y Mynydd, rising up out of the village. This is an ancient farmstead that has roots back to 1361. The Butler family lived here followed by the Vaughan family and then by the Earl of Ashburnham, who came from Sussex.[37] His name lives on in the Ashburnham Hotel, Ashburnham Road and Ashburnham Golf Club.

One of the area's most distinguished politicians, Denzil Davies, lives on the Links, an upmarket area which also has connections with Brian Trubshaw, who led the team of test pilots for the Anglo-French Concorde project.[38] Davies, the son a blacksmith from Cynwyl Elfed, filled another blacksmith's son, Jim Griffiths' vacant seat after he retired in 1968.[39] When Davies entered the Commons it is unlikely that he would have had quite the fuss one of his predecessors enjoyed in Pembrey in 1835 when 'a new Member of Parliament found himself in a chair as part of a procession that included two Marshalls, a Band, Constables, Portreeve, Flags and Banners, the Electors and Gentry in columns, three abreast. Stavemen and Constables; the Chair, supported by six men each side, appropriately garbed, with gilded leeks in their hats, a crowd of about 1,000 of all grades. The Chair was exceedingly neat, with a canopy, dressed with red and lilac colours, interspersed with gilded leeks.'[40]

One of the most extraordinary sights from the golf course would have been seen in December 1948, when a coal-fired Norwegian steel ship, the S.S. *Tungeness* of about 1,800 tons, ran aground on the Hooper Bank, right opposite the plantation on the 12th fairway. This huge ship, grounded because the master would not accept a local pilot to take her in to Llanelli, would have been enough to put any golfer off his stroke.

The coastline hereabouts began its retreat from the foot of Pembrey Mountain some 6,000 years ago.[41] The Iron Age has evidence of human occupation of the land, with hill forts dating from around 200 B.C.[42] Roman pottery remains have been unearthed in the oldest parts of the village. Evidence of an early Norman motte and bailey castle has been suggested close to the village square and buildings remain in the village from later Norman times. Most of the village of Pembrey was created during the eighteenth and nineteenth century coal mining boom, when Pembrey was a port. Pembrey Mountain or Mynydd Penbre was thoroughly mined by both Welsh and English companies for about 100 years and some reserves are said to remain underground.

Above the church, on an outcrop of rock, legend has it that wreckers lit false beacons to lure ships to crash on shore. Wrecking was a way of life along the sandy shore between Pembrey and Cydweli and their habit of carrying saws, nails and hatchets gave rise to the term *Gwŷr y Bwyelli Bach*, or people of the little hatchets. Hundreds of ships were wrecked here even without the

deceits of the wreckers as the waters of the Burry Inlet are notori-
ously treacherous as we've seen when visiting Cefn Sidan.

Pembrey was obviously a wild place at one time. The centuries
have tamed it, but you can still see the occasional brigand gleam in
the eyes of some of its inhabitants. Who'll be listening avidly to that
weather forecast no doubt....

PEMBREY AIRPORT

It's nothing fancy. A bungalow that used to be owned by Eastwoods
Poultry farm now has a door on the left side marked 'Flight
Operations' and another on the right which leads into the Amelia
café, named after the transatlantic airwoman Amelia Earhart, where
they serve a mean chicken pie. A squat building nearby is marked
'Customs' and 'Arrivals.' There's a basic control tower, a pair of fire
tenders, an H reg. airport police car and a runway that needs to be
extended to take jets. It's almost finished.

Pembrey Airport currently has a staff of six fire officers, four air
traffic controllers and a further six people working in the restaurant.
They're all part-timers and mainly volunteers but there are hopes
that some will be able to convert to full time work in the future. At
present most of their business comes from refuelling military aircraft
but the airport is trying to gear up for a new commercial phase. The
dream is to create the Pembrey International Airport, a magnet for
inward investment and clean industries. It's all happening because of
one man's vision, not to mention a lot of his own money. A real case
of blue sky thinking.

Machynys-born Winston
Thomas used to come here on
his bike when he was a boy, to
look at the aircraft at what was
then Pembrey Airfield. He
then went off to live a full life.[43]
When he acquired the site in
1996 he was taking over a
large tract of land complete
with its own air of dereliction
and a runway which had
turned to rank grass.[44] But he
wanted to employ air transport

to regenerate the area, envisioning planes connecting Pembrey with the rest of the world. For him this was no airy, fairy labour of love. He could see that all towns of the UK were competing for work and there was a missing part of the infrastructure in Llanelli that made it less attractive to inward investment. Winston lists all the attractions of the Llanelli peninsula, as he calls it, from new golf courses to upmarket housing. And air connections with Europe, he avers, would allow one to tap into a market of 600 million people, more than Russia and the U.S. together. These are points he makes with enthusiasm.[45] He goes to Dubai up to four times a year to make the same points. It's paying off. Emirates Airlines have been down twice to have a look at the place. Not that they tell him exactly what they're thinking.

Winston takes me out to see the new runway extension which he wants to finish before racing starts at nearby Ffos Las racecourse in June 2009 as he knows that Irish owners and trainers will be keen to jet in from that racing-crazy land and wants to be ready to welcome them with a new swathe of blacktop. He points out that, when finished, the tarmac, stretching away towards the dark sitka green of Pembrey forest will be the same length as London City Airport. From there they fly the Airbus 318 to New York. He makes the trans-Atlantic analogy to underline the potential of the place. He's steeled against disappointment, having already been part of the effort to establish a national airline for Wales, Air Wales, a brave idea at the wrong time.

When Winston revisited Pembrey during a trip home from America he thought it would make a 'nice project.' He also brought with him that American belief that a place without an airport is either too small or doesn't exist. By 1997 the Secretary of State for Wales officially opened this new airport. A lot of people remained skeptical of Captain Winston's efforts. But he's kept on dreaming the dream.

He has his own airline ready to go once the runway is ready. The new uniforms for the Southwestern Airlines staff are hanging in the offices. In one of them, a white board is already marked with a simple flight timetable. There's an aircraft ready, too. He's also identified some interesting routes. Such as flights to Brest in Northern France. 'I didn't realize that were so many people commuting to Brest, to work on the French fleet, including aircraft carriers, so demand for engineers there is very high.' The authorities in Brest want him to fly on to Paris. He's investigated other options, too, connecting with Birmingham or Shannon, with onward flights to North America.

He also knows that locally there are 2,500 commuters who want to get to London. Lots of people even want to pay in advance. Before he even owns the ten-seater aircraft he's had enquiries from folk wanting to book seats to know they were on the flight on Monday morning, heading for Biggin Hill or London City airport.

The proximity of the local RAF range is no problem he maintains. 'We will be gone before the military start. By the time they start in the morning we'll already be in London and we'll be getting back after they finish. Strike Command has agreed up to nine civilian movements a day out of Pembrey.' In the past the nearby range was a problem but all that's been sorted out with the men in blue eager to please. Winston sees them as an asset. At Pembrey, he maintains, military and civil aircraft work well together. As if on cue, someone from the RAF rings him to book in a night flight. They co-operate to the extent that they will hold up a military aircraft if needs be. 'We get a lot of helicopter traffic,' he told me, 'which is ideal for us and a big revenue earner. They come for training, as it's near to Castlemartin and Brecon. Because I'm ex-military and because of the skills of the people who work here we can do rotors-running refuelling. A Chinook can land here at night and put on two and a half tons or 4000 odd litres of fuel and we can get him back in the air within seven minutes. They can't do that at Cardiff as they'd have to shut the place down.' He knows that in order to become a commercial success he'll have to instigate new developments such as departure lounges, but asserts that the airport is pretty much unique in having plenty of room to expand. Standing in the control tower with Winston, as he surveys the future

in his mind's eye you can see surviving hangars from the days when this was Pembrey Airfield – so called 'F sheds' converted by a farmer into a cattle feeding facility.

Ever since the outbreak of the Second World War, RAF Pembrey has had an active and colourful flying history.[46] Construction of the airfield started in 1937 and by September of 1939, the RAF's No. 2 Air Armament School was stationed at the airfield. Trainees would sit in the turrets of Whitley bombers, setting their sights on targets towed by Wallaces.

By June 1940, Fighter Command was using Pembrey as a base for the numerous fighter squadrons caught up in Britain's 'finest hour....' During this period Pembrey gained honours as a Battle of Britain Airfield.[47]

Spitfires which had seen action over Dunkirk came here to keep the skies safe above the industrial zones of the Midlands, south Wales and Bristol, where the Luftwaffe used cover of darkness and cloudy days to attempt to drop their grim payloads. As if the dangers of encountering and neutering HE 111s, Dorniers and Junkers wasn't bad enough, landing Spitfires with their narrow undercarriages was a dangerous affair. When the Spitfires moved to Biggin Hill at the height of the Battle of Britain in September, No. 79 squadron, made of Hurricanes blew in to patrol both sides of the Bristol Channel. It is believed that 25 official kills were accredited to aircraft flown out of Pembrey during the war years.

Between 1941 and 1945 Pembrey was also host to the RAF's Air Gunnery School, after which its activities relaxed a little and it became an air crew holding unit for war-weary crews being demobbed.

Fighter Command once again took over as custodians in 1946, and remained there until their final service days and the airfield's eventual closure on the 13th July 1957.

Probably the most famous incident in the war had its funny side and involved a Focke Wulf, which sounds as if it was created to be laughed at. But the RAF took this new German aircraft very seriously and wanted to mount an operation to capture one. But as things transpired they didn't need to.

One Oberleutenant Armin Faber of JG2 Richthofen left Germany in June 1942 to engage British Spitfires and did manage to shoot one down, but in the aerial melee Faber got confused and mistook the Bristol Channel for the English Channel. He even thought that Pembrey was his home base and performed a series of aerobatic feats to celebrate his homecoming before landing in an enemy airfield with a brand new German plane for them to appreciate and study! Apparently he was captured by the Pembrey Duty Pilot, one Sgt. Jeffreys who grabbed a Very pistol, ran from the control tower and jumped onto the wing of Faber's aircraft as it taxied in. An arresting moment followed. Ironically, Faber was piloting the very latest enemy fighter, the Focke Wulf 190A, a type the RAF had only ever seen flying over France. The depths of Faber's despair at providing his enemy with an intact FW190 can be gauged by the fact that he subsequently attempted to commit suicide. As news broke of his landing in Pembrey, Fighter Command despatched pilots to photograph and return the aircraft to the Royal Aircraft Establishment at Farnborough. The RAF finally had an FW 190!

Over the years new British weapons and aircraft were trialled at Pembrey while some, such as the substantial B17s and Liberators used the site for emergency stops to refuel.

The Korean War brought fresh urgency and new planes to Pembrey, with Vampire FB 5s, Meteors, Mosquitos, Tempests, Chipmunks, Hunters, Tiger Moths, an Oxford and a Balliol all stationed here.

And the military still plays a part here. One afternoon I saw a Chinook come in to land at Pembrey Airport, the sound of its rotors lifted from any number of movie soundtracks. It had spent some time hovering over the dunes of Cefn Sidan, looking for all the world like an enormous cockchafer beetle. The team refuelled it double quick. They see it as part of the war effort. They're doing their bit.

CYDWELI

We are heading into Cydweli for my godson Owain's eighteenth birthday,[48] swinging by the castle which is hauntingly illuminated at night, washed in blue light. Sturdy, repelling, its turrets and gatehouse are an essay in conquest written in stone. And mystical, too, in this blue wash of light.

As we turn into the castle car park I keep an eye out for black cats. There's one on the town's coat of arms. Legend has it that the cat was the first creature seen alive after the Great Plague hit the town and is honoured as a symbol of salvation and deliverance.[49] I really don't want to run one over. That really would be bad luck. And I've got new front tyres.

The imposing castle, built to subjugate and dominate, consists of a square inner bailey defended by four round towers, which overlook a semi-circular outer curtain wall on the landward side, with the massive gatehouse next to and overlooking the river. The river prevents this from being truly concentric in shape, however a jutting tower protects the riverside walls. In the mind's eye it still exerts an iron will, conjuring up an image of a mailed fist. And an arrow in some poor dab's eye.

The castle was created to face down the Welsh and was changed many times over the years, often embracing the latest military advancements. The ringwork castle, set on the upper tidal reaches of the river Gwendraeth Fach, still dominates the town today. It was built by Roger, Bishop of Salisbury, as part of a chain of such fortifications commanding vantage points overlooking river crossings and harbourages: there are others at nearby Laugharne, Llansteffan and Loughor.

Cydweli fell to the Welsh many times in the late twelfth and thirteenth centuries and in 1159 Lord Rhys burned it to the ground; he reputedly rebuilt it in 1190. In the mid thirteenth century the Chaworth family took possession and embarked upon substantial building work, creating a concentric bastion, with both inner and outer walls of defence. The castle passed by marriage in 1298 to the Earl of Lancaster, who upgraded the accommodation to reflect his own status. He built a large first-floor hall, established a chapel in a tower and built a sacristy. In the fourteenth century the mighty outer defences were erected, including a stone curtain wall punctuated by a series of mural towers. Trouble was in store at the start of the fifteenth century. There had been prophesies. Owain Glyndŵr had written a vaticinatory letter to one Henry Dunn of Cydweli in 1401 saying that he had been appointed by God to release the Welsh from bondage to their English enemies. Perhaps the most imposing feature, the mighty gatehouse, took a century to complete, and was unfinished when Glyndŵr laid siege to the castle during his uprising of 1403, assisted by soldiers from Brittany and France. Extensively damaged, it was rebuilt at the order of Henry V, and subsequently

designed to be held independently of the rest of the castle. It sported an array of defensive features including machicolations, through which missiles could be dropped, and a substantial drawbridge along with numerous arrowloops.[50] The last major addition to Cydweli castle was a large hall built in the fifteenth century, most probably by Rhys ap Thomas, after the place was gifted to him by Henry VII.

The town was created shortly after the castle, but a Benedictine priory was established here in 1114.

For those with a taste for British surreal humour, Cydweli was used as a location for the film *Monty Python and the Holy Grail*: the place appears in the very first scene, just after the titles. After our first view of King Arthur and Patsy, a very misty establishing shot shows Cydweli as their destination. However, the following close-up filming was done at Doune Castle in Scotland. Fleeting fame, but fame nevertheless.

We leave the castle and head for the party. Godson Owain's do is being held at the Princess Gwenllian Centre, a leisure centre opened in 1991. He meets us at the door wearing a hat adorned with burning candles – battery operated for safety. He's an exceptionally person-able young man and I feel more than a twinge of guilt that I haven't seen him all that often during his growing up. But it's a relief to see that he's become a popular guy, as the cameraderie of his fellow sixth formers attest. They clearly love his company and he repays them with smiles. His default adjective is 'awesome.' Which suggests an optimistic bent.

The party's a chance to catch up on what young people in Cydweli are listening to nowadays. The disco sounds resound tinnily against the brick walls. Welsh soulster Duffy is obvious in the mix, so too Girls Aloud but the real karaoke gusto is reserved for songs from *The Rocky Horror Picture Show*. The chocolate fountain, serving straw-berry fondues and the like keeps the performers sugared up. I enjoy a few chocolatised fruit myself and catch up with Gareth Harries, Owain's dad and the oldest friend I have. There used to be three of us who played together all summer long. The third was Simon Thomas, a musician, but in those days he was a goalkeeper, standing between the conveniently spaced apple tree trunks in the little orchard at the bottom of the Harries family's long garden. On match days and every other day I wore jeans that had been patched too many times and now had to be held together with safety pins. It antic-ipated punk but without the menace.

Over chocolate this and chocolate that Gareth and I catch up on family news, now touched with illness, passings, the stuff that happens to us when we get older. But I can still see us in that perpet-ual summer. When what the playwright Dennis Potter described as the blossomest blossom was on the trees. And the sun always shone on the three ragamuffins playing football with all the vigour of the Cameroon's national squad.

As the young people of Cydweli bop till they drop it's moot to imagine what Gwenllian would have made of this centre named after her. She was the polar opposite of Amy Winehouse. Gwenllian was the daughter of Gruffydd ap Cynan, the prince of Gwynedd, who became the wife of Gruffydd ap Rhys, the prince of Deheubarth and the Lord of Ystrad Tywi.[51] He was a brave man and a scourge of the Normans, harrying them constantly. One of them, Maurice de Londres was an implacable enemy who swore he would kill Gruffydd and gathered an army for the purpose. Hearing of this Gruffydd decided to travel north to seek the help of Gruffydd ap Cynan. He left his leaders in charge and set off, taking his eldest son Rhys with him.

On March 1st 1136 a watch party above Mynydd-y-Garreg, which overlooks the castle, heard that a substantial army had landed in Glamorgan and was therefore only two days' march away. Gwenllian suggested that she should thwart their efforts to cross the river Loughor and dispatched the greater part of the army to intercept the Norman army while she would concentrate on ensuring that Maurice de Londres couldn't leave his castle. But by some means – some suggest treachery – the Norman army managed to avoid the Welsh interception and soon they were behind Gwenllian's small force. At the same time Maurice's horsemen charged out of the castle and so she and her men were trapped in a pincer movement. A fierce battle ensued and Gwenllian was finally captured. Her son Morgan was killed and another son Maelgwn was taken prisoner. Eventually Gwenllian was beheaded on a field which is still known to this day as Maes Gwenllian, Gwenllian's Field. You see what I mean about Amy Winehouse. She just about manages to keep her head.

Cydweli stands on the edge of the Gwendraeth estuary which is, quite simply, one of my favourite places on earth. Some of my best teenage days were spent birdwatching here. There's a tang to estuarine air which is seductive and homely. Light reflected by mud and river water has a shimmering, ethereal quality.

To get out there, into the saltmarshy expanses it's best to follow the Bank o' Lord. The Great Marsh between Pinged and Cydweli was often unpassable, as the two rivers, the Gwendraeth Fawr and Gwendraeth Fach, are tidal and estuarine waters reached far inland.[52] You'll still see huge swathes of water on the northern side of the main road after a high tide. So, in 1810, the Earl of Ashburnham raised an embankment to keep out the tide, and it still carries his title if not his name. Later a bridge was erected at Porth y Rhyd, with flood doors underneath to control the passage of waters. Water here is insistent, wilful, sinuous as eels. It creeps in unannounced.

On the face of it this isn't a place where wildlife displays itself at its most plentiful. You have to work hard to find the birds. Navigate creeks and runnels where the mud is so glutinous that it will suck off your boots if you're not careful and maybe do so even if you are. Ford tiny steams where crabs scurry for cover. Walk over swathes of purslane and sea-lavender. But it's all well worth the effort – when a flock of bar tailed godwit scatters in the air or wigeon ducks strike up a whistling chorus, which sounds like the very epitome of a wild place, or the sound of an emphysemic collier. To the west, at Salmon Scar rocks, you can find great numbers of oystercatchers and occasional eider ducks. In Cydweli Quay one might see curlew sandpipers during migration or overwintering warblers. Seek and ye shall find.

One May day I found a fine drake garganey duck, newly arrived from Africa, sitting on the small pond south of the railway line you have cross to get to the Bank o' Lord. One September afternoon, back in 1974, a white-winged black tern made an appearance on Cydweli Marsh, as did an egret, and a smattering of black terns, exotic and dainty, which made the place look like the Rhone delta.

On the forestry side of the estuary, near the RAF bombing range, you'll often flush snipe, which ziz zag away with an angry 'creech,' or the rarer jack snipe which rise silently. I once found myself wandering on the range when the jets started bombing, which raised the blood pressure a bit, especially as clumps of marram grass exploded in the dunes. An irate RAF man who subsequently picked me up on the beach was puce with rage. I'd never seen anyone's face that colour before. I was sorry to have wound him up so much. But he didn't say much after his original flare-up although he did keep on saying 'Range clear chief, range clear' into his radio, like a mantra.

You'll find both fowl and fish hereabouts. The biggest fish to swim up the Gwendraeth did so in November 1889, when it was recovered from the Gwendraeth Fach river just beneath the town bridge, trapped by timbers at the water's edge. It had previously been sighted swimming in the Gwendraeth Fawr, near Commissioner's Bridge. The fish was taken, appropriately enough, to the Pelican hotel, where people paid an admission fee to view the specimen which was almost ten feet in length and seven in girth. It was a tuna fish, a long, long way from its Mediterranean home.

In small towns events tend to magnify in importance very quickly, whther they involve a big fish or a big cheese. One of the most notorious aspects of Cydweli's history dates back to 1920 when a local solicitor, Harold Greenwood, was accused of poisoning his wife with arsenic.[53] She had died in June 1919 with the death certificate noting heart disease as the cause of death. She was buried in St. Mary's Church and in October of the same year Greenwood married one Gladys Jones, the daughter of a local newspaper proprietor. Tongues starting wagging and rumours multiplied and by the end of the month the solicitor was being interviewed by the police. Some six months later Mrs Greenwood's body was exhumed and by the summer Scotland Yard had begun to investigate. Within a week the Coroner's Jury had certified that the lady had died from arsenic poisoning, administered by the husband who was swiftly arrested and taken to Llanelli jail. By July he was committed to the next Carmarthen assizes to stand trial for murder. It took until November for the trial to start at Carmarthen Guildhall but in less than a week the jury had returned a verdict of not guilty.

There hasn't been an arsenic poisoning, or hint of one ever since then. Cydweli keeps itself to itself ever since the bypass was built. It's a little bit sleepy but friendly and simply steeped in history. That's a good mix for an ancient Welsh town.

notes

1. Paul Rees, writing in the *Guardian*, 24th October 2008.
2. Why are Llanelli people referred to as Turks? There are many possible answers, mainly apocryphal, none of them definitive. So pick one you fancy.
   – It's said that there was once a dock strike in Swansea and a Turkish ship tried to come in to port. The Swansea dockers refused to unload it and it sailed on to Llanelli.
   – At the time of the Great War the Fourth Welsh Regiment recruited a lot of people from Llanelli. They were sent to Palestine and during that campaign they defeated the Turks.
   – In tinplate works such as Old Lodge and the Marshfield works men wore turbans or towels on their heads so they best resembled Turks.
   – A more recent part of Llanelli apocrypha has it that in Welsh one part of the shoe is known as the *twrc* and when people were getting boot money in rugby it was 'under the turk.' This, I suspect is the most fanciful.
   – On a recent train journey the historian Peter Stead (from Swansea) suggested that it's a reference to the way the Turks were troublesome during the Ottoman Empire. Peter also reminded me that Llanelli's Cricket Club is one of the oldest in Wales and has produced a fine roster of Glamorgan players.
3. Recalling the moment he scattered his father's remains on the famous Stradey turf in 1989, Mr. Davies said:'I think the Scarlets had stopped the practice of scattering ashes on the pitch as the players were a bit put off at the thought of diving in someone's remains. But I remember saying to a friend of mine Jeff Lee, who worked as a groundsman in Stradey, that I had

my father's ashes in my car. He told me to go for it, so I scattered them on the try line and said a little prayer. It was just me there but the family approved and it's what my father would have wanted. I was shocked when I heard Stradey was going, especially with my father there. It wouldn't be so bad if it was being turned into a park, but to have houses built there was quite upsetting. When I heard that they were taking a token bucket of soil to the new stadium I was happy. I thank the Rev Phillips for deciding that such names should be read out.' The full story can be found at

   http://www.thisissouthwales.co.uk/news/9-000-mile-trip-pay-respects-Stradey-Park/

4. Sosban Fach's origins lie in a song called *Rules of the Hearth*, composed in 1873 by Mynyddog, the bardic name of Richard Davies of Llanbrynmair. In 1895 some comic verses were added by Talog Williams, a Dowlais accountant at Llanwrtyd, but one Rev. D.M. Davies also claimed these as his own. Many people went from Llanelli to Llanwrtyd for holidays and they embraced the new song, especially as the Stamping Works had been opened in 1892. This version of events has been challenged, with letters to the *Llanelly and County Guardian* claiming it was written by Owen Rees of Lakefield Road. Whatever, it's a song that stuck, and can still stir the blood. As the *Cambrian Leader* put it in 1896: 'Sospan fach does seem to have an extraordinary effect upon the Scarlets. The crowd began to sing the ballad of the Little Saucepan…and instantly the old spirit of the Scarlets began to reassert itself and before the strains had melted away, they were over with what had seemed like an impossible try. It was another testimony to the efficacy of the epic of the withered finger and Llanelly's splendid pluck.'

5. Paul Rees, in the *Guardian* obituary published on 2nd November, 2007.

6. ibid.

7. The Llanelly Steel Works were established in 1898 and operated by the Llanelly Steel Company Limited until 1907 when they were incorporated as the Llanelly Steel Company (1907) Limited. The works were then operated by the Iron and Steel Corporation of Great Britain from 1951 until 1960 when they were taken over by Duport Limited. Llanelly Steel works finally closed in 1981 when Duport went bankrupt.

8. Innes, John, *Old Llanelly*, Llanelli and District Civic Society, 2005.

9. What effect do closures have on a town? Paul Sheridan, team leader at the Wallich Clifford in Llanelli describes the social changes wrought in the town. Unemployment can lead to drug misuse:

Communities that grow up around heavy industries, be they mines or steel works see a culture grow where men going out to work each day – macho work, very hard work – with a support network of workingmen's clubs or pubs where they could meet up after work. Women would be at home looking after the children and they would have their own support from other women. At the core of it was the industry – either the pit or the steelworks. Now take away the steel works or take away the pit and then you have the large majority of the men at home now and not working. So the women are then less able to go to other women's houses because they've got the men home. The man is used to drinking in the evenings after work but now starts drinking in the day because he's bored. So the fabric that held the whole town together is starting to deteriorate. You have men who were very skilled, hard working men ending up working up in service industries, places like B & Q. Roles were being reversed as women were starting to go out to work. Men, because they'd worked in heavy industry didn't want to work in somewhere like B & Q or perhaps later in life they didn't have the motivation to retrain because perhaps they were proud of what they'd done all their lives. So now children were growing up with mum at home, clearly defined roles, men were getting confused about what their roles were, women were going out to work now, so the fabric starts changing, and heroin is a very useful tool for some people, in that it can be used to blame for the destruction of a community but in my opinion heroin fills the void, there's a huge void in the community and heroin or any other substance like that can fill the void very quickly.

10. The name Stradey is derived from the Welsh *ystrad*, meaning a level area, a vale. It's a name that recurs quite often in Carmarthenshire, with an Ystrad near Carmarthen and one near Llanwrda. At Stradey the rivers Dulais and Cwm-Mawr meet on a low plateau.

11. In Elizabethan days the word 'park' was used to denote an enclosed field or area, and this might well have been the enclosed meadowland which later became part of the demesne around the residence of the Mansels.

12. Sir David Mansel Lewis is the longest serving Lord Lieutenant in Britain. He followed the traditional trajectory through Eton (where he sang as a schoolboy) and Oxford to join the Welsh Guards in 1946 and became a lieutenant in 1948. He became High Sheriff for Carmarthenshire in 1956 and in 1973 became Her Majesty's Lieutenant, a title which changed to Her Majesty's Lieutenant of Dyfed the following year. He was invested as Knight Commander, Royal Victorian Order (K.C.V.O.) in the New Year's Honours List of 1995. Sadly Sir David passed away as this book was going to press.

13. Interview, *Llanelli Star*, July 16th, 1998.

14. Jeremy Musson, architectural historian and *Country Life* journalist. Quoted in an episode of *The Curious House Guest* on BBC 2 in which he visited Stradey Castle. An invaluable watch for writing this chapter.

15. In the sixteenth century the windows would have been made up with lots of little leaded panes but in the 19th century everyone wanted the latest thing – one big pane of plate glass – which George Gilbert Scott, the architect of St. Pancras station called 'the most beautiful and useful invention of our age, calculated to bring cheerfulness to the elevation of a house.' This number of large windows was only affordable because both excise duty on glass and window tax had been abolished in the 1880s.

16. Literally, people of the stalks.

17. The Burry Port & Gwendraeth Valley Railway was built in the late 19th century primarily to carry coal from collieries in the Gwendraeth Valley. In 1909 it was officially converted to carry passengers (though it had done so illegally for a number of years previously). Passenger services eventually ended in 1953 but the line remained open to serve collieries until 1996 when it was closed. Tracks are still in place for most of its length from where it branches from the West Wales line to Cwm Mawr, though in many places the tracks are now completely covered with shrubs and weeds.

18. Loose translations run as follows: Bank of the Wave, Sound of the Wave, Marsh Shore, Edge of the Sea, Sea Breeze, Sea Side, Anchorage, Crest of the Wave, Gower View and Wave Cliff.

19. See chapter on National Wetlands Centre, built at Penclacwydd.

20. 'Cil' is probably derived from the Irish suffix, and is found in other locations nearby such as Cwm Cilferi near Trimsaran and Ciliau Gwyn near the village of Furnace. My thanks to Ian Morgan for this information.

21. The stone has been largely overlooked by historians and antiquaries. It was dug up in the kitchen garden of the house during building works in the early 1900s and was initially thought to be an old gate post until the incised cross was noticed. Lady Howard Stepney then had it set upright in front of the house. Northwest of the building is an enclosure known in the schedule of tithes as 'Cae Main' or 'Stone Field'. This enclosure is the kitchen garden where the pillar was found. Lady Stepney translated Cilymaenllwyd as 'Retreat of the Sacred Stone'.

22. Edwards, John, *Llanelli: Story of a Town*, Breedon Books, 2007.

23. ibid.

24. This is Holy Trinity Church in Pwll.

25. My own memories of the place are rather painful. Back in the 1980s when I worked as currrent affairs journalist for HTV I covered a story involving an old man who was in a nursing home at Cilymaenllwyd. He'd been tied into his chair using bandages and was left to feed himself. The chair fell over and he choked to death. In order to make the

programme a local woman had to turn whistleblower and risk losing her job, which she did.

26. Opened at the end of the 1950s the Carmarthen Bay Power Station cost £25 million and was designed to generate 300,000 kilowatts of electricity.

27. A great deal of the historical material in this chapter was gleaned from D.G. Lloyd Hughes' charming eponymous book about the Burry Port Reading Room and Club. I gratefully acknowledge Mr. Hughes' book as a valuable source.

28. Davies, Russell, *Secret Sins: Sex, Violence & Society in Carmarthenshire 1870-1920*, University of Wales Press, 1996.

29. George Elkington and his brother Henry are still regarded as the pioneers of electro-plating, securing a number of patents between 1835 and 1845.

30. The Burry Port Smelting Company added a Lead Works to the Silver Works, so that both lead and silver were produced at the same site. It was known locally as the Blue Lead Works.' A White Lead works, making material to be used in the production of paint, etc was built in 1870.

31. The crow thinks its chick is white.

32. The Burry Port Smelting Company added a Lead Works to the Silver Works, so that both lead and silver were produced at the same site. It was known locally as the Blue Lead Works.' A 'White Lead' works, making material to be used in the production of paint, etc was built in 1870.

33. Hughes, Gareth, ed. *A Llanelli Chronicle*, Llanelli Borough Council, 1984

34. The stimulus for the creation of a racing circuit at Pembrey was the closure of the motor racing facility at Llandow near Cardiff. In 1981 the Welsh Race Drivers Association (WRDA) was formed with the expressed intention of developing a new race circuit in Wales. At the same time the former RAF airfield was acquired by the Borough Council, which had been used a chicken farm. Following a representation by the WRDA the decision was taken to construct a racing circuit at the venue. The first race meeting was held on the 21st May 1989, and the winner of the first race at the circuit was Nigel Petch in an MGB. In 1990 the British Automobile Racing Club signed a 50 year lease to operate the circuit on behalf of Carmarthenshire County Council. The circuit has hosted the British Touring Car Championship twice, in 1992 and 1993 at which time the championship was the most popular motorsport series in the UK outside Formula One. The circuit has seen the likes of Ayrton Senna and Alain Prost testing McLarens here while Arrows, Jordan and Benetton have also trialled cars at Pembrey.

35. Thomas Lloyd, Julian Orbach and Robert Scourfield, *The Buildings of Wales*, Yale University Press, 2006.

36. Some of the shipping was for pleasurable purposes. A steamer, the *Usk* ran to Tenby from Pembrey in the summer months.

37. Ashburnham is a peerage going back to 1689 with a Bertram Ashburnham being beheaded by William the Conqueror.

38. The subsonic booms caused by Concorde would have been as nothing to the enormous bang heard in Pembrey in 1882 when seven died as a load of dynamite exploded.

39. Jim Griffiths became the MP for Llanelli in 1936. He was to become the first Secretary of State for Wales.

40. Hughes, Gareth, ed. *A Llanelli Chronicle*, Llanelli Borough Council, 1984

41. I never thought I'd find myself quoting Wikipedia but there had to be a first time... http://en.wikipedia.org/wiki/Pembrey

42. ibid.

43. Winston is an amiable, neatly turned out figure and seems the sort people would like to do business with. He's crammed a lot in before coming home to Wales. After an early appren-ticeship in electronics, he then did his National Service with the Welsh Regiment which took him to a tense Suez, fractious Cyprus, and Kenya during the Mao Mao rising, then B.O.A.C.

before it became British Airways, a stint as a commercial pilot for Royal Worcester ceramics in Tonyrefail and then, when he'd racked up sufficient command time flew for a subsidiary of American Airlines out of their Dallas hub. When the Boeing 747 came in, causing a glut of pilots, he was furloughed, as American business euphemistically puts it. He then went back to electronics and ended running his own firm called Celtic Engineering, which was fortunate to have contracts with telecommunication giants such as AT & T, Bell telephone and Nortel.

44. http://www.pembreyairport.com/?page=history
45. At the end of the Second World war the Carmarthenshire Joint Planning Committee discussed the possibility of developing a transatlantic airport at Pembrey, although a site in Glamorgan, now Cardiff International Airport, was also in the frame.
46. Ivor Jones' *Airfields and Landing Grounds of Wales: West*, Tempus, 2007 was an invaluable source for the history of Pembrey Airfield. It's clearly the work of an extraordinarily well informed enthusiast.
47. Considering Llanelli's recent growth as a centre of Polish immigration it's appropriate to note that No. 315, the Polish City of Warsaw squadron was formed here in February 1941 and equipped with Hurricanes. The squadron was dogged with trouble, from inadequate training and ground personnel to deficiencies in the equipment. One of the biggest problems happened to be the guy running the show, the British Commander, Squadron Leader Donovan, who found fault with everything, down to the way the mechanics wore their scarves. Dutch squadrons followed the Poles as the site developed as a centre for gunnery training, with a range of aircraft stationed here, from Battles to Lysanders.
48. Owain is sister to Eleri and they're the fabulous children of my oldest school friend Gareth Harries and his wife Cerys. They live in the Old Vicarage in Cydweli and I don't see them half enough.
49. In what has to be the least academic footnote in this book I have to record that I gleaned this information from the back of a mug I found in the kitchen. It was given to me many years ago when I went to give a talk to Cydweli Rotarians. I knew it would come in handy some day.
50. For much more information look at http://www.castlewales.com/kidwelly.html
51. http://www.bbc.co.uk/cymru/deorllewin/papurau_bro/cwlwm/newyddion/mehefin03.shtml
52. Odd name, I know. Pinged, which means wet grassland, is still set amidst mainly wet grassland today. Pyngettes is a word that occurs in the Muddlescombe deeds in the 15th century.
53. Hughes, Eric, *Kidwelly: Memories of Yesteryear*, self published, 2003. An invaluable source of local history.

NORTH

FFOS LAS

It's not the most obvious use for a former open-cast coalmine. Most of the ones I've visited over the years have been returned to low-grade agricultural use after the coal has been scooped and scraped out. But at Ffos Las, near Trimsaran, pretty much half way between Llanelli and Cydweli, they're creating a race course. And it's not just a bit of grass fit for trotting races, either. This will be the real McCoy – Wales' third proper racecourse and the first National Hunt Racecourse to be built in the UK for eighty years.[1] Try out the litany. Goodwood. Kempton. Cheltenham. Taunton. Epsom. Ffos Las. It sounds like a different proposition.

The one-mile, four-furlong oval track will host both National Hunt and Flat Turf racing and was five years in the planning before the diggers moved in last year. But now they're off. Almost. The first phase of the scheme includes a 1,000 capacity grandstand, a parade ring and a winner's enclosure. While ensuring the public can see everything but are kept away from horses as they are dangerous animals. At Ffos Las there will also be hotel facilities and new housing. It's a vision located firmly at the bold end of the spectrum. Following the grand opening, racecourse training facilities and an equestrian centre will be built – and used as a training base for competitors at the London 2012 Olympics.

The course utilizes the old 600 acre opencast mine site which operated between 1983 and 1997. I remember watching the outsize trucks carrying their huge tonnages around the snail's horn roads which ran along the sides of the enormous maw of the

excavations. They looked like Tonka toys, built to last. Then the land here was black and grey and dusty. Now it's turf green. When I visited the site they were coming into the final furlong to use the parlance. Building work was cantering along and racecourse chiefs hope to establish a Celtic festival at Ffos Las around St. David's Day 2010 to attract the Irish horses and punters in the build-up to the Cheltenham

Festival. Ffos Las' proximity to the Welsh ports that link with Ireland means the huge Irish racing following is just a ferry boat away, not to mention the untapped market of west Wales. But business starts long before that with first meeting on June 18th. And a grand opening in high summer. So they still have to crack the whip.

Sixteen meetings a year, sanctioned by the British Horse Racing Board, have already been scheduled for the course, which will create up to 100 permanent jobs in the area. Initially the idea was to have the course nearer to Pembrey but that didn't work out for various reasons, from funding flow to the proximity of the site to an active M.O.D. area, with the attendant volume of noise.

Being a racehorse owner, Walters' Group boss David Walters had picked up on the fact that there isn't a racecourse in west Wales.[2] He knew the business case made solid sense, but he needed a good site for it. Serendipity was on his side. The group happened to own the area of land originally owned by Celtic Energy, which Walters had acquired early in the new millennium. He saw the bright dawn of a big idea when he realized that they had a former open-cast mine in an area close to Carmarthen and Llanelli, convenient for the M4 and for the Irish ferries which come into Pembrokeshire, and all in a lovely setting. All they had to do was fill, fill, fill that hole. Well, not quite.

The scheme was on the drawing board for five years and was unique because no one had built a course from scratch. In the past a course might have started with someone putting up rails in a farmer's field, the place accreting as bits were added on over time. Because they had a *tabula rasa*, a blank canvas, it gave them an interesting advantage. They could design it to work for animals, jockeys, punters and turf accountants. The British Horseracing Authority have had a big say in the layout of the buildings and the track, and there's been specialist advice from Mark Kershaw, who used to be the managing director of Newbury, and before that Ayr.

In such a rainy area drainage is a key factor so they built from the ground up and tested as they went, adapting the drainage system according to what they learnt. Nick Rolfe is the project manager, commuting three hours every day from his Cardiff home. He's relished the task of taking a filled-in quarry and turning it into one of the premier racing surfaces in the country. For him and his team this is a different sort of job and he had precious little knowledge about horse racing when he started. Nick would barely pause on the channel if he came across horse racing on TV but now he lingers a while, looking at how they've set up the parade ring and so on. Powell Dobson, the architects of the site, probably don't have that many race courses in their portfolio. They're not two-a-penny jobs.

Nick had only ever been to one racecourse, at Chepstow. There, he recalls, the horse disappears from view for much of the time. "Here we've got a very flat surface with a very even going although it is cambered for drainage. Wherever you stand in the enclosure and the grandstand you can see everything. The sun is always behind the visitors, so they're not looking into the sun for the home stretch."

In one sense this *is* just another construction job and Nick apologizes for sounding cold when he explains it's the same as if they were building a road in a circle or a hospital. Yet this one has grown on him. 'Motivation is a massive factor in construction – working outside in Welsh weather isn't that much fun. If you get a unique project it does get under the skin: no one's done this for eighty years. I'm immensely proud – everyone I know will come here. I just love it, I love the place and can't wait for the pressure to be off and for the place to open.'

And the pressure is most certainly on. His deadline is race day. He says they'll make it, even if he has to pick up a hammer and a saw himself to make sure. Nick points out that much of the work they've done here will be invisible to visitors. They may end up spending between £20 and 25 million on the project, but the buildings and grandstand only cost £3 million, so there's another £22 million that people won't realize has been spent.

Nick suggests that the great benefit of site, and thus of the course, is the natural bowl and amphitheatre. Well, sort of natural. Three million tons of earth were moved to form the shape of the place. Then

140,000 tons of topsoil had to be imported from Pembrey to put on the surface of the track and 30,000 tons of sand placed on top of that. They had to cross the river Morlais, which flows away towards Llangennech. This meant building two bridges, running the river under the racecourse with two tunnels: all in all a massive engineering project. Thirty-five kilometres of drainage was installed beneath the track so

every seven metres there's a drain running sixty metres across the track. 'There's also another drain running at right angles to those every two metres which isn't even included in the 35 kilometres so I don't even want to add those up really. There are two kilometres of roads that all have gas, water, electric and telecoms in. There's 18 acres of housing we've sold, there's an area set aside for a hotel, pub and commercial complex. We've created river walks, we opened bridleways which had been closed for twenty years, and made two wetland lagoons. All the water that falls into the drains is harvested into those lagoons, then we pump it back to irrigate the track. We harvest all the water that falls in the buildings and car parks into those lagoons. We've brought gas to the edge of the village of Carway so it's a commercial prospect for a developer to run gas in.' Phew! Take the weekend off.

Along the way there were lots of unexpected tasks. They had to collect reptiles and amphibians such as slow worms, grass snakes, toads, lizards and move them in buckets into an area that was not being developed. This was to clear a big area to be turned into a roundabout. In order for building work to continue they had to have five 'reptile clear' days. First catch your reptile. They placed roofing felt on the ground because the animals like the heat there. Ffos Las' own ecologist let them know when there was nothing under the felt anymore and thus the days were reptile clear.

There was other wildlife to protect as well, such as the orchids which bloomed hereabouts. And sometimes compromises had to be made, such as scaring birds away so that they couldn't nest. Lapwings had bred at Ffos Las, so they had to put up a bird-scaring fence and even had people chasing birds on quad bikes to make sure they nested in the area set aside for them. Should the birds have nested on the construction site itself then the workers would have had to down tools. Other environmental work involved installing resting pools for sewin to come up a river that hasn't seen this fish for many years.

To invest this much time and energy needed faith and a clear sense that if they built the course people would come. It was clear that the horse racing audience was already well established. If one attended races in the south west of England you would see and hear people from south Wales. West Wales is, indeed, an area with a great deal of interest in racing, but in the past there'd been no local racecourse to go to, the nearest being Chepstow, which is a fair run, if you pardon the weak pun.

Interest in racing is running particularly high at the moment as

Welsh trainers have been doing very well. Fifteen or twenty years ago a venture such as Ffos Las would have been reliant on trainers bringing quality horses from England and from Ireland but now people like Peter Bowen, Evan Williams, Tim Vaughan and a lot of trainers right across south Wales can bring quality horses. It also means interest is high among the west Walian, the local public, because they take an interest in local horses.

So it wasn't a case of fill in big hole, then plant grass. 'Getting the layout of the track right was crucial,' general manager Jon Williams explains, 'so we've gone for a big galloping track really, which means big long straights and wide bends and that means that it's going to appeal to more trainers, horses and jockeys than a lot of other courses. We had to import some quality topsoil and mix the soil with sand to get the drainage right because fifty inches of rain falls here in an average year. This is exceptionally high and in racing it's important because if you get water pooling on the track it becomes too dangerous for the horses to run, which is why you see abandonments because of weather.'

They're keen to make visiting Ffos Las a social occasion, though I imagine it won't be as swanky as Ascot. There won't be the same sparkling freshets of champagne, or the hampers in the boot of the Rolls. You can tell I've been there. Just the once. Found the accents laceratingly troubling.

Ffos Las aims to offer more traditional race meetings: a fifty-fifty split between the enthusiasts who follow horses every day, know the trends, who's successful and who's not, and the other less knowledgeable folk who enjoy the buzz of having a bit of a bet, don't go overboard but enjoy a bit of a flutter. They aim to make it a social occasion with their friends – a get together. And as it's a compact site, people don't have to traipse too far, a good thing in this leisure age.

There will be betting, of course. There'll be the peripatetic bookmakers who move around from Chepstow to Kempton or Wolverhampton or wherever, racking up the road miles. Bookmakers based in south Wales will see Ffos Las as a Godsend because it's only an hour down the road. There has been a lot of interest more generally in the industry as influential trainers such as Nicky Henderson and Barry Hills have beat a path to Ffos Las, greeting what they see with enthusiasm.

On the course punters will be able to place bets in the traditional way with on course bookmakers positioned in front of the stand and in the so-called betting ring. There'll also be a betting shop in the stand, just like the high street shop where you can place bets on other races in the country or on the football going on at the time elsewhere. There'll also be pool-betting run by the Tote. This is a bit like the Lottery: everyone who's on the course bets on a horse but the money goes into a pool.

Jon Williams gives me the lowdown, as it were. 'People who are used to having a bet would tend to go to the ring to look for the best price, the difference between 10 to 1 and 9 to 1. If you choose pool betting you get a nice lady behind the counter. It's less brash, a softer bet, if you like.'

I ask Jon what the Unique Selling Proposition is of Ffos Las. He readily admits that there are lots of nice courses up and down the land such as glorious Goodwood. Cheltenham has its rolling hills. Chepstow is blessed with an attractive setting in the Wye. But he maintains that Ffos Las is unique because it's in a bowl, surrounded by hills. 'You can look up the Gwendraeth Valley or down to the Carmarthenshire coast. People who visit here are astounded when they find out that it was former open cast mine. We're an hour and a half's drive from any other course so in that sense we're on our own. We have an opportunity therefore to reach people who have never gone racing before. The other thing is that we're going to try to emulate or generate an Irish style atmosphere – such as that you find at Punchestown. We appreciate that we're in a part of west Wales that's very proud of its heritage. We'd like to help underline that.' He's proud of such a big project that has worked without public finance, yet will still create jobs.

Jon Williams admits the chill economic winds that currently blow will be an extra challenge and concedes that they wouldn't choose to be opening a brand new attraction in a recession. But he suggests that the fact it's a new attraction might mean they'll be in a financial bubble.[3] He also knows they'll have a lot to learn in the first year, that until they put a few thousand people in the enclosure they won't know how the whole place works. But already they have achieved a heck of a lot. And done so at a gallop.

TRIMSARAN

The name of the village explains its location perfectly: 'trum' means mountain and 'sarn' means road,[4] and this village is set alongside a road that rises up over the crest of a mountain, or least what passes as a mountain in south Wales. It would be a hill in Scotland, but rise like Kilimanjaro above Lincolnshire, say.

Once an agricultural community, all that changed with the advent of coal, which led to the creation of almost forty collieries in the area. As with so many villages in Wales, coal was king and colliers its willing servants, and the black diamonds created the village we see today. Mining ceased at the Trimsaran Colliery in 1954 after eighty years and many of the old mines disappeared under the garagantuan Ffos Las open-cast development, which scooped out and buried, among other things, the site of Trimsaran Hall, once a stately presence in the landscape going back to the Age of Princes.

As the land hereabouts was rich in underground deposits, ironworks were started here. In 1843 the Trimsaran Iron Works were established, attracting a substantial workforce from Staffordshire. A brickworks in the village, opened in 1984, was renowned for the durability and hardness of the bricks it manufactured. These were used to build Fishguard Harbour and the network of tunnels at the Tre-cwn military site in Pembrokeshire. Another aspect of Trimsaran industry was the Patent Fuel Works, which opened in 1883.

But coal shaped things. And where there were miners there was thirst and where there was thirst public houses mushroomed. In 1871 the village of Trimsaran had seven public houses, the Colliers Arms, the Miners Arms, Trimsaran Arms, Royal Oak, Star, Pelican and the New Inn. Later came The Bird in Hand, which had a pub sign summing up this relationship, showing a collier carrying a canary. The bird was used in the era before the Davey lamp, to warn of methane underground. My collier grandfather kept them, cross breeding them with captured greenfinches and linnets. They sang piping symphonies and chattered like diminutive fishwives.

Disaster came in other guises. Ten lives were claimed in 1923 when the spake at the Trimsaran Colliery, carrying eleven carriages and eighty people, broke free. It must have been a terrifying death, hurtling to ground zero in pitch dark.

The village has produced quite a few people of distinction, such as the journalist Owen Picton Davies,[5] but it is really famous for its rugby players. It's a factory, squirting them out like sausages, which are then used to feed the Llanelli squad. One of the first Welsh internationals to come from Trimsaran was Les Williams, who was brought up in Llandab cottages.[6] His first game for Llanelli was against New Zealand in 1945 and he went on gain five rugby union caps and fifteen caps for rugby league. Another luminary was Derek Quinnell, who was raised in Garden Suburbs – an area which was also home to

Jonathan Davies and Garan Evans. Derek joined Llanelli Youth in 1964 and continued to play for the Scarlets for eighteen years, during which time he racked up 366 premier games, scored 44 tries and captained the side. He also played for Wales on twenty-four occasions, both played for and captained the Barbarians, and went on three Lions tours. His sons have followed suit, playing rugby like the sons of a lion.

Just to prove that Trimsaran is a factory when it comes to rugby players, Nigel Davies is also a son of the village, a man who played 360 games for Llanelli, taking part in a record eight cup finals. He also won twenty-nine caps for Wales as well as taking the captaincy.

And nowadays the village is synonymous with the name Jonathan Davies, the rugby fly half who started his rugby career here. His father Len had played centre for both Llanelli and Swansea and was made captain of Trimsaran RFC. Even as a young lad Davies had showed promise, playing sevens at the village primary school under the tutelage of his teacher Meirion Davies. Despite his size he proved to have stature, a point not lost on Carwyn James. Soon Jonathan was representing West Wales in the Under 12s competition at Cardiff Arms Park.

All young boys have heroes but he had one in particular: 'I had so many heroes when I was growing up, with Wales being so successful in rugby. Georgie Best, Maradona, John McEnroe, Muhammad Ali – people like that who, when they did something in sport, brought me to the edge of my seat. If I were to pick one person over and above those, because of my upbringing and background, it would be Gerald Davies who played on the right wing for Wales, the Lions and the

Barbarians. He came from a very, very, very small little village called Llansaint, and every time he had the ball he was fantastic. We came from similar backgrounds, and are of a similar stature.'[7]

After leaving Gwendraeth Grammar School the pint-sized Jonathan became an apprentice painter and decorator, signing for Neath RFC in 1982 and 35 games later being asked to don the Wales shirt. His first game was against England where he scored two tries and was named Man of the Match.

He recalled the feeling when he donned the Welsh top with a mixture of pride and exhilaration: 'I think when you represent your country at any sport it is a magnificent feeling. It's first of all a surreal moment – you've dreamt of it as a little kid – I was Gerald Davies, I was Gareth Edwards in my back garden. I listened to Bill MacLaren commentating on them and then you're listening to them commentating on you. When I gave up playing I was fortunate enough to share the microphone with Bill so it's been great.

'But nothing ever replaces, or comes anywhere near, the first time I played for Wales. Running out against England at the Arms Park, all my family and friends and people who'd coached me from the age of eight, the dinner ladies in the school to the women and wives in the rugby club, people who marked the pitches and cleaned the changing rooms; they were all there supporting me. I felt they were all a part of my success and when I ran out it in the red jersey it was just a very emotional, exhilarating feeling.

'My father died when I was 14 and he wanted me to play rugby and enjoy it, and I thought of him then and how proud he would have been, so it was just a magnificent feeling playing for Wales.'

The Neath captaincy followed on from Davies' Welsh debut and he played an important role in the 1988 Triple Crown success. Between 1985 and 1997 he won 37 rugby union caps.

In 1988 Davies switched codes, leaving Llanelli to play for Widnes where he experienced winning the World Club Championship. Three years later he swapped hemispheres and moved to Australia to play for the Canterbury Bull Dogs. A year later he was back in north west England, having signed for Warrington.

Personal circumstances forced him to move back to Wales when his wife Karen was diagnosed with cancer. Jonathan joined Cardiff RFC and in 1996 he was awarded a MBE. Sadly, his wife died in 1997.

He ascribed his success to one thing: 'I think attitude is the main thing. Having not been successful in getting any recognition at any schoolboy or youth level, I just wanted to show people I could do it, irrespective of honours at a young age. And I kept on training with my village, Trimsaran, and had the kind of attitude that wasn't going to fail me really. I always knew I had something, even if other people couldn't recognise it. I just trained and trained and the opportunity came, and once that opportunity came I took it. It was maybe the fear of failure, but I put it down to a real mental toughness, that I wanted to be successful and try to overcome every obstacle that was put in my way.'[8]

After his playing days were over Jonathan became an effective and popular broadcaster, with his own light entertainment show in Welsh and regular slots covering rugby for the BBC, where his sharp opinions gained respect. After what must have been some dark emotional days and years he married Helen in 2002, with his long-time friend Ieuan Evans as best man.

Trimsaran is a traditional coal mining community that's seen the mining drift away. It's greatest legacy is its rugby players, men as hard as anthracite and shot through with flair and passion. And so many of them, too. Must be something in the water.

FURNACE

I had arranged to meet local historian and Furnace enthusiast Lyn John in the car park of the Stradey Park Hotel, a place with some unfortunate memories for me. When I was in secondary school I worked here as a waiter – even did silver service – though I suspect they seldom actually broke out any real silverware. I was taught some important things early on, such as how to take change back to parties of drunks in the form of as many coins as they could spare at the bar. Invariably the tipsy drinkers would wave the tray away, which you could then exchange for notes. It was a fairly lucrative way of skimming cash and my natural boyish appearance stood me in good stead. So I liked waiting at table. But then, one night, I had an accident, managing to pour an entire tureen of scalding soup down a woman's back. My plaintive offer of complimentary sherry did nothing to stifle her screaming and sobbing or placate the anger of her fellow diners. Standing in the car park brought it all flooding back.

Lyn, who works as an electrician at Trostre, told me how the Stradey Park Hotel stands on the original site of a mansion house called Bryn y Môr, home of the Raby family, which played a pivotal role in the early industrialization of the town. As we walk out the hotel's main entrance he shows us houses to the left of us that would have been stables and intimates that the river Gille is flowing underneath our feet.

Pre-industry the village of Furnace was known as Cwmddyche, where there was a farm of the same name. The name is said to mean pleasant or useful valley. Lyn and I pass the location of Ynys y Cwm, a smaller mansion, originally built as part of the furnace complex in the village which included a weighbridge-cum-railway station for the iron and minerals which would be brought down the valley. We then follow the main road leading to Five Roads and Pontiets, which was created relatively recently, about 150 years ago. Before that the main throughfare cut along Penyfai Lane, now a well-to-do enclave. Along our brief route we note a wall which is all that remains of a house called the Dell. It was owned by the Stepney family and at one time was called Furnace House. It was said to have been built by Alex Raby, and was demolished in 1972 or 1973.

Alexander Raby Sr. was an ironmaster who originally worked iron in Cobham in Surrey and other parts of eastern England, making iron goods such as barrel hoops, knives and wagon wheel rims. At Cobham he mainly manufactured rolled iron and had to import pig iron, so he thought he'd cut out the middle man and make pig iron himself. Llanelli was ideally suited to supply it.

Coal was the other magnet. Raby dealt with the Mansel family, working numerous coal mines in, or rather under, the Mansel estate, such as Caemain, Cae'r Elms and Caebad. His son, Alexander Junior was a shipbroker, dealing with the shipping trade in Llanelli. You can appreciate how felicitously sited Bryn y Môr house was, with a commanding vantage point over the Burry estuary, so Alexander Raby could see ships coming in along the channel and know when his goods were going out.

Legend has it that when Raby Senior arrived in the town in around 1796, he crossed the Falcon Bridge in a wagon train bearing his family, his possessions and a large chest of gold. He certainly had the Midas touch when it came to his early ventures, although later speculations saw him come somewhat unstuck. He was described as 'tall, handsome, high-minded, eccentric, always doing strange acts of kindness'.

As we clamber over a fence into a woodland which is dark green in early morning light, Lyn explains that he has lived in Furnace for the past twenty-four years and finds it exciting that this is where Llanelli's industry started. He thinks it extraordinary that some people who live in the village don't even know there's a furnace here, let alone where it is. This was the epicentre of transformation: Llanelli was a fishing village until Raby brought his industrialist's energy to the area, creating a demand for housing and attracting other industry.

We are heading for the very birthplace of the industrial revolution in Llanelli, following the route taken by the trams that brought down quarry rock to build it. The river in the valley is only mildly boisterous after nightime rain. Part of this valley was formerly dammed and was known as Furnace Pond, gathering water to supply energy to the furnace, but the waters were drained and the dam deliberately breached because of the dangers of its collapsing and flooding parts of the village downstream.

The furnace wasn't the only building of course. There were lime kilns near the site, and numerous other buildings associated with iron making, but they're long gone. There were also roasting houses to roast coal to make coke. North east of the site there used to be another house, now called Cae

Mawr cottage – quite a large building – owned by Raby's other son, Arthur Turner Raby, who went into business partnership with his father. And in order to bring the minerals from Castell y Garreg near Llandybie and Cross Hands, Raby decided to build a railway connecting with the Carmarthenshire Dock, later to become the first operational mineral railway in the world under Act of Parliament.

Lyn explains how the furnace came to be built: 'Two gentlemen, Thomas Ingman and John Gevers, had borrowed money from Raby to build the furnace but he foreclosed on them eight years later in 1796 and took over the furnace. He then built a second furnace at a boom time for furnaces toward the battle of Trafalgar and the French Wars before that. There had been a threat of invasion and there was a great demand for the cannon and shot which he made for the Board of Ordnance. He may also have been making cannons and cannonades, small short cannons firing heavy rounds, known by some as "smashers"'.

The furnace itself is something Coleridge would have approved of, draped with such shrouds of ivy it looks like a Gothic ruin. But although nature has reclaimed much and eroded the fabric of the building it has also hidden and protected the furnace from vandalism. There have been many attempts over the years to restore the furnace but costs have proved prohibitive.

In reality it was a sort of big oven, heating up raw ingredients such as iron stone or iron ore, using carbon in the form of charcoal or coke and also employing lime which was used to purify the metal, to get rid of the slag. The resulting iron came out from what was called the tweer at the front.

Lyn shows me the working end of the furnace, namely the hearth. Iron would be tapped at bottom and run out into channels, and then into sub-channels on the side which resembled the sow suckling piglets, which explains the term pig iron. Ingots were then formed. They were then sent to a forge to be rolled out to make workable iron, and the impurities squeezed out so that it became wrought iron.

The hearth would be working day and night. Once lit, the furnace had to be kept going for a month, or even two months because once they started a so-called 'campaign' it couldn't be allowed to go out. Twenty people were directly employed on the site but it also generated work for nearby coal mines, for the wagoners bringing the coal down, for carpenters and stone masons.

The exterior of the furnace is pierced with holes, like arrow slits, designed to penetrate the stone lining of the furnace and thus release excessive heat, mortar steam and assorted vapours, otherwise the furnace would explode. One couldn't build a furnace right next to the rock because moisture would get in and cause explosions, so to be doubly safe the furnace is built off the quarry face.

The inside was lined with refractory bricks, able to withstand great heat. You can still see the firebrick lining. Even though the furnace at Furnace was blown out just after the battle of Waterloo the original firebricks are still here. A tribute to the brickmaker's craft.

We look at where the furnace was 'charged', or loaded, and here the people who would be working were shielded from the elements. 'To the side,' Lyn explains, 'there would have been a huge set of bellows, driven by a water wheel. The mill was continuously driving the bellows to supply oxygen. You'd blast the furnace with air to produce the heat.' Hence the name.

At one time there were four furnaces in Llanelli working day and night to make ordnance. Some made cannons marked A.R. The iron was taken to where Sandy Bridge stands today. At the back of the present day White Horse Inn stood a forge, employing workers who used to live in small hovels, one up one down. They were demolished in the 1930s. As the work expanded so too did demand for workers' accommodation. The history's still there in the names. Pentrepoeth – literally hot village – grew to house Raby's workers. His forge gave its name to Forge Row, and there is Raby Street, in town. At one time business was booming for Raby to the extent that people said that his workers 'eat pound notes on well buttered sandwiches.'

We walk along a bridlepath, heading north now to Trebeddod – Town of Graves. Early Victorian historians said there were burials here. Lyn tells me that the name goes back to the fifteenth century. 'We know that further up the valley toward the north east there was an ancient chapel – there were ruins there in 1835 – the area up the top of the valley is known as Eglwys y Cwm. There was also a place called Tŷ Du where there was reputedly a battle between the Romans and the Ancient Britons, although there is no hard evidence for this, just old, old hearsay. To the east of the reservoir there's a field called Cae Fynwent. Maybe the dead were buried there.' The reservoir is known locally as Furnace Pond. It's a place treasured by coarse fishermen, judging by the number of rods set out early in the morning.

The reservoir was created at a time when there was no healthy water in Llanelli and some of the wells were sited below graveyards.[9] Outbreaks of cholera and typhoid were not uncommon. In the mid-nineteenth century the townspeople realized they could make money by charging ships for clean water. The town had grown too big by 1870s so Swiss Valley reservoir had to be built.

We stop along the way to look at the setting for a gypsy camp which was painted by the Llanelli painter J.D. Innes, and also seek out the imposing rockface in his dramatic painting of Furnace Quarry. We find it with little trouble, although getting to the actual place where he set his easel it looks as if we might need a freshly honed machete to slash our way through.

Lyn is also very knowledgeable on the subject of the Rebecca riots. Though seen as rural these troubles affected Llanelli too. Many people were aggrieved because they were paying money for roads which weren't improved, so they attacked the toll gates under cloak of darkness, sometimes dressed like women.

One night the Rebecca rioters hit Sandy gate – destroyed it – and then Furnace gate was attacked where they hit the keeper in the face with a blank charge from a shotgun. Lyn talks about such matters with enthusiastic passion. I can almost feel the foment of trouble, hear the shouts in the night and the cantering of hooves.

On we walk, with Lyn polishing nuggets of information at every turn. We pass the Castle colliery, or Gille colliery. A local hero, Rees Thomas from Llwynhendy, displayed considerable bravery when he rescued a man here. They'd laid charges underground and withdrawn but one man hadn't come out, so Thomas went in and got him out as the charges went off. The man died, but the Edward Medal was awarded to Thomas, for his sheer selflessness.

We meander past the Mission church, built in 1878, and then the

Furnace rugby club, which stands on the site of the old colliery complex. We used to meet here for underage drinking. Everything was sweetened with blackcurrant in those risky days. Cider and black. Guinness and black and, God help us, Southern Comfort and black. Sophisticated tipple. Appropriately for a village with its own coalmines the Colliers pub is just across the street and Lyn maintains you can't get a better pint of Felinfoel. I underline this in my notes. A man has to have priorities.

The other Furnace pub stands nearby. The Stradey Arms is where Bonesetter Reese was born in 1855, a famous osteopath who treated many Americam politicians, footballers, boxers and film stars. There's a whole book about his bony adventures. It's called *Child of Moriah*.[10]

For less alcoholic drinks you might seek out the site of a local well, Cae Ffynnon Elli. A map of 1814 map shows it, above Furnace rugby field, although it could equally be found at a site down the road. Maybe there are two wells. We pass the former community school which in 1914 had fifty scholars, but is now the local primary school. Now we're walking along a cycletrack which follows the route of the Carmarthenshire tramway created in the 1880s to take advantage of the minerals in Cross Hands. It's now operated by Sustrans. A green way, not a freeway.

We pass the site of Cae'r Elms where there was another colliery operated by Raby and adjacent there were the hovels known as Cae'r Elms cottages, before they were knocked down in the 1930s. We note the entrance to the old Mansel estate and as we go under the Sandy Road bridge we arrive at what used to be old coastline of Llanelli. The river Lliedi used to enter the sea at what is now the Sandy Water Park, but it was diverted to scour the Carmarthenshire Dock. There's a street name here which confirms this: Cae Bad, Field of the Boats near Banc y Llong, the boat bank.

We part company at *Pownd Twym* on the edge of People's Park. This pond was built during the nineteenth century to cool the Old Castle Works, and the island in the middle is the site of an old motte and bailey castle. It's a place where people like to pause awhile to feed the ducks. The water is bottle green. Out in deep water tufted ducks plop under the surface, their ripples like full stops, slowly exploding.

This is a place to pause and consider post-industrial Llanelli. It was a tumultuous birth at Furnace full of noise and ambition followed by a life of hard work and danger. Decrepitude naturally

followed and there are still some buildings which formed part of the Old Castle Works that are yet to be bulldozed, their slates creaky on their rafters. On our walk we have seen glimpses of so much history, so much graft and enterprise, money and misery. Lyn is a time traveller, who's managed to show me some centuries in a couple of hours. A perfect guide.

SWISS VALLEY

Leaving Felinfoel there is a path, muddy and muddier that can take you along the river to the optimistically named Swiss Valley, site of the municipal reservoirs. Or you can go along a better route that follows the old railway up from Pentrepoeth. The name conjures up Julie Andrews singing in alpine meadows and the extravagant aerial shots at the beginning of *The Sound of Music* but the reality is a little more prosaic. There are two pretty and substantial areas of standing water, with trees along their shores, and ducks dabbling the margins. But before we go to Swiss Valley I should mention one building just outside Felinfoel.

During the Civil War one of the prominent Royalists was the Deputy Sheriff of Carmarthenshire, Francis Howell, who lived in an imposing house at Cwm Llethri, or Cwmllethryd, above Felinfoel, which is now Cwm Llethri Farm. The place still has a unique feature, being the oldest building in the county to still have the date of building visible on the outside. Whitewashed over by paint and the centuries the inscription is faded now, but detective work has shown that it carries the initials of F.H., his wife, E., and M.H., his son and the year Anno Dom 1665. Sited on a slope this is a 'whitewashed house with a big upper end chimney. Next to which is a stone stair, lit by small windows with dripstones.'[11]

Possibly the first reference to Cwmlliedi as Swiss Valley came in a work of fiction, *Mary de Clifford*, by Madeline Jones in 1847. This novel centred on the town of Melton, a vile place of dirty streets and thick with coal dust. But Swiss Valley was a very pretty valley. It's a make-believe name, although the lakes formed by the reservoirs, with woodland reaching down to their shores, is pleasant enough a place, fit for a chocolate box cover. Lindt maybe, with a ribbon. I used to hear cuckoos here in the spring, regular as clockwork. But they're gone now as the countryside empties of birdsong. And what happens to poetry then? Will there be no more odes to nightingales? No verse about skylarks? No couplets about cuckoos? When I used to come to Swiss Valley as a young man to do some birdwatching I wouldn't think twice if I saw a song thrush. Now seeing one makes for a red letter day. Dramatic change in less than four decades. It's sobering. Will I be able to show my children the things that were common in my childhood or will they have slipped into extinction? Enough, now, of my ecological concerns, lest I get you down.

Water was, of course, a much needed commodity in Llanelli, both for a burgeoning population and expanding industry. Because the population of the town doubled in the thirty years between 1851 and 1881 and tinplate works seemed to be breeding, a new source of water was needed to replace the Trebeddod reservoir at Furnace. So the site at Cwmllieidi was inaugurated in 1869 but there were many complications as three mills, Felinfoel, Upper and Lower Town Mills, were bought up so the reservoir – three quarters of a mile long and holding 160 million gallons of water – wasn't opened until 1878. The Upper Lliedi reservoir was opened in July 1903 with a capacity of 200 million gallons and at a cost of £38,000.

One effect of creating the reservoirs was to diminish the flow of the river Lliedi, such that it was no longer powerful enough to drive the

machinery of mills downstream, and in 1902 its owners had to install a gas engine at the Felinfoel Mill to drive its machinery. Sadly for a village named after a mill this last mill was demolished in 1973.

One of the most interesting buildings in the area is to be found north of the Lower Lliedi reservoir. The remains of Tŷ'r Heol are those of a single storey farmhouse and byre of a long-house type.

When it was inhabited people would have to enter the house from a cross passage at the top of the byre. Under its tin roof straw rope was used as under thatch.

Swiss Valley is a man made idyll but it's not an Emmental, Sertig or Sernftal. You'll never hear cow bells tinkling here, or be able to walk barefoot through alpine flower meadows, but it's peaceful enough, when the wind blows through the willows and dabchicks dive underwater trawling for sticklebacks. Bring Toblerone.

FELINFOEL

Famed for its beer, the name of the village may derive from a bare mill or a bald mill, although in 1709 there was a Voyle's mill, but whether this was an Anglicized version of the Welsh or whether there indeed was a mill owner called Mr. Voyle is lost in history's mist. Hungover sots refer to the beer made in the village as Feeling Foul. It's unkind but true, but it all depends on how responsible you are with alcohol.

There is some suggestion that there might have been a medieval corn mill hereabouts. There was certainly a mill and mill pond here in 1815 and the various mills that sprouted on the banks of the Lliedi were used to make cloth and grind corn, along with grist, wheat and flour. One of the farms, Glan Lliedi also had a mill, used to power a threshing machine.[12] Coal was only mined at one site, the Llanlliedi colliery, now Pwll Bach farm, which worked the Bushy seam between 1837 and 1842 and was later incorporated into the Gors/Bryngwyn complex in Dafen.

You might easily miss the baptismal pool for Adulam Chapel, or dismiss it as a simple lip or weir in the river but it's worth pausing awhile – just after the fine fish and chip shop and the little round-about opposite the King's Head – to consider the matter of souls, and the cleansing of them in bright waters and how Llanelli was ablaze with Christianity at one time.

There were occasionally enormous crowds to witness the ceremonies at this pool. In 1936 no fewer than a thousand people converged to see the immersion of six candidates, converted by the efforts of one Beryl E. de Vine, the Tasmanian ex-dance hall girl evangelist. The pool was moved in the 1940s to allow the road to be widened.

A few hundred yards away

the most striking thing about Holy Trinity church is the verdigris, the green patina which has covered the copper cladding of a spire that looks as if it might have been airlifted in from Bavaria. It was built in the mid nineteenth century and designed by the architect R.L. Penson for the Nevill family. Before this they had held services in their family homes at Westfa and Felinfoel House. In the graveyard there's a sheltering angel tombstone by Antonio Maraini of Florence: the wings spreading beneficently over the grave of one Ivor Buckley who died in 1921. It's a peaceful place, with the history of the village there for all to read in the inscriptions on the gravestones. Young deaths. Local names. Where they lived. Who remembers whom.

Across the way is the monumental Adulam, a chapel and a half which was designed by a minister from Briton Ferry, the Reverend Henry Thomas. This was the mother church for the other Independent chapels in Llanelli and it has that sort of Welsh mam authority about it – solid and dependable. In the seventeenth century local Baptists had to meet to worship in secret, meeting in houses or even in caves. One such cave was at Goitrewen near Felinfoel.

Then things changed and they no longer had to be so secretive. In 1689 an Act of Religious Tolerance was passed which allowed Baptists to worship openly. Twenty years later, the first Baptist chapel in Felinfoel was built, know as Tŷ Newydd, the New House. It was rebuilt in 1840 when it took the name Adulam. Plain to the point of austerity on the outside it apparently has some fine ironwork inside, with the gallery railed continuously and the *cadair fawr*, or great seat also made of metal, along with the pulpit. Here celebrated preachers such as the dynamic one-eyed Christmas Evans orated. He visited in

1794 and although he was described as looking like a scarecrow his sermon was delivered with fire and zeal. The schoolroom next door is equally imposing in size. It was built by J & B Evans of Llanelli in 1932 and seems big enough to accommodate all the kids of Carmarthenshire in one big noisy Sunday School.

So, Felinfoel, a place for cleansing away sins and establishing chapels. It's not hard to imagine how upset the old ministers with their warnings of eternal flames and brimstone endings would be to know that the village is synonymous with beer. It would leave a bitter taste in their mouths. But then again they had their day, of rapt audiences and religion spreading like gorse fire. You can't drink the past. Onward to the brewery.

FELINFOEL BREWERY

The three liquid wonders
Of this remnant
of the Isle of Britain:
Buckley's Best, gusty as the blood
of Carmarthenshire foxes;
Brains SA, the cosmic urban
Skull Attack;
& Felinfoel Double Dragon.
brewed at last
to transcendent perfection
by Cheesewright the Sais,
one of the three most beneficial
White Settlers who ever came
to this thirsty remnant
of the Isle of Britain.[13]

There's something reassuringly old fashioned about visiting the

Felinfoel brewery, an overwhelming sense of things not changing much unless they have to. Which explains why I love their beer. It's *consistently* delicious. Set against the backdrop of brewery closures and disappearing pubs, it's a bastion against change. And, to boot, you can make a meal of one of their pints. They are champion pints, quite literally. The real Glory Year for the business came in 1976 when Fred Cheesewright was the brewer. Felinfoel won the equivalent of the World Cup of Brewing, gaining not one but two Gold Medals for the best exhibited draught beers.

Felinfoel Brewery is a company with deep Welsh roots, with a heritage going back over 125 years. It's run very much as a family business. They employ forty-four people with a turnover of £6 million. They never have to advertise jobs here as people think that everyone gets to do some sampling and quality control! At least that's what they say. My name's down.

It's a very stable company and proud of its Welshness. Welsh beers are quite a rarity nowadays, with only two major brewers in Wales, and they're also standardbearers for tradition. Felinfoel is also pretty south Wales-centric and although the company's appointed distributors in north Wales to try to capture some of the market there, their core business pretty much focuses south of a line running between Aberystwyth and Brecon. They own 83 pubs in south west Wales though they haven't bought a pub for some six years. It's a valuable property portfolio.

I've come to the brewery to meet Philip Davies, the joint managing director, and later I've been promised a tour in the company of the brewer. It's a salivating prospect. This is after all the home of the National Ale. And I'm no stranger to its delights. Philip isn't a family member but joined the firm fifteen years ago having previously worked in accountancy with British Coal at Betws Colliery in Garnant. He's been general manager, director and is now managing director. Wood panelling in his office gives it an air of British Rail waiting rooms, circa 1950.

'A lot of the characteristics of the beer are down to the actual process and plant,' Philip explains. 'Obviously seasonality and ingredients have a little bit of an impact but basically a lot of the national brewers have moved plant and tried to replicate a beer afterwards and failed abysmally. A lot of it is down to the characteristics of the fermenting – even the shape of the fermenting vessels which impart characteristics into beer. The vessels we use haven't changed much over the years so a lot of the character of the beer is constant, really.'

Philip points out that the process here is heavily reliant on gravity. It's a tower brewery with few concessions to modern technology other than in matters of food hygiene, such as utilising stainless steel instead of the old copper vessels. The water for the process no longer comes from the river Lliedi but they do have an aquifer that's a hundred and twenty feet down that supplies water for the process.

Double Dragon is their mainstay. They've deviated into a few seasonal beers but they're geared up to fairly large volumes. At the moment they're only working to a tenth of their capacity, so to experiment with small niche beers is pretty difficult for them. The brew length – the size of copper that the boil takes – is about 155 barrels. These are the old brewers' barrels holding 36 gallons each, so it's a substantial brew. Currently they're producing 10,000 barrels in a year, but they're capable of producing much, much more.

The brewery founder, David John, owned iron and tinplate works around Llanelli when, in the mid-1830s, he bought the King's Head opposite his home in the village of Felinfoel. This was no ordinary pub but an important coaching inn with its own blacksmith's shop to service the horses. It also had a more worrying feature. Alongside the building, which stuck out into the road, was a toll gate. At the time this gate was like a red rag to an angry bull. The Rebecca rioters, the hard pressed tenant farmers who bitterly resented the road charges on their wagons and animals, were rampaging through Carmarthenshire, destroying toll gates. Feeling was running high against the authorities. David John decided to abandon the king and renamed his tavern the Union Inn.

Like most pubs of the time, it brewed its own beer.[14] It proved

popular and soon his Felinfoel ale was being sold to other houses. As demand increased, he erected a larger brewery in 1878 opposite the pub in the grounds of his house, Pantglas. The imposing stone brewery was erected on his orchard, right up against the road.

The premises became a focal point of the community, employing about fifty people. A villager later recalled, 'nearly every family kept a pig in their garden. When the butcher was booked to kill a pig in the back yard, large cans of hot water were carried from the brewery to scrape and clean the pig. Some people living in the vicinity even carried hot water for their weekly washing. Ladders were borrowed, tools sharpened, any excuse to go into the brewery for a drink.'

On brewing day, farmers from the surrounding area came for the 'sog', the spent grains from the mash tun, to feed their animals. Gradually the brewery built up trade throughout the old counties of Carmarthen, Cardigan and Pembroke, buying pubs as they became available. When David John retired from his business interests, his sons David and Martin took over the running of the brewery, with Llewellyn John looking after the Gorse tinplate works in nearby Dafen. The brewery was registered as a private company in 1906, and in addition produced mineral waters under the Trebuan Spring label, the water being piped from a source above the village.

The family also had mining interests, and in 1908 these almost undermined the brewery. Sinking a well at the brewery to find an additional supply of water, workmen struck a two-foot thick seam of coal, some 12 yards below the surface. But, after due consideration, the John family decided not to work the seam, as it would interfere with the brewery.

Another family joined in the running of the brewery when David John's daughter, Mary Anne, married John Lewis, the manager of the Wern Ironworks. This was later to lead to a serious split in the company, and the initial marriage was little happier. John Lewis was a compulsive gambler, prepared to risk everything on the turn of a card or a throw of the dice. He is reputed to have lost a tinworks on a bet, and would probably have gambled away the brewery except that his wife controlled the shares. He was little luckier in his business life, once buying a worked-out mine into which heaps of coal had been carted to fool potential purchasers.

In the 1920s, the strain became too much, and he shot himself while alone in the brewery office. Undaunted, Mary Anne, a formidable woman, carried on with the business. Her visits to the brewery made a deep impression on the staff. She carried a big stick, and if she was unhappy with the performance of any of her employees, she hit them with it! The stick still hangs in the brewery office today.

These were troubled times at the brewery, but the company's close connections with the tinplate industry were to alter that. Many types of meat, fruit and vegetables had been canned in the nineteenth century, the first food canning factory being established in London as early as 1812. By the end of the century, the can was becoming a common sight on the kitchen shelves. The 1895 edition of *Mrs Beeton's Book of Household Management* includes a picture of a huge array of tinned provisions, including liquids like condensed milk and soup. But tinned beer was another 'can of worms', entirely. Well, not worms exactly, but you know what I mean.

Many brewers were sceptical that drinkers would ever accept beer in a can. Customers expected beer to be on draught from a cask, or in a glass bottle. Advocates of the can pointed out that ale had been enjoyed in pewter mugs for centuries, but few were convinced.

The weekly *Llanelli and County Guardian* recorded the historic moment on 3 December 1935, under the triple heading: 'Canned Beer Arrives', 'Epoch-Making Process at Felinfoel Brewery', 'New Hope for Tinplate Industry'. The paper's report said that the first can of beer was turned out 'without a hitch' in the presence of chairman Martin John, brewer Sidney John – 'who has pursued much research work in connection with the new idea' – and representatives of other brewing and trade interests.

The conical cans were filled on adapted bottling machinery and sealed with a standard bottle top (known as a crown cork). The 10oz cans of pale ale were the equivalent of half-pint bottles. They were then packed in cardboard containers, holding two-dozen cans, ready for dispatch. The newspaper reported: 'One of the most impressive features of the process was its simplicity and speed. Girls, who in the past have handled many thousand of bottles, adapted themselves to new conditions with apparent ease and, once started, the cans were filled and corked with unbroken regularity.'

After trial batches Felinfoel began to produce canned beer for public sale from 19 March 1936. A month later the steel firm of Baldwins issued thousands of leaflets to its workers in south Wales urging them to buy their beer, cider, fruit juices and milk in tin containers instead of bottles, in order to encourage others to follow their example and so stimulate the tinplate trade.

Felinfoel is famous for travelling well. I've had great pints of 'Foel in Dylan's Bar in the Mission District of San Francisco, and remember drinking it with gusto in the Sun public house in Lamb's Conduit Street in London when I was a student. The taste and appearance of Double Dragon exercise many drinkers' minds and cause many to reach for the dictionary or, after a few, for two dictionaries. A quick sample of comparisons and adjectives employed to describe Felinfoel gives you some idea.[15]

Dry as a desert bone
Hint of oak
Caramel malt
Sweet and sour
White fluffy head
Good cap and lace
Diacetyl?
Amber, sweet grain
Citrus taste
Dark and malty
Dark copper and clear
Sourness follows on from the swallow
Mouthfeel slightly soapy
Floral hops
Pilsner/noble hops at first
Then a butter sensation
Then a toastiness
And a lingering bitterness
Ripe fruit or fruitcake
Slight toastiness in the aroma
Slight tea-like spice
Classic English ale mustiness
Hints of sulphur
Chestnut colour
Dusty aftertaste

And it really is all of these and more. Trust me.

Even though the company will always be a real ale brewery and cask beer is important to them, their bread and butter is keg beer. Over the years the company has really refined its filtration processes, which improves the longevity of the beer, filtering down to a few microns. Unlike many other brewers they don't pasteurise their beer so even the keg beer retains many of the characteristics of real ale, but still gains the added shelf life that filtration brings.

The economic downturn has hit them, but not too hard. 'We're weathering the storm better than most,' explains Philip. 'We're down about four per cent on our volumes. If you spoke to some of our competitors they'd be very pleased if they were only down that amount, to be honest.'

The core Felinfoel pubs are what Philip describes as backstreet boozers, very traditional spit and sawdust outlets really which were traditionally built around the heavy industries in the area, where beer was seen as a liquid replenishment for the people who came out from the steel works and so on. It helped promote weaker beers at that time, because drinking five or six pints of strong ale would have had you falling down.

Traditionally the beers of Felinfoel have been slightly sweeter than their English counterparts. They don't use the same hop rates as some of the English beers and the ales themselves are of lower gravity. Not only do you not fall over as often but for the brewer weaker beers mean they can benefit from the Chancellor's Small Brewer Duty Relief Scheme, which can mean paying up to half the normal duty rate, depending on what production volumes are.

The ingredients are pretty straightforward, as Philip explains: 'There's malt which is partially germinated barley which has gone through a malting process – we tend to use the same varieties of malt. Hops from Hereford and Kentish hops – we also tend to try to source as local as we can. We even tried growing our own barley but the greenhouse effect hasn't kicked in enough to make that viable yet. There's a lot of body in the beer, very much of a meal as much of a drink – we haven't cut back on ingredients as some of our competitors have done. It's pure malt so that imparts quite a flavoursome beer – it's quite moreish really.'

John Reed, the man in charge of the brewing, isn't a qualified brewer as such. The last qualified brewer was John Kenny; Cheesewright[16] was his predecessor, who followed on from Graham Kay. John says he got the job because of the principle of dead men's shoes. He'd been at Felinfoel for thirty odd years and picked it up as he went along.

Leaving the office I'm faced with a heck of a climb, a real heart pumper, to start our tour at the top of the tower where the whole process takes place. Gravity runs the show with pumps to augment things. Sacks of malt are lifted up to the malt room by hoist.

The barley smell is seductive. John cracks open some husks to show the white powder they extract from them. On a good day two and a half tons – that's forty bags of barley – go into a hopper.

He maintains the taste of tradition. 'We're using the same old recipes. The way we brew today, apart from the heat exchanger, is the same as it would have been in 1878 when the brewery opened. The coppers have been replaced by stainless steel which is lucky because the coppers were a nightmare. You had to secure the lid when they were boiling. There was a terrible accident once when someone fell into a vat of boiling water, dying three days later.'

He shows me how they use pale malt and crystal malt to give the final colour, and talks about the length of boil and when they add sugar: the longer you boil something the darker it gets.

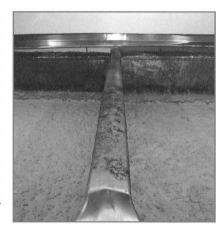

We pause to admire the mash tun. I've never admired a mash tun before and the novelty is disarming. 'It's a simple fusion masher with a rake in it. On the day of brewing we start at eight and we heat this up by sparging hot liquor or hot water through these sparging arms. It's like a garden sprinkler really. We heat it up to 160 Fahrenheit. We'll use two and half ton of malt.'

The tour is like a lesson in a foreign language, all worts, icinglas, gravity, and runnings. I realize we're inside a huge chemistry set, with pipes everywhere. There is even a stage in one of their brewing experiments where they use something called finings – the swim bladders of tropical fish to clarify the traditional beer. I kid you not.

At the end of the tour there's the chance to taste a new pint. I sip it as the Gods do their ambrosia. It's nutty and can make you nutty. A fabulous ale. A sourness follows on from the swallow.

Llanelli Pubs of Old

No more …

Waxing lyrical at *The Half Moon*
Mixing with the *Oddfellows*
Getting bladderwracked at the *Marine*
Getting bitter at the *Beaufort*
Shitting at the *Bull*
Ironic republicans at the *Prince of Wales*
Fishy tales at the *Mermaid*
Getting off yours at the *King's Head*
Gin at the *Bryn*
Roistering at the *Britannia*
Seeing eye to eye at *The Lord Nelson*
Taking in the *Sea View*
Pasties at *Cornish Arms*
Greetings at the *Salutation Hotel*
Getting stuck in at the *British Tar*
Celebrating the *Union Inn*
Being half mast at the *Ship*
Spending more than *Three Crowns*
Malts at the *Marquis of Granby*
Whiskies at the *Wellington*
Drinking at the *Dimpath Inn*
Knocking one back at the *Smiths*
Hoving into the *Dock Hotel*
Feeling morose at the *Trevose*
Wandering the *Globe Inn*
Dancing with the *Old Red Cow*
Friendly jousting at the *George & Dragon*
Laying siege to the *Castle*
Having a ball at *Union Hall*
Riding a *Black Horse*
Surveying the *Royal Park*
Glugging at the *Glanmor*
Weaving your way to the *Cardigan*
Battling for a beer at the *Trafalgar*
Stop tap at the *Albion*
Bringing the *Sailors Home*
Stepping out at the *Stepney*

Racing for the *Greyhound*
Cutting a swathe at the *Barley Mow*
Beating about the *Bush*
Swapping stories at the *Royal Exchange*
Storming the *Dynevor Castle*
Roaring at the *Black Lion*
Evaluating a *Bird in Hand*
Taking pride in the *Golden Lion*
Indian Pale Ale at the *Malabar*
Thwack of willow at the *Cricketers*
Croaking at the *Raven Inn*
Carousing at the *Clarence*
Face to face at the *Bres*
Consorting with *Queen Victoria*
Clearing the pipes at the *Northumberland*
Racket at the *Steam Packet*
Seeing double the *Harbour View*
English ale at the *Rose and Crown*
Whiskies at the *Whitstable*
Drowning in booze at the *Neptune*
Three rums for *Three Mariners*
Pissed at the *Penrhos*
The newt at the *New Inn*
Billiards at the *Biddulph*
Oloroso at the *Old Castle*
Feeling mellow yellow at the *Tŷ Melyn*
Shipshape and *Bristol fashion*
Inebriation at the *Ivy Bush*
Sly ones at the *Swansea Castle*
Meeting old dears at the *Stag's Head*
Sampling the wares at *New Market House*
Sighting the *Welsh Star*
Running *Whitehall*
Battling at *Waterloo*
Rolling home from *Rolling Mill*
Sampling the *Fruit of the Vine*
Locked in the *Pemberton Arms*
On track at the *Railway Station*
On course at the *Railway Hotel*
Getting merry at the *Melbourne*
Getting axed at the *Foresters Arms*

Sinking scrumpy at the *Apple Tree*
Heading for the *North Gate*
Finding *Dead Centre*
Cocktails at the *Cambrian*
Beery *Brecon*
Shining *Star*
Lushing at the *Lamb and Flag*
Pig out at the *Boars Head*
Carousing at the *Crown and Anchor*
Felinfoel at the *Farmers Arms*
Saintly *Thomas Arms*
Fountain of beer
Long way to the *Drovers*
Secretive *Masons*
Heraldic *Rose and Crown*
Weighty *Anchor Inn*
Vodka at the *Vale of Neath*
A busy bar at the *Bisley*
A half at the *Hope and Anchor*
Lush *Green Field*
Ministering *Angel*
Serene *Swan* and *Theatre Vaults*
Mystical *White Hart*
Prosaic *Stevenson's bottling stores*
Losing your bearings at the *Square and Compass*
Imperious *Princess Head*
One last drink at the *Saddler's Arms*
Exploring the *West End*
Marrying the *Ship & Pilot*
Meeting *Friends*
Drinking at the *Dillwyn*
Running the *Ship Aground*.[17]

PARC HOWARD AND HOLLYWOOD

This is where we, as a family, came on summer days to enjoy Walls ice cream and pretend to be rich. The large Italianate mansion sits in its own perfectly arranged and manicured gardens on the road from the town centre to Felinfoel, a gift to the townspeople from Sir Stafford Howard in 1912. When I say perfectly arranged I don't include the new spider web kids' plaything which totally spoils the aspect of the standing stones on the slope facing Pentrepoeth. It was clearly put there by someone who doesn't even know how to spell easthetics.

Once known as Bryncaerau Castle, Parc Howard was erected between 1882 and 1886, using Bath stone, to plans by J.B. Wilson. The architect was related to the Buckley family and his father had rather predetermined his son's architectural course as he himself had been building villas in Bath itself between the 1850s and the 1860s. Like father like son.

In architectural parlance it's roughly a square, two storeys with a very imposing porte cochère. There are balustrades on the roofline decorated with urns and piliastered walls with big plate-glass sashes. One of the most dominant features is the big belvedere tower and inside the main rooms open off what is known as a spine hall. The ghost of a First World War soldier has been seen here along with other ghostly visitations, often glimpsed at day. During the Second World War the mansion was a home for Belgian refugees.

Inside Parc Howard there's an exhibition of Llanelli pottery, including cockerel plates painted by Sarah Jane Roberts, a short dumpy woman known as 'Auntie Sal' who always dressed in black. The fact they were painted in a slapdash manner makes each one unique and they are avidly collected. The most famous painter of plates and cups was Samuel Walter Shufflebotham, who worked at the pottery between 1908 and 1915. His stuff is on display as well, along with a variety of paintings by various artists, which explains

why some of the windows are blocked off to protect the art from the ravages of sunlight.

All municipal museums have one killer story, an account of an unexpected hero. And in Parc Howard the hero is Gareth Hughes, a local boy who made good in Hollywood before becoming a missionary, on what was then known as an Indian reservation before political correctness blew across the prairie. There are photographs of him with his Native American charges and arrays of polished stones he encouraged them to produce. They're absorbing displays.

Gareth Hughes was baptised in Dafen as William John Hughes in 1894 and went to school in Coleshill in Llanelli. At the age of sixteen he decided to tread the boards, touring the UK under his new name, Gareth. In 1914, he crossed the Atlantic in the company of a group of Welsh players, and within two years of setting foot on American soil, he had become one of the youngest, most celebrated and sought after stars on Broadway. In fact he became not only a major player on the stage but also the first Welsh film star.

The more he acted the more the plaudits poured in. The *New York Globe*, reviewing his lieutenant in *Moloch* cited it as 'one of the best performances of the evening, or, rather the whole season.' The *New York Times*, after seeing his Caliban in the city's Shakespeare Tercentenary Celebration noted how the crowd bayed for him. With evangelical zeal Mary Madden Fiske said 'I can believe in acting as an immortal act when watching the glow of a performance by Gareth Hughes', while David Belasco thought his acting 'among the most magnificent that I have ever seen on the English speaking stage.' In the photographs of him on show at Parc Howard the word 'dapper' seems obligatory and 'foppish' doesn't lurk far behind. Indeed, Fulton Ousler remarked that here was 'the charm boy to end all charm boys.'

In *Sentimental Tommy*, made in 1921, his acting was a revelation, said Gilbert Roland, who described it as a role never to be forgotten. This almost gained him a casting as Peter Pan, although he lost out to Herbert Brenon for the starring role in the Barrie classic. He moved to Hollywood in the early 1920s where he became Metro Pictures' boy star. This had a lot to do with his height, standing tall at a mere five foot five. As he weighed only eight and a half stone at the peak of his career it's little wonder that he himself described his speciality as juvenile leads.

As a matinee idol of the silver screen Hughes appeared in no fewer than 45 silent films and two talkies, such as *The Christian*, appearing in a range of movies such as Albert Parker's 1919 feature *Eyes of Youth*, *Mrs Wiggs of the Cabbage Patch*, and *The Chorus Girl's Romance*. At his peak he made $2,000 a week and a home for himself in the legendary Laurel Canyon, which he called Brynmawr. In 1929 the Wall Street Crash stripped him of much of his wealth and to compound his difficulties his accent worked against him in the talkies. In the late 1930s he resurfaced as the director of the Shakespearean and Religious Drama for the Federal Theatre Project of Los Angeles. His last role was Shylock at the Hollywood Playhouse in 1938.

In the early 1940s Hughes experienced a 'calling' to serve God, and after two failed attempts to take Holy Orders he accepted a post as a lay missionary on the Pyramid Lake Indian Reservation at Nixon, Nevada. As Brother David he devoted the next 14 years of his life to the spiritual, physical and financial welfare of the Paiute Indians, although he did return to help in film, coaching the great Bette Davis in the 1945 film *The Corn is Green*, based on Emlyn Williams' three act play from 1938. There had been signs of religiosity earlier in Hughes' life, from his habit of collecting Bibles, to his love of jewels that suggested resplendent altar cloths and stained glass windows.

It wasn't an easy move, as one Bishop Lewis recalled in a letter:

He has a true Celt's emotional approach to other people. He has had a very chequered career attempting to find a vocation in religion subsequent to the end of his Hollywood days. He got far off the beam at one point, but has come back the hard way and accepted work as a lay brother, ministering to our Indians from whom he has a devoted and truly saintly love. He still has some of the faults which spring from his background and there are times he can drive any administrative officer crazy. The ordering of his own work is one of the greatest weaknesses, as he is quixotic and changeable in his plans. It is very hard to get him to build a progress as the sociologist puts it.

On the other hand he is the only white man I have ever known who seems to win immediately the unreserved affection of the Paiute people. He scolds them, cajoles them, and he is fiercely partisan on their behalf. He is the most effective teacher of the simple essentials of the Catholic faith that I have ever known. He is a tireless worker and one of my concerns is that his devotion to his charges will undermine his health. He is still remembered with love and respect by many of those he taught there as children.

But Hughes would sometimes admit that he was nothing more than a ham, even in this priestly role. That said, his life was sufficiently interesting for RKO to suggest a biopic about him in the 1950s. Struck by a late dose of *hiraeth*, Hughes moved back to Llanelli in 1958. But rainfall in Llanelli, which most resembles the sort the Scots call *mirr* got to him. Hughes had grown accustomed to the endless sun-drenching of southern California and he moved back pretty sharpish. He died in the Motion Picture Home in California, where he had his own cottage, on 1 October 1965 and was buried in Reno, Nevada. Just before he died he had baptised the silent film star Clara Kimball Young. He had been accepted as a religious man.

There is also an exhibition at Parc Howard devoted to the invention of the 'revolutionary' Stepney Patent Spare Wheel for motor cars, which is exactly what it says on the tin. In the 1900s the Stepney Spare Wheel Company pioneered in the field with an invention that was 'patented in all civilized countries' with offices in Llanelli, London, Berlin, etc.

Famous people used these spare wheels, including the Czar of Russia, the King of Spain, Andrew Carnegie, the Princess of Wales and the Duke of Oporto.

The advantages of the tyre were listed as follows:

1. It can be fixed to a punctured wheel in one minute, thereby saving the difficult, unpleasant labour, annoyance and loss of valuable time entailed in removing the dirty, damaged tyre, and the substitution, thereof, of the spare tyre. 2. There are no levers or tools of any kind required to fix the Stepney Wheel; it is secured by two simple thumb screws. 3. There is no pumping required on the road, as the Stepney Wheel is always carried pumped hard, ready for use.

I've been told that people in India still refer to the spare wheel as a Stepney. In the same way that people in the Khasi hills in India, who were influenced by missionaries from Wales still say they *cwtsh*, or cuddle their children. It's odd how language works, moving across continents, imported or exported. So before I leave Parc Howard I'll tell you a quick story about language as it's something I discovered quite by accident in Llanelli.

I've worked off and on in television for much of my adult life so was interested to learn that in order to find a Welsh word for television a magazine called *Y Faner* held a competition and the winning entrant, who suggested the neologism *teledu*, won the *Dictionary of Welsh Biography* or some such star prize. One rainy afternoon in Llanelli Public Library I found myself looking through the *Oxford English Dictionary* (as you do when it's raining a *mirr* in Llanelli) and found that the word teledu already existed in the English language and it had as its definition 'a stinking badger from Java and Sumatra.' I could hardly wait to go and tell Geraint Stanley Jones, who was running S4C at the time, what he was in charge of. A herd of badgers? Stinking, certainly. What's in a name?

Notes

1. The two other Welsh racecourses are at Chepstow and Bangor-on-Dee.
2. The man and the money behind the scheme is racing connoisseur Dai Walters, whose portfolio of racehorses is trained at Peter Bowen's renowned west Wales yard and Helen Lewis' Hollies Stables in Cardiff. Walters owns the Walters Group, a 250-man plant hire and civil engineering firm with a £50m annual turnover.
3. Early signs were encouraging. They had annual membership badges for sale and had sold three hundred after just a couple of weeks.
4. The components of the name have changed over the years, as happens with so many names. It's interesting to note that some modern names in England and Scotland derive from the Welsh initially. Dover comes from *dwfr*, the Welsh word for water. Stratford sits upon an *afon*, or river which then becomes Avon. And in Scotland Strathclyde comes from the early Welsh *Ystrad Clud*, the Valley of the Clyde.
5. Owen Picton Davies 1882-1970
6. http://trimsaranrfc.8m.com/halloffame.htm
7. http://www.bbc.co.uk/wales/southwest/halloffame/sport/jonathandavies.shtml
8. http://www.bbc.co.uk/wales/raiseyourgame/pages/jonathan_davies_heroes.shtml
9. Trebeddod reservoir was built behind an earth dam in 1854 to supply water. It was 24 ft deep and had a surface area of 3 acres and held five million gallons.
10. David L. Strickland (1984), *Child of Moriah: A Biography of John D. Bonesetter Reese*, 1855-1931.
11. Lloyd, Thomas, Julian Orbach and Robert Scourfield, *The Buildings of Wales: Carmarthenshire and Ceredigion*, Yale, 2006
12. Felinfoel Heritage Guide. This was invaluable as was walking around the village with one of its compilers, Hugh Morgan Lewis.
13. From Nigel Jenkins, *Acts of Union*, Gomer, 1990.
14. Historians tell us that in the old days the inn brewed its own beer, but only during the winter months. The keeping qualities and the strength of the beers, therefore, were of

prime importance and the popularity of 'Felinfoel Beer' led to this pub brewing for other inns in the locality. This, in turn, led to the present brewery being built in 1878 to accommodate demand.

15. All these descriptions and more can be found on websites such as: http://beeradvocate.com/beer/profile/1310/7403   and http://www.bottledbeer.co.uk/index.html?beerid=592

16. Fred Cheesewright, who was head brewer from 1951 to 1982, claimed that when he arrived the brewery was on the brink of collapse. 'When I first came here, Felinfoel had a terrible name. In one year the brewery lost 30 per cent of its trade. Some houses were selling as little as one kilderkin (18 gallons) a week. We were close to bankruptcy.' It took a long time to turn the brewery round, as the plant and the seventy to eighty pubs had been neglected for some years, the war starving the company of investment. In Cheesewright's period Felinfoel won some of the biggest prizes in the brewing world, a golden age. For much more about Felinfoel visit the brewery's own website.

17. This is based on a list of public houses in Llanelli in 1897 kindly sent me by Huw Morgan Lewis. Not all of them are shut, but in the currrent climate where a pub closes somewhere in Wales every week the future isn't rosé.

CENTRAL

THE CIVIC CENTRE

It's perhaps my favourite building in Llanelli. The old Town Hall is a bit of a stately old lady. Not too well heeled, but heeled certainly and reflecting a time when the town was blessed with a combination of civic aspiration, money and pride. The German writer Goethe said that architecture is frozen music (to which the science fiction writer Michael Moorcock replied therefore music must be defrosted architecture). In the case of the old Town Hall one imagines the music as a roundel, an elegant dance, and the Town Hall as a crusty dowager, whose clothes have a patina of moth dust as she creaks around the floor on spindly legs.

In September 1891 the Board of Health – which predated the council – chose a site between Moriah and Tabernacle chapels to build the new town hall. The original plans had not only court facilities and a council chamber but also a 2,000 seat public hall, but that part of the plan was jettisoned, despite a groundswell of public protest. Twenty-five plans were submitted, the winner being an Edinburgh firm, with a local firm William Griffiths of Falcon Chambers, coming second. The Board then had a change of heart and plumped for the plans submitted by the local firm – who knows under what pressure. Thirteen tenders then came in for the building work, which went to T.P. Jones of Station Road for £11,000. Built of Bath stone in the free classic style of architecture, it was sturdy enough a building to withstand an earthquake in 1906 when the clock tower was seen to sway visibly. Its main features are attractive without being O.T.T. The portico's fluted pilasters, the beautifully carved and

enriched cornice and two carved lions above the pediment standing on either sides of the blindfolded figure of Justice add decoration without being too rococo. To the south there is a raised balcony, ideal for rabble rousing, although the decline in local and indeed national political engagement has put paid to such things.

Civic life grew with the rise of the middle class and the

shopocracy – there were over 1,063 premises registered with the Borough Shops Inspector in 1917, along with four hundred residents of private means. The town already had its own *Who's Who* by 1910, listing 180 local notables from shipbrokers to surveyors, from publishers and preachers to phrenologists. One of the latter was nothing short of a miracle worker, granting the gifts of sight and hearing, or so the

adverts for David Williams, a former steel smelter, claimed.[1]

In the grounds of the town hall there is a war memorial from 1921 by the eminent sculptor Goscombe John, along with another memorial to those fallen in the Boer War in South Africa. The war ended in 1902 and the sculpture was unveiled in 1905 by Earl Roberts, Commander in Chief in South Africa. Designed by a Newcastle artist, F. Doyle Jones, it's a simple symbol, a lone soldier with rifle in hand, and was paid for by local subscriptions. There's another similar figure in West Hartlepool. When Earl Roberts came to unveil the Llanelli sculpture it was a day of torrential rain but not sufficiently so, one hopes, for him to have failed to see the statue of himself in tin, sat on horseback riding through a tin arch, erected opposite Trubshaw's tinplate works.

Also in the same park you'll find the Ivor Rees memorial. The Victoria Cross was awarded to Ivor, a twenty-three year old Felinfoel man, and member of the South Wales Borderers, for an act of extraordinary gallantry in 1917. It's worth citing the official commendation in full so you can see what this local superhero did, all by himself:

> For most conspicuous bravery in attack. A hostile machine gun opened fire at close range, inflicting many casualties. Leading his platoon forward by short rushes, Sergeant Rees gradually worked his way round the right flank to the rear of the gun position. When he was about twenty yards from the machine gun, he rushed forward toward the team, shot one and bayonetted another. He then bombed the large concrete emplacement, killing five and capturing 30 prisoners, of whom two were officers.

The bandstand nearby was designed by George Watkeys and was opened in 1889, similar in design to that in Cwmdonkin, the Swansea park made famous by Dylan Thomas. In its shadow is buried Sosban, the first regimental goat of the 4th Battalion, Welsh Regiment, interred there with full military honours, after a slow procession through the town.

Opposite the Town Hall, in what was then known as Spring Gardens, there used to be a steam mill which was used as Tŷ Cwrdd, the meeting house for Baptists connected with Adulam Chapel in Felinfoel. You can today find the Christian spirit represented by the YMCA in the same area, the first to be raised by subscription from working men and opened in 1911.

Across the street from the old Town Hall is the far less graceful new Town Hall, or Tŷ Elwyn, named after Elwyn Jones, one of many eminent politicians from the town.[2] He was the Labour M.P. for Plaistow, and son of Fred and Elizabeth Jones of Old Castle Road, both tinworkers in the Old Castle Works.[3] After an education that took in the Llanelli Intermediate School, Aberystwyth and Cambridge, he trained as a lawyer, wrote books warning about the dangers of Hitler's Reich, and was to serve as a prosecutor at the Nuremberg trials. He later became Attorney General in the Labour Government and ended his career as Lord Chancellor in the House of Lords.

Tŷ Elwyn is the architectural equivalent to flat pack furniture: functional, basic, it works. The five storey council offices are fundamentally unremarkable other than for the excellent carved lettering by the Ammanford calligrapher Ieuan Rees and the etched glass

doors by Brian Gardiner. It occupies the site of the old two thousand seater Regal Super cinema,[4] opened in 1929, but which had closed by 1960 and later burned to the ground.[5]

The town coat of arms which decorates the entrance to these civic buildings, later gained the motto 'Ymlaen Llanelli'.[6] There's even a song which takes these words as its chorus, once recorded by actor Emyr Wyn as boy soprano, with full male voice choir on backing vocals. Look for it on eBay, but don't spend too much.

As I'm in the vicinity I decide to drop in on the mayor. Not the current mayor, you'll understand, but rather Stefan Chrinowsky, the first Ukrainian mayor in the UK. He lives near the swimming pool. A chatty octagenarian, he tells me his story in an accent which declares the many years he has spent in Llanelli, although with an east European undertow.

Stefan was brought up in a Ukraine, which was divided into zones of various influence – Russian, Polish, Hungary and Romanian. He lived in Western Ukraine under the Poles, so his school was Polish and they had two languages, Polish and Ukrainian. His education ended early because World War Two broke out and the next thing, the Russians came into his part of the Ukraine. Within a few months Russia was at war with Germany. Germans moved in and took a lot of forced labour to Germany and Austria with Stefan in their number. He escaped once. The next period of his life was all about being taken to labour camps, escaping and being taken back again. Once he was accused by the Gestapo of being a ringleader. A sticky moment.

He was taken to a huge transit camp, then put with others into cattle trucks – with only half a loaf of bread and some salami to eat. There were thirty of them lying on straw in each carriage as they were taken as far as Czechoslovakia. The Red Cross were there on the border serving very welcome coffee, and then he was taken to Austria, where a farmer took him on as a worker. Stefan had never worked on the land or handled a scythe. He broke a couple of scythes and the farmer wasn't a very happy man. One suppertime he asked if he could have a lettuce, but there was a snail in it. When Stefan complained the unhappy farmer, 'a real Nazi', hit him in the face.

Then the Russians moved in, stealing everything. Stefan was forced to become an interpreter. He had one near escape from death. One day he was up a cherry tree, having been told he could help himself to the fruit. Next thing he could hear voices – a Russian and a Ukrainian girl. When they spotted him he came down from the tree and started running to the sound of the Russian firing his gun. He told a new farmer he was working for, who told him to go hide in the woods and they'd feed him until the Russians left. He was in the forest for a week and the farmer and his son brought him food.

The Russians withdrew and were replaced by British troops, the Corps of Royal Electrical and Mechanical Engineers who built storage facilities. Stefan worked for them in the capacity of local guide, so they gave him two lorries and twelve men to fetch coal and timber. Meeting the British soldiers and working for them was the catalyst for his moving to Britain and he landed in Market Harborough, where he was billeted in a training camp for Displaced Persons – people with no state. There they were given a choice of somewhere to work – either a farm, mine or steel works. He chose steel, which brought him to Llanelli, where he started off in the Sandy sheet mills. It was a 'vision of hell. It was very hard hard work. My shirt was full of salt – when it was dry it was white and stiff. We had to take tablets to replace the salt we were losing. I started as a scrap boy taking the sheets for the shearer to cut. I used to sit near the furnace with the scaler to help load the steel which would be rolled until it got to size.'

At this stage he didn't speak anything other than rudimentary English, yet he had enough to meet the girl he would eventually marry, Gwenda Richards, a Welsh speaker, just to complicate things linguistically. They met at the Ritz,[7] Stefan impressing her with his skills as a dancer. 'I met a lot of girls, dancing, dating, and in those days I went to Porthcawl practically every Sunday on the bike. Gwenda was working at the Co-operative stores and I met her and we became friendly, we got engaged after I'd met her brother, her parents, a very nice family. All Welsh-speaking.'

When Stefan came to Llanelli there were lots of Ukrainians here along with other foreigners, so he could have stayed with his own kind, as it were, but he felt that if you came to a new country you should obey its laws and observe its customs. He became a Liberal Democrat councillor even though this was a town where reputedly monkeys could be elected if they were Labour monkeys. Imagine an orangutan wearing a red rosette swinging on a liana. In those days there were a few communists in Llanelli and they would ask him why he wasn't going back. Stefan used to tell them about Stalin starving people to death, a fact that even Churchill found hard to credit. The reds wouldn't credit it.

'I hated Stalin so I joined the Liberals. When I stood as Liberal councillor my wife said who's going to vote for you? But I told her I was going to listen to people and work for them. It seemed to work.' He was a councillor for twenty years, having first joined the Liberal Party in 1975, and became chair of the local branch in 1980. He then became the mayor of Llanelli between 1993-94, indeed the first Ukrainian mayor in the UK. He's worked very hard in various industries during those years – after working at the Sandy sheet mills for five years he put in eleven years as a maintenance engineer for British Rail in the big depot. He did a brief stint at Fisher and Ludlows and then worked at Trostre for eleven years, where he gained a new trade as a mason working on the floors and the furnace.

He's now lived in Llanelli for longer than he's lived in the Ukraine. It's now the place this eighty-three year old calls home. This Ukrainian ex-mayor of Llanelli.

Along from Tŷ Elwyn there's another civic building dedicated to a very different local hero, but this time a master potter. It's situated between Tŷ Elwyn and the town's police station. It houses the Terry Griffiths Matchrooms.

To win your second ever professional event is something special but when that event is the World Snooker Championship it is nothing short of sensational. Terry Griffiths did precisely that in 1979. A Llanelli man through and through, Terry had been playing since he was a teenager, winning the Llanelli and District championship when he was sixteen. He did not play seriously however until he was twenty-five, when he entered the Welsh Amateur championship. When I was growing up he was a hero as much as the town's rugby players and watching the smoke filled rooms of the various championships, often sponsored by the fag companies was a matter of nail biting tension and flashing pride.

Terry Griffiths went on to win the W.A. title in 1975, ushering in a glittering amateur career. This was followed by a quarter final in the world championships. He went on to win the English Amateur title in 1977 and 1978 but, as a Welshman, he needed his national title to qualify for the 1978 world amateur event. He failed to do this, losing out to Steve Newbury in the quarters and so he decided to turn professional, having tried his hand at various jobs.

Terry Griffiths' first professional event was the UK championship and in the qualifying round he led Rex Williams 8-2, but eventually lost 9-8, and so it was on to the 1979 Embassy at the Crucible. Victories over Perrie Mans and Alex Higgins were followed by a

memorable semi-final against
Eddie Charlton, which Terry
eventually won 19-17 in the
early hours. When the presenter David Vine approached him
for an interview he uttered
those immortal words, 'I'm in
the final now, you know!' The
cool Irishman Dennis Taylor
was his opponent, also in his
first world final, and Terry won
convincingly 24-16, becoming
world champion. Griffiths
proved this was no fluke by

reaching the UK final a few months later, losing to John Virgo, and
then winning both the Masters at Wembley and the Irish Masters.
Like many before, and since, he fell at the first hurdle in his world title
defence to a certain Steve Davis, one of the coolest and most clinical
snooker players of modern times.[8]

And talking of modern times, before I leave the civic centre I
should note the existence at least of the magistrates court and the tax
offices, essays in drab concrete block.[9] It makes the place look like the
Stalingrad theme park. Let's leave it at that.

COLESHILL TERRACE

There is, on the face of it, little to warrant an entire chapter about
Coleshill Terrace, to set it above any other streets of comparable
length or age in the town, other than for one remarkable man. More
of that later. But we can start at the seemingly off-the-peg Tabernacle
chapel, an offshoot of Capel Als, which had already thrown out three
other branches, namely Siloah, Bryn and Park Congregational.
Looking out at the town hall this imposing place of worship was
designed by John Humphreys of Morriston, architect of the famous
Morriston Tabernacle. Llanelli's version is similarly a grand building
in the Corinthian style. When the memorial stone was laid a procession which went through the centre of town brought no fewer than
1,500 faithful to witness the act. Next door is the registry office, for
all your birth, marriage and death needs. But that's not why I linger
on the terrace, even though that's where we went to register my dad's

death. Just after the funeral director offered us a choice of coffins. In ascending order of price we could have chosen the Lincoln, cheap as cardboard, the Exeter, a cut above, the outlast-his-sons Durham model or the top-of-the-range, brass handles 'n' all Dyfed. How could we bury a Welshman, who lived in Dyfed, in anything but?

So to the killer fact. It will surprise many that Donald Swann, one half of the quintessentially English comedy duo Flanders and Swann, came from Llanelli. He opens his autobiography with just that fact and reflects on the fact that despite only spending two years in the town, once born in Wales, one is taken on board as a Welshman. He was a composer, pianist and entertainer. The shows he performed with the wheelchair-bound, deeply suave Michael Flanders, *At the Drop of a Hat* and *At the Drop of Another Hat*, ran for over eleven years in Britain, the United States, Canada, New Zealand and Australia and sold well on records. Songs such as 'Mud, Mud Glorious Mud' and 'The Gasman Cometh', with its insistent refrain etched deeply in the British consciousness. One of their songs, 'The Slow Train', remains a favourite of mine, up there with Aretha Franklin's 'Say a Little Prayer' and the Manic Street Preachers' 'Motorcycle Emptiness'.[10] 'The Slow Train' is, in effect, a long list, sung in stately, chugging and forlorn progress, of many of the stations axed by Doctor Beeching when he closed down huge parts of the rail network in 1962.

I met Donald Swann a couple of times in the 1980s when I was working on a TV chat show, *The Chris Stuart Cha Cha Chat Show* – it happened to be produced by a man with a pronounced stammer, which always gave us pause about the show's name. Swann, a dapper, sprightly and clever man, was a total delight, especially as he led the

studio audience in a resounding and spirited chorus of what was known by many as 'The Hippopotamus Song', in Russian! 'Mud, mud, glorious mud,' sang the audience, as if they liked nothing better than a wallow in a hollow.

Swann's flair with the Russian language is explained by the history of his family. He was born in Coleshill Terrace on the 30th September, 1923 and the backstory of how his parents got there is exotic stuff. His great-grandfather, a draper named Alfred Trout Swan – at the time spelled with one 'n' – left Lincolnshire in 1840 to go to Russia, a country clearly in need of drapers at the time. He married Sarah Hynam, whose clockmaking family had also been attracted there by the Anglomanie which set great stock on English craftsmen, and changed his name to make it easier for German customs to pronounce as Schwann. His grandfather worked for the Russo-American India Rubber Company. His father was caught up as a young medical student in the great sweep of the Russian Revolution. One day a peasant threw a stone through the window of a car he was travelling in, a shattering portent of the trouble that lay ahead. He was sent to England for a holiday by a father who probably could read the signs. Ironically, he arrived in a country which had just found itself involved in a war. He joined the Red Cross and did the same when he returned to Russia, with a great deal of work to do in the Ukraine as wounded soldiers came back from the fronts. A team of Tartar doctors and nurses from Ashkhabad came to augment them, and Donald's father, Herbert, met and fell in love with Naguime Sultan Piszova, a Muslim from the desert beyond the Caspian Sea, accompanying her on the piano as she sang gypsy songs. Their escape from Russia was like a missing episode from Pastarnak's novel, *Dr. Zhivago*.

They arrrived in Tilbury as paperless and penniless refugees and after Donald's father retrained in medicine he was offered £500 to work as an assistant to a Dr. Davies in Llanelli, where in 1921 Herbert and Naguime got married. Work wasn't easy, especially when all the other members of the practice were taken ill and he had to deal with the long and troubling roster of patients, many of them suffering from TB. A great deal of colour was injected into their lives, and that of the town, when Donald's uncle Sokolik arrived at Coleshill Terrace, entertaining everyone by singing rousing songs and playing the guitar, the balalaika and dancing exotic Eastern dances involving whirling sabres and knives. I wish I'd been there.

When it came to religion the Swanns were a dizzying mix to rival Sokolik's antic antics. Together with the muslim part of his mother's side, his sister married to a Jew and his uncle became a devout Russian Orthodox. Donald had plenty of choice. He started off immersed in High Anglicanism and then became a Quaker.

A blue plaque has yet to be erected to mark Donald's sojourn in Coleshill Terrace. In the meantime listen to *At the Drop of a Hat*, one of the all-time classic recordings of Swann with his urbane comedy companion Michael Flanders. He may not sound like a Llanelli man, in fact anything but, yet he sure made you laugh, sure as eggs is eggs.

THE PARISH CHURCH

Nowadays skirted by the traffic of Gelli Onn and with the Verandah Indian restaurant as a neighbour, the most striking feature of Llanelli's parish church is quite obviously the church tower, which is 77 feet high and measures 27 feet across the base.[11] You need a clean bill of health to climb the hundred spiral steps to reach the top. Even more striking, in the literal sense, is the peal of eight bells hung in their oak frames and the window of the ringing room containing six pieces of medieval glass. The clock is 230 years old. It says it's twenty five to nine. Always. You can set your watch by it. Twice a day. Frozen in time, or rust. There was probably a spire, or little tower as well as the main tower, but that was demolished in the nineteenth century. And it's to the church that Llanelli owes much of its basic shape as the medieval commote, Carnwyllion accreted around it, like an oyster.

The church is dedicated to St. Elli and is said to have been founded on the site of the cell in which St. Elli prayed in the sixth century. It was always a substantial church, although what you see today is mainly the restoration of 1904-06 by E.M. Bruce Vaughan. At least one Roman visited the spot as a Roman coin from the reign of Diocletian was discovered in the churchyard in 1855.

Llan means an enclosure and Elli is a saint mentioned in the *Book of Llandaff*, which chronicles the so called Age of Saints. When I grew up in the town I remember being told that she was a female saint. As with so many saints the truth of their lives is wreathed in a swirling Celtic mist. There's a story told about her that she was the virginal granddaughter of Brychan Brycheiniog, ruler of the kingdom of Brecknock, who didn't want to accede to her father's wishes that she marry a particular prince. In order to avoid wedding him she took

the drastic step of killing herself, and with her martyrdom came sainthood. So you have a choice in the matter, although it's likely that the Elli in Llanelli was a miracle-making disciple, possibly the son of Cadog who ran the monastery at Llancarfan in the Vale of Glamorgan. It is told that Elli took over the running of the monastery after him. One local historian, John Edwards, points out that much of this could be made up. That being said Elli's saint's day is 23 January. So we know the day but not the year!

The first reference to the church is found in the *Book of Llandaff*, *Liber Landavensis*, and relates to the time of the Norman Conquest. 'In Lannelli Umel was priest, afterwards Uchtryd, afterwards Ionas, afterwards Gwasdwyn, afterwards Aeddan.' Later accounts describe a place of worship that's gone to rack and ruin.

A reply to an official questionnaire in 1684 about the state of the church gives a picture of a place in tatters and disrepair. Spiritually things were rent and torn, too. There was a single curate for the parish and he also had to take Llangennech under his wing. The sexton was accused of sheep rustling, not something of which the Lamb of God would approve. Sunday was no holier than Saturday or any other day of the week so ball games were regularly played on Sunday in the shadow of the great church tower, to the extent that the area gained the moniker Cwrt y Bêl – the Ball Court.

The churchyard used to function as a marketplace, with cockles being sold around the cross and butter under the sycamore near Raby's tomb, the tombstones themselves making excellent flat stalls to display produce. Nearby Church Street was so crammed with boot and shoe shops that it was known as Heol y Sgidie, or Shoe Street. It was never going to last. Sorry. My paronomasia gets the better of me sometimes.

My redoubtable native guide, Huw Lewis gets me to pause awhile in the churchyard to ponder the grave of Ebenezer Morris, the town's most pugilistic parson. It's appropriate that he's buried facing Llanelli House, with its connections with the Queensbury rules – but more of that anon.

The Thomas Arms was built by Rees Goring Thomas and leased to Vicar Morris and it opened in 1830. The county's magistrates were all invited to an evening that would end in uproar. After the meal an argument broke out which so piqued the Vicar that he stood on a chair and assaulted one John Edward Saunders of Llandyfaelog, a man handy with his fists and prone to anger. He was beaten senseless by the Vicar and it was lucky that Saunders' friends intervened and stole him away to a bedroom to avoid the enraged vicar. But that wasn't the last time Vicar Morris went a-brawling. When the Bostock and Wombell Menagerie came to town in 1832 Llanelli Pottery owner William Chambers and some friends were given a private viewing, when a drunken Vicar stumbled on the scene. He demanded to be let in, insisting with his fists and knocking the showman to the ground, letting in a crowd and then giving an impromptu lecture in which he compared Chambers with some of the animals. He even followed Chambers home, kicking him on his own doorstep. The so-called 'fighting parson' was subsequently fined and bound over to keep the peace.

Wandering the church is a more sedate affair.

The interior of the church contrasts green-grey Bridgend Quarella stone walling with red stone dressings, under a fine series of roofs. Let's note some of the church's highlights as we undertake a virtual tour of the place. Imagine what follows as a 3-D computer simulation of the church interior. So through the main doors and there's a thirteenth century font which stands on the stones of a sepulchre found during the renovations of 1905. Approaching the altar you'll notice a beautiful stained glass window. Close-up. It depicts Christ as the central figure, with Mary and John at his side. Naturally. Another window, letting in a bit of typical rain-showery light shows the figure of St. Elli holding the tower of the Church in her arms. Heavy burden. For the patriots among us St. David makes an appearance, too, complete with a pair of peaceful doves on his shoulder. There are other creatures to spot, too. Tucked away in the grand scheme of things are thirteen carved mice, though finding them all needs infinite patience. The patience of a saint indeed.

The reredos includes a carving in pink stone of the last supper by Harry Hemms of Exeter, while the carved oak altar shows St. Mathew, St. Mark, St. Luke and St. John. The gospel full set. To the right of the altar is a piscina, a relic of the church during pre-Reformation times. It was used by the clergy to rinse the vessels used during the Eucharist. At that period there was a sanctus bell in the small tower above the chancel, which would be rung during the communion service. Note well, then move on. Note if you will, the choir stalls, beautifully carved from Austrian oak, and also the barrel roof, which was renewed in 1906. Pause to admire.

Ladies and gentlemen, the bronze memorial on the north wall of the sanctuary is to the memory of James Charles Murray Cowell, who died at the Battle of Inkerman in 1854 and is commemorated by Inkerman Street in the town. This is by Baron C. Marochetti and is a copy of a marble cenotaph in St. Paul's Cathedral. There are many other monuments in the church dating back to the seventeenth century, such as one to Walter Vaughan dated 1680. Others include John Vaughan Stepney, Sir Stafford Howard and Emma Chambers.

On the north wall you will find an aumbrey. Not a word you hear everyday, I'll admit. This is a safe which contains the blessed sacrament. Also on the north wall you'll see a brass memorial to Samuel Oakley Morris, who gave his life along with 359 others in a Royal Navy disaster. He was the son of the Rev. Ebenezer Morris, the boxing vicar. Let's take a minute to think about sacrifice, all those who laid down their lives.

As you leave the Lady Chapel you enter the north transept, with a white marble floor area, with the entrance to the vaults in which members of the Stepney family were interred. On the walls here you'll see monuments to the memory of Sir Thomas Stepney, Baronet, a relative of Henry VII. There is also a memorial to William Chambers, and his wife Emma. He was the squire of Llanelli, who lived opposite the church in Llanelli House.

In the south transept there is another beautiful stained glass window depicting the Nativity. This window is dedicated to one of the more eccentric members of the Cowell family, Sir Algernon Keppel Cowell Stepney, who worked for the Foreign Office, became an M.P, and died in Yuma, Arizona U.S.A. on the 2 July 1909, while out collecting beetles. He was buried in Llanelli on the 31 July the same year.

And last but not least behold the Compton cinema organ which came from the Dominion Theatre on Tottenham Court Road in London. It was installed in this church in 1959 by the Vicar, the Reverend Islwyn Davies, to replace a church organ which had bellows. And just a final point of interest. Alwyn Bowen Hurren, a former vicar's warden once recalled that when he was a young choir boy, a man known as 'Johnny the Organ' had the duty of keeping the bellows full of air by pumping a long oak bar. On rare occasions that they sang an English hymn or psalm, Johnny would refuse to pump.

So that's the church. Sanctuary and worship house. Locked doors most of the time because of thieves. Who'll steal anything. Particularly an aumbrey. Hard to fence, mind you.

LLANELLI HOUSE

Some buildings, like irritating politicians, seem to have the knack of dividing public opinion. That's very much the case with Llanelli House. This is an historic building on Bridge Street that attracts both praise and opprobrium. It was the subject of the BBC's *Restoration* show in 2003, in which viewers voted for the building they believed should be restored to its former glory. It didn't win but that was enough of a trigger to pull in millions for its redevelopment. Not that everyone is pleased. I spoke to one prominent person in the town who was pretty much spitting vitriol at the mention of the place. 'It's the home of the *crachach*, where people had to touch their forelocks even though there was cholera and shit running through the streets. So what are we celebrating by restoring it? Why put all those millions into it? I'd put a bulldozer through the bloody lot. It's not worth it. Better for a town to look forward than look back.'

In his new book the distinguished journalist and chair of the National Trust, Simon Jenkins, describes the house as 'barely noticeable in the surrounding dross, it is like a fine lady in a prison camp.'[12] For Jenkins the whole building has an excellent composition, reminiscent of the urban baroque of Thomas Archer in Covent Garden, and notes that the restoration is already revealing the original building behind the Georgian façade.

A stairwell has been unveiled which rises the whole height of the building, with the original balustrades and balconies unharmed by time. That term so beloved by estate agents, 'original panelling', is still plentifully apparent, as are fitted wall cupboards and plasterwork, along with over-mantel paintings which have been described as 'delightful.' There's a painting downstairs

of the British fleet at anchor off an idealized coast and is similar to one at No. 111 Main Street, Pembroke. Upstairs there is one showing Llangennech Park, seat of the Stepney family, which may have been painted by the peripatetic artist John Lewis around 1770. Although the house is mainly associated with the Stepneys other families lived here at other times. Before the Stepneys it was home to the Vaughan family and after them it was owned for a while by William Chambers.

When one turns to other architectural experts we find enthusiasm bubbling over for 'an extraordinary house...' set in a location which 'represents not so much an urban core but a lost village centre.'[13]

What you see today is the pre-Georgian, seven-bay house erected by Sir John Stepney on the site of the older mansion belonging to Thomas Lewis. Originally it was built on land which ran down to the river Lliedi which nowadays flows sullenly as what the Merthyr poet Harri Webb would describe as a 'sewered drab' under Stepney Street.

Work on the building was completed in 1714 when it became the family home, and that date is still visible on the cast iron down pipes at the front of the house, which also bear the family crest. Llanelli House has grand sash windows which are a little spoiled by later work, although experts reckon this is rectifiable. The house was the focus for much of Llanelli's early urban life. When the local eisteddfod was held here in 1856 a marquee able to accommodate 4,000 people was erected in the beautiful grounds. Indeed the gardens were so extensive that they reached as far as the present day market. The gardens were uprooted and became the main shopping thoroughfares of Cowell, Stepney and Vaughan Streets. In its heyday this would have been a chandelier of a building, full of social whirl and upper crust busyness and its gardens would have been well laid out and productive.

The Stepneys, from Hertfordshire, came to Llanelli via Haverfordwest. Sir John was the Member of Parliament in Carmarthenshire between 1717 and 1722. The house was only occupied by the family for sixty years, though, and when part of the house and latterly all of the house were put on the market there were no takers. So decay set in quite early and by the turn of the nineteenth century the house was in some disrepair. That didn't stop John Wesley, the proselytizing Methodist, from staying there on many occasions, and his visits to the town are commemorated on a plaque set in the library wall. In fact he preached here eight times between 1768 and 1790, standing in the small market place in front of the church lych gate.

Llanelli House was also the home of Llanelli's first Post Office in 1811,[14] before the P.O. moved thereafter to various inns, including the Falcon, the Ship and the Thomas Arms, with coaches leaving regularly for places such as Swansea and Haverfordwest but the coming of the railway in the mid 1850s led to their demise.

As we've seen Llanelli House has spawned a fair amount of verbal sparring in the town so it's appropriate that it has an interesting connection with the history of boxing. A new book about Wales and boxing makes it.[15]

The famous Queensbury Rules of 1867, which replaced the London Prize Ring Rules of 1838 and were meant to help replace savagery with skill and win back respectable if not royal patronage, were not devised by John Sholto Douglas, the syphilitic Marquess of Queensbury but rather by John Graham Chambers who went from Llanelly House to Eton and Cambridge. He helped stage the Boat Race, the first Cup Final and the first Amateur Athletic Club championships. This remarkable man was a champion walker of England, instigated championships for boxing, billiards and cycling, went in a boat to accompany Captain Webb as he swam the English Channel and found time to open a Welsh shop in Chelsea.

As you might expect this house has its ghosts. Reputedly a servant girl who had found out she was pregnant threw herself out of one of the windows and killed herself. To find out more I contacted Geraint Hopkins, a.k.a. Geraint the Snakeman from Ghost Watch Wales, based in Llanelli. He remembers when Llanelli House was a café in the nineties. As he recalls, 'the shop was fine but the cafeteria was odd' and he didn't feel alone. The fireplace drew him and the owner said everyone who sat at the table near the fireplace had the sensation that someone was looking down at them from the chimney. On the stairs Geraint had the sensation of a crinoline drifting against him. At one of the windows he had the feeling that someone was trying to pull him out and the sensation of falling.

Immune to such eerie events Geraint has even slept overnight in Llanelli House. The ghost most closely connected with the house in local legend was a servant, Mira Turner, who was meant to have taken laudanum and jumped out of the front window. On the other hand, Geraint, along with two other mediums, sensed something about the window at the back. In a séance they picked up a butler or servant called Wilfred as well, who also haunts the place. In the upstairs rooms children also come as visitations, and they're happy, but Mira is 'grounded', meaning she stays there. Still is, probably. We now have bookish matters to attend to: we'll hear more about Geraint and the local roster of spooks later. As we leave Llanelli House to the renovators – they've already redesigned the streets so that outside is now pedestrianized – we walk all of twenty yards. Across the street from Llanelli House is the library, which grew out of the Atheneum, which became the venue for the Mechanics' Institute, set up in 1840, an organisation which sought to educate workers after they had finished their shifts. They amassed over 1600 volumes covering subjects which ranged from history to commerce.

The Atheneum was a 'building devoted to the intellectual improvement of the inhabitants.' Finished in 1857 there was a grand ball to mark its opening in 1858, where Mr Ribbon's band was in attendance playing polkas and quadrilles.[16] There was a reading room where you could read six daily newspapers and twenty-four weekly titles, a geological musuem donated by the Earl of Cawdor and a hall for lectures. One such lecture, about the American Civil War, lasted for three nights and was reported in the London press.

This library has played a pivotal part in my life. Both my brother and I set off of various mental adventures here and whenever we followed various new enthusiasms the library would always, and I mean always have the books we wanted. I might be on an American poetry jag and be looking for Hart Crane or John Berryman and they'd have plenty in stock. My brother, Alun might be feeding his hunger for obscure military histories and they'd have more than enough to keep him going. It's a place with fond memories but more importantly it made us feel a part of the wider world, in touch with the best ideas.

Diametrically opposite Llanelli House is the place where the TV presenter and comedian Griff Rhys Jones' great grandfather died during a drunken brawl, a fact he discovered while making the BBC programme *Who Do You Think You Are?* For a hundred years the family had believed that the great grandparents had died in a train crash. This Victorian disaster had orphaned his maternal grandmother, Louisa Price, who was then adopted by distant cousins. Or so the family history had it.

But investigations for the BBC show revealed different deaths for Griff's relatives. Daniel, a steam-engine driver, cracked his head open on the pavement outside what is today the Verandah restaurant after a drunken altercation. Furthermore the coroner's report revealed him to be an alcoholic whose liver was severely damaged by too much toping. The man who fought him was tried for manslaughter but acquitted while Daniel's widow, Sarah, had to raise four children alone. As it transpired she wasn't up to the task and gave up two of them, Thomas and Jane, to special boarding schools for truants. A third child, William, was sent to America. The fourth, Griff's grandmother Louisa, was lucky enough to be adopted. In a newspaper article Griff talked about his experience of having to revise history: 'I thought the poor man had been set upon by a thug. They went to trial and the the judge didn't feel this at all. When you look closely, it appears he was the thug.'

Father of two Griff pitied the poor widow: 'Poor Sarah was left with these children. She went before the union to try to get some relief and they told her to go the poor house. I thought, poor woman, she probably died and her children were sent to orphanages. But they weren't orphanages. They were approved schools for children running around uncontrollably and refusing to go to school. For one reason or another she was a very bad and unsuitable parent and didn't manage to cope at all. It left me feeling pretty miserable.'[17]

Sarah's troubed tale reminds us that Llanelli people are a varied breed. They are tough or terrible when times demand; learned when time allows and sometimes, like John Chambers can box clever. They live with ghosts, decay, optimism and a singular lack of planning. They also live with a lot of history, which can make us wise.

THE TOWN CENTRE

The old heart of what has, on occasion, been referred to as the 'Llanelli Shopping Experience' is more than a trifle sclerotic now, with empty windows and 'For Lease' signs jockeying for attention with the dwindling number of businesses competing for a slowly drying trickle of visitors. At the very centre of things, on both sides of the entrance to the Santes Elli Centre, two shoe shops are closing down. It's down at heel, pardon the pun. Diametrically opposite, the Topshop has bottomed out and consolidated in Swansea. I've heard locals refer to the way the place is 'rotting from the centre' and 'dying on its feet.' There's an enormous task facing those charged with regenerating a town centre which has lost out to out-of-town development. One of those involved in this Sisyphean task is Andrew

Shufflebotham, the town centre manager, who's been involved in retail since he was sixteen years of age and delivered goods for his grandfather Arthur's firm in Neath. He describes himself as a beleaguered optimist, as he tries to stem the tide of shops leaving the main shopping streets. I'd give him a medal for trying. And another for maintaining his optimism. This is a story repeated in so many towns.

He says that no one could have conceived of the rapid change in retail. The competition for town centre traders is not just a matter of how much goods cost, or ease of parking, but the out-of-towners are open for forty more hours a week and reflect new shopping habits which include Sundays and Bank Holidays. He admits that what the multiples offer has certainly affected the footfall of shoppers in the centre. He thinks a correction in the rates paid by the independent traders will help. They, after all, put their profits back into the local area, which isn't true for the big boys.

That said, it's still an improvement on the Llanelli of yesteryear. During the industrial era the criticism was sometimes savage: 'We want more attention paid to architecture in Llanelli than has hitherto been the case. The place is unattractive enough already, when we consider the black smoke, coal dust, broken streets, puddles, want of street crossings, drippings, its sewage carts and sewage works, without making it worse through the want of architectural taste in the construction of its houses.'

More recently the blight has been mainly in planning, or lack of it. Robert Lloyd, former editor of the *Llanelli Star* reckons 'it's difficult to date the beginning of the demise. In urban planning terms the town's a disaster.'[18] As a Carmarthen man who used to come to Llanelli to watch rugby and have lunch at the Blue Orchid or a pint at the York or the Camelot he remembers a vibrancy on match day when the people were all wearing supporters' scarves. He bemoans the fact you don't get that nowadays. He opines, 'Llanelli's really been knocked about and it is a real catastrophe in terms of planning. The rot set in when Tesco moved out of town and there was a rider to the contract that said they couldn't open another food store on that site and that signed Llanelli's death warrant.' That codicil was, indeed, to have far reaching effects.

Another death knell sounded when Marks & Spencer decamped to the Trostre Retail Park. This was a personal blow for me as my mother had worked there for years and both my brother Alun and I had had satisfying and lucrative holiday and Saturday work in the store. Indeed, the company saved my mother's life by paying for her to have private health care. In jumping the queue to have a hysterectomy they discovered a tumour which they got rid of in time. I know this smacks of privilege but I'm still grateful to them.

I have an abiding memory of working there. M & S used to have a policy of not prosecuting shoplifters because of a belief that it generated negative publicity by having the company's name in the court pages. So there'd be a lot of lifting, and when I worked on the menswear section it was incredible to note the chutzpah of thieves who'd saunter in, try on a new velvet jacket and walk out, leaving the old shitty one hanging on the racks. One day I saw a woman stealing a chicken and as she'd seen me seeing her I felt obliged to ask her to accompany me to the manager's office. It was some small moral consolation to know that all she would get was a telling off, but I still felt bad about it. As we waited in the office an extraordinary thing happened. The woman's face started to melt. It was as if there was a fire in Madame Tussaud's and all the waxworks were beginning to deform. When the manager arrived he asked her to remove her hat and it transpired that she had two pounds of butter under it.

While the litany of loss of town centre shops – W.H. Smith, Woolworths, Topshop – seems to lengthen by the week, some things remain pretty vibrant. Cathryn Ings, until recently the editor of the *Llanelli Star*, reckons 'the market is one of the most exciting ones in Wales', and as the current editor of the *Carmarthen Journal*, a paper covering events in a town blessed with its own fine market, that's praise indeed. The old market was established in 1866, with no fewer than thirty-five butchers' stalls but the Market Pavilion – the so-called Crystal Palace of Llanelli – was knocked down in 1968. I have a young boy's memories of it with live poultry and rabbits in cages and the jostling legs of many grown-ups.

The present day market still sells meat and does have fantastic fresh vegetables grown on Gower, and a fine fishmongers, and individual florists, and one of three Jenkins bakeries outlets in the town selling the best Cornish pasties this side of St. Ives, veritable three course dinners wrapped in pastry. The cabbage from Panthywel farm glistens with dew so fresh is it, and it is indubitably one of the most wonderful things you can eat this side of the Pearly Gates. Ambrosial greens, that's what they are.

Andrew Shufflebotham remembers some of the jaw droppingly big orders the David Jenkins baking company would place with his grandfather's firm. Once he had to double check that they actually did want no fewer than 150 dozen half- and one-pint pudding basins from them, until he realized that they used to give the basins away with their Christmas puddings. David Jenkins is still one of the business success stories in the town centre and they have one shop near the entrance to the market, two others in town and one near the station. Try those pasties. A Sunday lunch wrapped up in pastry. Delicious. Totally.

On a good day the market is full of electric chatter, the friendly sound of commerce and gossipy exchange. Here you can get Mexican food, Penclawdd cockles, infernally difficult jigsaws and chat to the people selling the stuff to you. It's more personal and personable than Asda, which is part of a global empire. Anyone who's seen the movie *Wal-Mart: The High Cost of the Low Price* will know that, will have had a glimpse of its vexing philosophy. But for now Llanelli has both market and supermarket, living cheek by jowl.

A great enthusiast for Llanelli market is Barrie Davies, who runs a shop in the market precinct and a stall in the market itself. The business was founded by his mam and dad in 1947 after his father changed direction, having previously worked in the Llanelli tinplate and stamping works. His father always used to tell him that if you could make a success in Llanelli you can make a success anywhere. His mother, Gladys, now 84 years of age, still works in the shop and always 'tells people she's the boss.' In one site they sell 'hardware, cookware, a smattering of ironmongers' equipment and gifts ranging from a couple of quid to Doulton figurines at £135 and Ainsley China at £ 249.50', although he cheerily admits he'll knock off the fifty pence. They sell an enormous amount of enamelware and what Barrie describes as an astonishing number of bakestones for making Welsh cakes. On the stall in the permanent market they sell toys, Welsh souvenirs, hobby stuff and people will travel good distances to buy 'this and that and such and such for model railways.'

For him it's 'not been a big surprise' that Asda hasn't brought about the demise of the small businesses which he thinks 'run along-side the supermarket picking up the crumbs off the table, if you like, while Asda gets the main meal. Take curtain track. Customers will worry about saving money on lengths of this but the big stores don't stock the additional gliders you need. We stock the spares the big stores like Asda and B&Q don't.' And before I leave his Aladdin's cave of a shop he gives me a parting gift, an overheard remark which seems to say a lot. He heard someone say 'I'll see you later on in a minute now.' There's Greenwich Mean. Pacific. Eastern Time. And Llanelli time. Beyond even Einstein's grasp.

On Cowell Street, which connects with one side of the market, there used to be gentlemen's outfitters and jewellers and the upmarket Pugh Brothers store – which gave a glimpse of how the other half lived – with its weightily price-tagged furniture and a sure sense of style. I say this as someone who shared with a family of four a living room which was some ten foot by ten in a house with no inside lavatory and, because of a complicated standoff with my grandmother, had no access to a proper bath, even though there was one in the house. Pughs was fantasy island in that respect.

Cowell Street houses the offices of the *Llanelli Star*, a hundred years old this year. It's a fine local newspaper, packed with events and insight into a town which is changing fast. Former editor Robert Lloyd agrees it's a good patch to work. Read the paper and you'll find out how one café in the town has had to stop putting out metal spoons as the junkies always steal them. I had to laugh when I read in a recent issue about a man who was caught stealing a bottle of port and a cocktail mixer. Live it up, man.

On a Monday morning Cowell Street is witness to one of the saddest spectacles of Llanelli life – the snaking queue, sometimes up to fifty people strong, waiting to get their names on the list of appointments at the Citizens' Advice Bureau. In contrast, the street also has an interesting pop music connection. Ronnie Cass, son of local jeweller Saul Cass, who used to own a shop on this drag, was an actor and all-round entertainer who worked with the likes of Harry Secombe and Tom Jones. He won the Ivor Novello award for composing the music for Cliff Richards' hit singles 'Young Ones' and 'Summer Holiday'.

At the junction of Cowell Street and Stepney Street it's well worth craning your head upwards to enjoy the architecture. This has been home to both the Randell Brothers bank and the South Wales Union Bank Ltd. It was designed by James Buckley Wilson in 1891. Part of the building projects outwards and is decorated with hanging tiles and beautiful deep-toned Ruabon strawberry coloured bricks. It's

worth looking out, or up for.

On the other side of Stepney Street is the Stepney Arcade, designed in 1894 by William Griffiths, which is a delightful short galleried arcade, mainly in painted timber. You can be tattooed here or buy the latest Dafydd Iwan CD or the new novel by Wiliam Owen Roberts at the wonderful Llyfrau'r Ddraig, a quiet readers' enclave and now the last place you can buy new books in the town centre, although there are discount chains where you can buy remainders. This arcade used to abut the Lliedi, which was only canalised in the 1930s. Here you found a slum area around Kings Square and Spring Gardens. You could approach the arcade via a steel bridge but a job creation scheme in the 1930s culverted the river. This part of Lower Stepney Street lost its west side to the Town Hall Gardens. The York Palace was the old Llanelly Cinema around 1920 but it's lost its white ceramic façade. This building used to have an Art Nouveau tree by way of decoration but time has cut that down. Things erode fast around here. Somewhere in the town there's always an axe swinging, hacking away the past.

There are other shopping streets which snake away from the town centre, such as Thomas Street. As you start the gentle climb up here you pass what remains of what was once the very considerable brewery complex at Buckleys.

Llanelli has a long history of brewing, and a maltster called Henry Child founded a brewery here around 1760. His business was handed on by the marriage of his daughter Maria to the Reverend James Buckley, the only Methodist minister to be made famous as a portrait on a beer bottle. The firm expanded by taking over the Bythways

brewery, situated near Emma Street and later acquired the Carmarthen Brewery, becoming the biggest brewery in West Wales. It was a successful company and won the Gold Medal at the Brewers' Exhibition in London – open to all brewers in Britain and the Empire – in 1906 and took the Grand Prix and Gold Medal at the Paris Exhibition of 1911. It was eventually taken over by Crown Brewery of Pontyclun in 1989, when beer production ceased in Llanelli and within ten years the Pontyclun firm had itself been acquired by Brains. I've downed my fair share of Buckleys' products in my time and still miss their sweetly bitter beer. 'Lemon top' was a traditional way of drinking it, with just the merest soupcon of lemonade added. Just to make it sweeter still.

The site of the former Falcon Estate Agents was the old Falcon Inn, where magistrates used to sit. Sentences could be very harsh, as three boys found out when they were whipped through the town for stealing apples. A fraudster got sentenced to a month on the tread-mill. That is tough justice.

The Falcon Inn was an early transport hub, from which the the daily coach, the Royal Queen, would set out each day for Swansea. The Falcon Bridge could be a noxious affair. Walking over it 'you would be nearly suffocated by the stench of a hundred pigs, and the evaporation of steam from large boilers preparing their food; pig styes behind every house; great heaps of manure, and even the emptying of cess-pools and water-closets, to be seen at almost every house in town.'

On your left is Gelli Onn, now a slow chicane of roads, but with a name which derives from the earliest Methodist chapel and Sunday school in Llanelli, dating from the eighteenth century. Thomas Charles, the founder of the Sunday School movement, came here from Bala to visit.

On the right, going uphill, as you walk past pubs such as the Masons and the Drovers, not to mention representatives of the radiant glut of tanning salons, you'll come to the fine Georgian Caeffair House, now a nursing home. The name means 'Field of the Fair' and refers to an era when cattle and horse fairs were held on the site, which helps explain the name of the Drovers pub, as they would stay here and at the nearby Thomas Arms.[19] In the 1890s this hostelry could see some fine dining indeed, as when a representative of Roederer champagne producers hosted a dinner which included real turtle soup, prairie hen, pigeons and a liberal supply of French beans, peas and new potatoes, not to mention pineapples 'of rare and choice growth.' The town's Post Office was located at the Thomas Arms for many years.

Head back down to town and veer left, past the old Tescos which now houses Tinopolis television, and you'll see the ongoing blitz of the East End development and banners protesting the demolition of the Island House pub. They used to worship more than just hops here. Island Place was the first worshipping place for the Mormons in Llanelli. They arrived in 1847 and two years later they had built up a congregation of 180, poaching members of nonconformist chapels such as Zion and Capel Newydd, and eventually many of them were to emigrate to Salt Lake City, Utah.

I was sad to see the wrecking balls smash into the former Ship and Castle, later known as the Stepney, as the demolition gang, which seems to have been permanently at work in the town, went about the business of razing it to the ground. This was where sixty gentlemen once convened to celebrate the opening of the new Llanelli Pottery. The memories settle like dust in the rubble. There are plans for this part of town. A cinema and hotel on the drawing board. This town is anything if not mutable. It feeds off change. Even though this diet leads to the architectural equivalent to rickets. Five minutes walk away from this building site is Capel Als. This is the oldest Independent chapel in the town and there are various explanations for its name. It may derive from a woman called Alys who had a well here, while local historians posit it came from the word *als*, or rock cliff, referring to the solid rock from which the site is hewn. One of its most arresting ministers was David Rees, a literally broad-shouldered editor of *Y Diwygiwr*, the Independent denominational journal whose radical outspokeness was nowhere more evident than in its motto 'Agitate, agitate, agitate.'[20] And agitate he did, even fomenting rumours that he was suspected of not only supporting the Rebecca rioters and their night-time attacks on iniquitous toll-booths, but of being one himself. He was castigated in the *Times*, no less. Questions were asked about him in the Commons. The Home Secretary was told about a man *Blackwoods* magazine described as 'a sort of bishop in his dirty diocese of colliers and coppermen.' Both kinds of workmen are rare as ibis in the town nowadays, especially with the last of the copperworks closing. And as the recession bites, work itself is a scarce commodity, sought after as platinum on these terraced streets.

MURRAY STREET

It's no Egyptian wonder, but Llanelli's pyramid at the St. Elli Centre is a central landmark. Asda lies at the heart of the enterprise, not that I darken its doors. Ever. At the entrance to the supermarket car park is a building that used to be part of the gas works company. The supermarket itself lies on the site of the former Bres pit, established in 1795, which supplied coke for the gas works and had a canal to connect with shipping at Seaside.

In 1835 five men were 'dashed to atoms' at the pit when the basket they were in crashed to the bottom, with one young boy miraculously escaping by clinging on to the other set of conducting chains.

Across the way from the Asda car park is Pottery Street, its name a remnant of a once proud local industry. The Llanelli Pottery started in 1839 and its owner, William Chambers Junior, ensured that his workers had decent places to live by erecting houses in Pottery Street and Pottery Row. This later became Pottery Place, atttracting former Staffordshire potters who arrived in the town via stints at Swansea's Glamorgan Pottery which had ceased production in the mid-1830s. Production started in Llanelli in 1840 under the aegis of manager William Bryant, who urged his workers to save to buy their own houses, and it provided work for artists, craftsmen and general grafters until it closed in 1923.

When I was growing up, the best feature of Murray Street was the elevated walkway which crossed it and linked two parts of the Co-op. I have to admit that just walking across it was a thrill. You could swear you lived in New York. It was that modern, that thrillingly urban, or at least to a kid from Pwll. The street is now mainly estate agents, solicitors and takeaways nowadays. There's also the Salvation Army shop. In the window they've had a copy of Magnum photographer David Hurn's book, *Land of my Father* for sale every time I've visited the town. I still wish I'd gone in to buy it. Damn.

When General Booth, the founder of the Sally Army, visited Llanelli in 1883 he was criti-cized for the coarseness of the proceedings, some commenta-tors referring to mountebank work and objecting to boister-ousness.

But I haven't come to Murray Street for a doner kebab, or some boisterousness. Rather, I've come to look at a house which has connections to a wonderful Llanelli artist, J.D. Innes, a man who died early leaving a legacy of

questions about how great he might have become had he lived longer. A bit like the poet John Keats, who spawned a lot of what ifs. Bear with me, as I've been reading and thinking about Innes for getting on forty years, so I've got lots to share.

Llanelli's most talented artist was born at Greenfield Villas on Murray Street on 27 February 1887, even though his life was to be cruelly and tragically short, as he died in 1914 at the age of twenty-seven. James Dickson Innes was the son of John Innes, author of *Old Llanelly*. His education included a stint at Christ College, Brecon in 1898 and between 1904 and 1905 he attended Carmarthen Art School, where his early style was developed. For clues to influences on him one need look no further than the fact he always carried a book of Constable's colour reproductions with him, and that Turner's water colours, then housed in the National Gallery, were his 'ideal and almost daily visitation.' He admired Turner for his light and his poetic effect. You can see hints of the influence in Innes' work.

One of his most dramatic local subjects, *View of Llanelly from the Furnace Quarry*, painted in 1906, shows sheer, vertiginous cliff edges to the quarry, overlooking smoke stacks and a wide bay. Very early on Innes developed the habit of working *en plein air* using the suppressed light of evening or dawn. He worked very fast on a small scale. Although Innes started as a watercolour artist he painted equally deftly in oils.

A year after the Furnace painting he was exhibiting at the New English Art Club where he met Augustus John, who was to be a great influence and boon companion.[21] John was twenty nine when they met, Innes nine years his junior and then living in Fitzroy Street in London. John was then a notorious bohemian who had six sons by two women and was already the subject of a cult. Innes loved John's over-the-top, flamboyant personality and the lyricism of his nude figures, even if a part of Innes' look was pthisis, a wasting away. He was to match the impact of John's appearance.

Innes was a remarkable looking young man, and dressed with a distinction which owed nothing to the rules of fashion. His pale and cadaverous face, with lank black hair, black beady eyes and large flexible mouth would arrest attention anywhere; attired in a long black over-coat and a broad brimmed Quaker hat, a voluminous silk scarf took the place of a collar, and he held a silver-mounted Malacca cane in his gloved hand. Thus his appearance possessed a unique style to which his speech contributed an elaborate English note, superimposed on the characteristic intonation of his native land.

Other descriptions of him note a less kempt figure, 'unwashed, with ill-fitting false teeth, paint stained clothing, and a foreign, sometimes melancholy, often dissipated look which would not have fitted into jazz-age society.' There are tales of his fighting policemen and joining John in brawling scraps when Innes was wounded in the head in a back street.

Innes vigorously enjoyed the wrong sort of company, from the innocence of known eccentrics and practical jokers to seedier drunks and fallen women. One day when he was travelling in a taxi with Augustus John and Horace de Vere Cole they talked about being blood brothers and Innes pushed a knife right through his left hand with John replying by stabbing himself in the leg. But he still found time to work amid the debauchery. In 1908 he won first prize in the Slade figurative competition.

Innes' real life as a painter began when he went to France with John Fothergill in April and May 1908, visiting Caudebec, Bozouls and on to Collioure where Matisse and Derain had sought inspiration only a few years previously. Fothergill was interested in Innes sexually as well as artistically. The southern light acted like a luminous touchstone on Innes.[22]

He attracted interesting companions for his journeys. He travelled to Spain with Lord Howard de Walden, and they both painted at Ronda, where the steep valleys and sharp inclines delighted the eye.

In 1910 Innes fell in love with Euphemia Lamb in Paris, and the couple made their way back to Collioure with Euphemia paying their way by dancing exotically in cafés. This was the year he started to see a lot of Augustus John and they shared an obsession with landscape, painting quickly in bright Mediterranean light, using high key colours as if they were recollecting their childhoods in Wales. They were looking for 'the reflection of some miraculous promised land.' John had an exhibition in Chenil; Innes had a one man show of water-colours that pleased John so much that he wrote to people telling them to buy some. Wales and the south of France attracted them both. Innes had been in trouble with the law and was not paying much attention to his appearance any longer. He was paint-bespattered, constantly ill and always out of doors as he preferred to live rough and have the stars to comfort him.

Come 1911, he rented a cottage with Augustus John at Nant-Ddu near Arenig, where he was joined by Euphemia Lamb and the painter Albert Lipczinski and his beautiful wife Doonie. His first sighting of Arenig was an act of immersing love. It became a sacred mountain for him and the slope of Migneint his spiritual home. On his visits here he shared his love of the rocks and crags with women. On the summit of the mountain he buried a silver casket containing his letters to Euphemia and would always conflate the two loves: she was Arenig, a fixed magnetising point in his life.

This part of north Wales gripped his heart. Not for him the much painted terrains of Pont-Aven, Newlyn or St. Ives, but rather the inhospitable, unpeopled tract of land that stretched between Blaenau Ffestiniog and Bala, and especially Arenig Fawr, which was to become his most engrossing motif.

The speed with which Innes painted was extraordinary, making quick sketches in oils on wooden panels he would have carried for miles over squelching and sucking moorland as he waited for that moment when the clouds parted and the sun poured in. He set the pace for John and he energetically followed. John also liked his fellow painter's artistic innocence, a naiveté that translated into simple colours, fluid lines.

Even though Innes rented a place in the bald Welsh hills both he and Augustus John were still in touch with the London scene, connected to the avant garde. John said

I think he was never happier than when he was painting in this district. But his happiness wasn't without its morbid side, for his passionate devotion to the landscape of his choice provided also a way of escape from his consciousness of the malady which already was casting its shadow across his days, ignore it as he might pretend in an effort of sublime but foolish self-deception. This is what hastened his steps across the room and lent his brush a greater swiftness and decision as he set down, in a single sitting, view before jewelled view of the delectable mountain he loved; before a darkness came to hide every thing except a dim but inextinguishable glow, perceived by him as the reflection of some miraculous promised land… and it might have been this too, that led him to seek at times in the illusory palliative of the brandy bottle some respite from the sentence under which he knew himself, though secretly, to stand condemned.

There were other loves, of course. Love like a linnet flitted in every so often. Innes had a mad fling with an Algerian carpet weaver. On one trip he was accompanied by a young woman known variously as Billy or Shelley, a period when he bought a gypsy caravan to travel in. In Corwen, near Bala, he fell in with a party of gypsies and in love with a beautiful woman called Udina. He gave chase to her across north Wales, and on the outskirts of Ruabon collapsed and was found in a ditch by a good Samaritan. He shared a love of hippy life with John but also had come under the influence of John Sampson, a leading scholar of gypsy lore and a librarian at the University of Liverpool.

In 1912 his health collapsed after a visit to Galway Races, enjoying the hospitality of Lady Gregory at Coole Park. When John met him in Marseilles he was seemingly going out of his head and stuttering uncontrollably. In Perpignan he was taken seriously ill and then in St. Chamas he took to his bed for a week, after which his friends took him to Paris and from there to London to see a doctor.

In 1913 he had a one-man show at Chenil which made over £700 but by this time friends thought that he was rather far gone. That same year he moved to Mogador in Morocco with Trelawney Dayrell Reed where 'he remained some weeks in a Moorish house, merely occupying himself… in experimenting with various combinations of tobacco.' I can't help the image of Robert de Niro in Sergio Leone's *Once Upon a Time in America*, settling into his old age in an opium den, though we have no hard evidence Innes was toking anything other than 'bacco. But old age was to be denied him. He died of TB on 22 August 1914.

After his death many pondered the question of talent as yet unfulfilled. One of those was Augustus John who said, 'he cannot be said to have fulfilled himself completely as he died too young for his powers to reach their full maturity – and for that matter does not everyone? But by the intensity of his vision and his passionately romantic outlook, his work will live when that of many happier and healthier men will have grown, with the passing years, cold and dull and lifeless…'

TINOPOLIS

Television in Llanelli has come a long way since Les John made a television set and got the first licence for a TV in the town, back in 1950. It's now home to a real media player. Tinopolis, based in the red brick building which used to house Tesco in the town, is now the headquarters of a group of companies that make 2,500 hours of programmes for 200 broadcasters, employing 450 staff across the UK, one of the biggest outside the M25.

Three years ago the company won more awards than any other independent television company. Companies in the group make *Question Time* and *Panorama*. Others such as Fiction Factory and Daybreak produce top end drama such as the *Sex Life of David Blunkett* or TV plays about the suicide or maybe murder of David Kelly in *The Government Inspector*. Sunset and Vine is their sports' specialist, best known for the fact that it reinvented the way cricket is televised, using state-of-the-art technology to track the ball, not to mention the fact that it makes all of the BBC's racing coverage.

I remember when its predecessor company was based in Swansea, with a TV studio in the middle of a shopping centre. I met Ron Jones, a Brynaman boy and the chairman of Tinopolis, in his rather outsized office in the Llanelli HQ. It transpires that the reason it's so capacious is that it used to be the store's trolley park. So why move to Llanelli?

'Fundamentally we went to Swansea as it was seen very much as the capital of West Wales. I've never believed that was sensible. What we should have been looking for is a presence in Welsh-speaking Wales. Llanelli is far from being a Welsh-speaking town but it remains

the heartland of Welsh-speaking Wales and therefore culturally and emotionally the company feels much more at home here. There's a band from the Amman through the Gwendraeth down to west Wales and they feel very much a part of that.'

Serendipity played a part in finding the site.

They had viewed a new warehouse in Dafen as they wanted to move the whole of their production – digital and high definition structures – and had been looking for suitable spaces. Ron and his brother Clem drove round on Sunday mornings for weeks looking for a suitable space. They drove into the centre of Llanelli, saw the old Tesco store, and his brother being his brother, suggested they should break in. It was derelict and completely boarded up, and it had been empty for many

years. The place was dirty, had burned out internally, all the fittings were taken, drug takers had taken it over and there was drug debris everywhere. As they moved towards the back of the building in total darkness apart from their torches, his brother was describing the building in fairly unkind terms and threw some debris into the air in disgust. The ceiling collapsed to reveal behind it eight metre headroom – precisely what they needed to build television studios.

Ron notes at this point that Llanelli is 'a dark town. It was clear that the building had been used as a drugs HQ for years and one Friday night the whole building was attacked by twenty-five youngsters who wanted to drive us out.' Today they have two of the largest television studios in the UK entirely because the building was constructed to accommodate the 850-car car park on top. This means they've been able to place their satellite farm at quite a high level.

There was a famous occasion when a Llanelli councillor was shown the plans for the building and said in frank terms that 'he didn't want a mini fucking G.C.H.Q. in his ward but by now local people accept it as a technological company, so satellites are essential.' I'm reminded of the story, apocryphally ascribed to Aberdare, which tells of a local councillor suggesting new improvements to the lake in the town park and suggests getting a gondola. Not to be outdone a rival councillor asks 'why don't we get a pair of them and then they can breed?'

There is more bandwidth coming into Tinopolis than you need to run a medium-sized country and as a result they have all the technical facilities to operate throughout the world. They make material which is shown in 180 countries, from *America's Worst*

Drivers on NBC to *The Hamburg Cell* on HBO.

They first began to work in new media back in 1999 and invested heavily in them. There were a few difficult years because they were probably too early and the markets weren't there for the products they were trying to develop, but since then the market has demonstrably arrived. They generate content in sport, education and learning which is distributed extensively. And here is a firm that's happy to go to the dogs. When the BBC decided it wasn't going to broadcast the Crufts dog show Tinopolis stepped in and broadcast it on the web. They had a million and a quarter visits to the website from all over the world.

Tinopolis is owned by its management and a private equity firm called Vetruvian Partners, who came in when Ron realized that the market was reaching a crisis point. He posits, 'television companies have never done well outside Wales and that's why we became acquisitive, buying the expertise and the presence in the market place. Now we're probably the fifth largest media producer in the UK, but that still makes us small in the market place and in international terms. Can we be international and keep our roots in Llanelli? That's too difficult to answer but we also have to accept that we're risking our identity. Identity and ambition are always in tension.'

Ron says the name is very much about identity, of nailing one's colours to the mast, 'I chose Tinopolis for a few reasons. When we moved here we were known as Agenda and there was a them and us situation. I wanted to take us to one side and take the identity away and make it clear that this was something new, was something more. I've never believed the rampant theory in Wales that we are permanently disadvantaged. It's the lack of ambition that kills us.'

Just as Llanelli used to export huge amounts of coal and metal so too does Tinopolis export tons of stuff. Well, megabytes of the stuff. Every week they produce a sports magazine programme for Proctor and Gamble and the boys in Llanelli press a button and it can be seen all around the world.

One thing that brings a smile to faces at Tinopolis is that they were recently working with the University of California on their postgraduate programme. If you were working as a middle manager in Silicon Valley and wanted to broaden your education you were hooking up to Park Street in Llanelli. Cool.

It's one of the few industries where geography isn't a barrier. Ron cites a visit to the HQ of Ben and Jerry's ice cream in the back of beyond in Vermont. It shows you can be world leaders while based off the usual map. In the same way producing education and entertainment content for many media there isn't a physical barrier. So a company based in Llanelli can compete against rivals pretty much anywhere.

Ron Jones has also been involved with Llanelli rugby club and especially the redevelopment of the site of the old rugby stadium. Nimbyism almost scuppered the plans which were developed as the club was running on empty, financially speaking. 'Local people didn't realize that the Scarlets were in the trouble – what saved us was that when they found out they clubbed together to get half a million pounds to keep us going. That allowed the rugby club to prosper. For eight of the last twelve years Llanelli had provided a team that has consistently been among the best in Europe. What is it about Llanelli that allows that to happen?'

Rugby offers a complicated metaphor for the town. 'This little town has delivered by any statistics one of the best teams in Europe. They go through one bad season and the fans desert them. There is something about the psyche that doesn't engender the sense of loyalty and reality you need. People don't go to Parc y Scarlets because they say it's too far out, yet both Stradey Park and Parc y Scarlets are equidistant from here. That sort of attitude is there in many aspects of Llanelli life and it's not useful. If you're going to move things on there will be steep gradients. Llanelli is a town with serious issues to confront and such development as Machynys and South Llanelli don't resolve it all.'

Sitting among the ghosts of shopping trolleys Ron takes visible pride in the positives, in the triumphs of both the television company and the rugby team and finds parallels in their respective journeys.

'The eureka moment was a game against Wasps at Stradey. They were the newly monied class of English rugby and they came down here expecting to trample us into the dust on their way to European glory and the team stuffed them. One little guy, our flanker Ian Boobier, in eighty minutes took apart, emotionally and psychologically, Laurence Dallaglio who was everything Wasps was going to be. And Boobier took him apart to such a point that at the end he was speechless and it's at those moments you realize there's something about local people and about this town that becomes extraordinary.

'Now in our case, I don't think Tinopolis is an extraordinary story at all. What's extraordinary about what we've managed to do in Llanelli is actually the ordinary. The people who work here are in the main local youngsters who've come in from school or college, sometimes with skills, sometimes without, who somehow have conspired to develop a skill set that allows them to compete outside and to compete equally. So when we do go to London to compete creatively or on the corporate side we're not seen as second raters – we're not seen as people coming to make up the numbers – there's a competitive edge in both rugby and television that for me are the high points of the last twelve years.'

As I leave Tinopolis the floor manager and the camerafolk are just getting ready to rehearse *Wedi 3*, one of many magazine programmes which come out of the Llanelli studios every week. There's that quiet buzz that anticipates all live programmes. Beamed out from where the fresh veg used to be.

BIGYN AND TYISHA

Near the highest point of the town it's worth wandering along to the site of the old Llanelli General Hospital, for which a building committee was established in 1883. Debts plagued it but an unlikely saviour was found in Henry Studt, the fairground operator, who gave two sums of £500. It was finally built in local stone and ashlar in 1885 to a design by E.M. Bruce Vaughan, who used the same blueprint for the Aberystwyth Hospital three years later. Nowadays only a part of Llanelli Hospital remains, and it has been converted into a private residence, but Gothic lettering still runs around the front door. It's an interesting place to live and an interesting way to keep some history intact. Luckily, before demolition, panels from 1900 depicting nursery rhymes were moved from the hospital to the new Prince Phillip Hospital in Dafen. There's new housing on the site nowadays.

'You can find my house easily, it's the one with the hearse parked outside.' Geraint Hopkins' home is on the site of the old hospital near the top of Bigyn Hill. He has variously been a gravedigger, an operating theatre assistant and escapologist – in fact his trusty bed of nails is still in the shed after he failed to sell it on e-Bay – but nowadays he and his wife Yolande run Ghost Watch Wales, taking believers and sceptics alike to experience the paranormal. He's already experienced some at Llanelli House, as we know. Geraint also exhibits and handles snakes and two African Royal pythons slither languorously around in a glass case in the front room where we're sitting. The room also houses the bardic chair of his late father, Glyn Hopkins from Hendy, along with various porcelain rattlesnakes and cobras. My tea cup shakes slightly in my hand. I have a phobia. In the corner a six foot high manikin of an undertaker in full funeral frock coat with a ghastly green face adds to the surreality.

Geraint tells me about his extraordinary inheritance. 'I got my psychic powers when my mother passed away. I was fourteen and the day that she died something very strange happened. I dreamed that they were opening her grave – this was before I knew she was dead – she was in hospital and I couldn't visit her because I was ill. Two weeks after that I was in bed feeling very low and I could smell flowers – like funeral flowers and then I could feel a flush of warm loving feeling from my feet up to my head and I didn't feel so bad after that. Before that I used to feel very uneasy in a graveyard – I used to see people and they weren't there.'

One day when he was sixteen he was going with his mates on their pushbikes to Pontyberem when this chap ran across the road and they all crashed and ended up on the floor. Geraint asked them if they'd seen the man but not one of the others had. He'd started to see things. His powers were growing.

Later he and his wife moved into a flat in Park Street and sensed something odd. 'My wife had a blind dog and one night it was howling and the window was open where it hadn't been. In the bedroom I saw an old lady and she was pointing to the attic and then she disappeared. I wasn't such a good psychic then – I hadn't developed. I smelled the flowers again and it felt as if I was being hugged by an invisible force. When I did go up the attic all I found was an old sweet jar.'

Over the years he's encountered all manner of paranormal events in new houses as well as old. They've cleared many places of their ghosts – police stations, a bank and no fewer than four fire stations. Not that they always clear ghosts. Some people want them to stay. Geraint will see apparitions anywhere. In Llanelli market he saw a ghostly woman with a parasol. In Llanelli town there was the ghost of a paedophile farmer called Tom – a malevolent spirit – which Yolande dealt with by uttering the Latin Mass. They don't use ouija boards, which Geraint warns against, but they do use the full panoply of ghost hunting equipment such as laser thermometers and electro magnetism meters. Not that he needs them, of course. This sort of equipment lets them see orbs which 'are often no more than dust but if you get orbs with faces they're spirits. Usually spirits manifest as orbs first.' Good to know.

As his pet Chihuahuas yap at my feet Geraint gives me a quick taxonomy of ghosts and spirits. 'Some scientists have investigated 'stone tapes' which are based on the notion that old buildings with stone walls absorb things and replay them every so often that they have residual energy. Some ghosts are grounded and there are others that visit from another dimension. Then you have malevolent spirits and demons. I did a house in Llanelli where a gentleman had ended his life in the kitchen. The owners had all sorts of things happen such as blankets were taken off them as they slept. We always videotape private investigations and when we played the tape back afterwards we could hear the words 'Get out' very faintly. I told the spirit we meant no harm and asked whether it wanted to come into the light. My colleague then saw a vase lift up and hit me on the back of the head.' In some ways Geraint's like Bill Murray in *Ghostbusters*, only without the outrageous guns.

Stand on Bigyn Hill, and you can see a great sweep of low lying plain. Imagine the ice age, before the glaciers' retreat. As the landscape defrosts into the middle Paleolithic this is a haunt of hyenas, reindeers and woolly rhinoceros, mammoths, bison, giant ox, Irish elk and cave bears. Nowadays it's a post-industrial panorama. Gone are the smoke stacks that rose like birch thickets from the marshland of Machynys to the edges of Pwll, not to mention the three enormous chimneys of the Carmarthen Bay Power Station to the west. Drink enough strong lager, as someone has clearly done judging from the number of cans I can see near a bench, you might well see those mammoths again. Waltzing on ice.

As you proceed down the vertiginous hill you'll come to the home of an actress who starred alongside movie stars such as Rex Harrison, who eventually became her husband, Albert Finney and Richard Harris, and appeared in films such as *Picnic at Hanging Rock*, Lindsay Anderson's *This Sporting Life*, played Brenda in Karel Reisz's landmark kitchen sink drama *Saturday Night and Sunday Morning*, and *Yanks*, not to mention a long string of stage appearances in the West End and on Broadway.

Rachel Roberts was born at the manse of Emmanuel Chapel in Tyisha Road on 20 September 1927, the daughter of the minister of the small chapel that still stands at the bottom end of New Dock Road. Although she picked up some tips from his preaching and was influenced by her mother's speaking skills, it was her paternal grand-father, Goronwy Rhys Owen Roberts, who shaped her stage and screen presence. He gave her a good voice and, genetically, a pug nose. She also had 'a tendency to gloom,' as one colleague put it. She was to end a terribly lonely life in Los Angeles, committing suicide in the Hollywood hills, still missing Rex, who had given her love, a champagne lifestyle, a retreat above Portofino, all in all a world far removed from life on this Llanelli street.

Along the way this graduate of Aberystwyth had progressed to RADA and played at Stratford. As the historian Peter Stead puts it, hers was 'the story of an actress losing control, of hopeless addiction to sex and alcohol, of a growing dependence on stimulants and prescription drugs, of a collapsing professional confidence and finally, of course, of loneliness. "You'll be left alone," her mother had warned in the way that Welsh mothers would.'[23] Her life was a catalogue of boorish drinking and messy and squalid hopelessness, yet Rachel, or Ray as she was known to her friends, kept it together sufficiently to act and to write superbly, whether in her journals or in occasional forays into fiction. She always turned up on time for rehearsals or performances, out of respect for her thespian colleagues who respected this aspect of her in turn. When she pulled out of an Athol Fugard play it was because the slope had become too slippery.

Other film stars were born in the town, too. Clifford Evans, whose parents lived in Capel Road, won a competition hosted by the Metropole Theatre in London designed to find 'one whose appearance and ability qualify him for a career in films.' Clifford was a finalist from among a thousand entrants. He went on to appear in Hammer Horror films such as *Kiss of the Vampire* and *Curse of the Werewolf*. Eleanor Daniels, from Pembrey Road, carved out a career for herself on Broadway as well as film and radio. She returned in triumph for the 1930 National Eisteddfod in the town. And we've already heard elsewhere about Gareth Hughes, the desert priest of Hollywood.

We've also detailed the astonishing success of the Stepney Spare Wheel. As you leave Geraint and his snakes behind we walk down Tyisha Road and come to the two-tone brick 1860s villa, Highfield

House, which you can glimpse behind a high wall. There's a blue plaque outside noting that this is where the owners of Stepney Spare Wheel Company lived.[24] The history of the wheel itself was described when we visited Parc Howard. The Davies brothers, Thomas and Walter moved into what was originally the home of J.S. Tregoning, Junior, the owner of the Morfa Works. Their former home is the ideal place to ponder the run of luck: how two men who started life running an ironmongery shop in Stepney Street, then a cycle shop in the Stepney Street Arcade, then a small cycle and motor repair works, before claiming a new world market in the early days of motoring, is still a great tale of entrepreneurship and luck.

At the bottom of the hill you come to the railway sheds built by Isambard Kingdom Brunel. As a boy I used to play here when I accompanied my father to work in the nearby British Rail offices, and would always be impressed by the scale of the engineering work and the smell of oils and unguents.

And on one occasion I was invited here to be presented with an award. A terrible gale in 1890 washed away the railway line between Llanelli and Burry Port, waves from the estuary taking away some twenty yards of track. As contemporary reports had it, it was lucky the accident happened at night. In the 1970s I was walking the same length of track, en route to do a spot of birdwatching, when I noticed the sea wall had again been washed away, leaving nothing to support the tracks of the main Fishguard to London route. I ran home as fast as I could and told my father, who in due course phoned to stop all trains. I was given a guided tour of the place where he worked and in the engine sheds the area manager formally gave me a copy of the

Collins Field Guide to British Birds as a reward.

Now the roofs are falling in, and time is eating away at the masonry, but these are still imposing structures which capture the confidence of the Victorian age. There were proposals to move the railway museum from Swindon to be housed in these sheds, but dillying and dallying by the council, married to nimbyism by local residents, apparently put paid to that idea. Now they molder and decay, testimony to another opportunity missed.

STATION ROAD

I'm walking down Station Road with amateur historian Huw Lewis, and as he's proved on other walks, he's a veritable mine of information. It takes us a meandering hour and a half to cover what would take five minutes at a brisk pace. First, we pass the first actual Post Office to be built in the town, now a bar called Stamps. Original name. First class. Dreamt up at a lick. We then stand near the site of a Roman camp, marked by one of the blue plaques Huw and his colleagues at Llanelli Community Heritage have put up. All voluntary work, but invaluable. You could do lot worse than to try to see all the plaques, collectively a guide to Llanelli's historical hot spots. I've done it and learned a great deal. Huw tells me that of the Roman fort there's very little evidence, a few coins found and tiny fragments of pottery. There is a slight rise in the ground which is believed to be the camp wall, shaped like a playing card around the Post Office. In the 1860s a map of the town had the area marked as a Roman camp.

At the top or the town end of Station Road there is an area marked on old maps as Pencastell – Head or Top of the Castle – where Station Road meets John Street and Murray Street. It was originally the name of a field, a part of the park which opened out behind Llanelli House. A doctor's surgery was latterly called Pencastell and you can still see Castle Buildings,[25] now housing La Caprice restaurant, a tattoo parlour and a tapas bar.

We pause at the corner of John Street. This used to be Salamanca Road, Huw tells me. This is where a horse died in about 1905 and the police officer had it dragged into John St because he didn't know how to spell Salamanca. I check my trouser leg to see if it's got bells on it. There are three tiny silver ones, made by elvish fingers. We move on.

Along this stretch there used

to be a clutch of Italian cafés which Hugh, now 58 years old, remembers with relish from the days when he was four or five, when he'd come here for a knickerbocker glory. I used to come here for peach melbas served in banana shaped glasses. Peaches were exoticism itself back then.

There are two Baptist churches along the strip. The Baptists have a long connection with the town, meeting at a house in Berwig as far back as 1650, when technically they were members of Ilston Church in Gower and would cross the Loughor at low tide to worship. There they attended services under the auspices of one John Myles, who organised the sect across a section of country from Hay-on-Wye to Carmarthen and was paid for out of Cromwell's purse, using the role of Public Preacher to disseminate public propaganda.

Diametrically opposite the Llanelli Entertainment Centre used to stand the Synagogue, on Queen Victoria Road. It opened in 1909, when there was a large contingent of Jewish people living in the neighbourhood. Immigrants have energized the town, coming in successive waves. Nowadays you see many signs proclaiming *Do Wynajecia*. To Let. There have been estimates that as much as five per cent of the town's population was Polish in recent years, though job losses at employers such as Dawn Pac in Cross Hands have left many of these industrious people without work.

The Polish presence in Llanelli nowadays is palpable, but they've not been attracted here by the *atrakcje turystyczne*, or tourist attractions. To find out more I met Halina Ashley, the project manager of the Polish-Welsh Mutual Association, or *Stowarzyszenie Współpracy Polsko-Walijskiej*, which shares its office space with Saveasy, the Llanelli and District Credit Union. She came to Llanelli twenty years ago although she came to Britain forty years ago. She was eighteen at the time and it was a different world. She'd been brought up in Poland and when she was given a passport at the age of eighteen she came to visit her auntie in Blackburn. It wasn't easy as the state put up lots of obstacles. It was meant to be just a holiday visit for two or three months but Halina decided to stay and had her family's blessing in this. This was a life-changing decision because in those days you didn't have the freedom of travel. Under the communist regime, Halina avers, you didn't have any kind of freedom. In Poland one had to fight for everything. Britain seemed to her to be the land of opportunities.

She eventually came to Llanelli because her son was growing up and both she and her husband wanted a safer and nicer place to live, perhaps similar to Halina's own childhood in the Polish countryside with its greenery. There were also many interests her son, Andrew, could pursue better here than in Manchester, such as athletics. He was to represent Wales in junior athletics, and generally enjoyed his Welsh childhood. It seems to have stood him in good stead for the future because Halina is a very proud mother. She has ample reason to be. Her son is a junior research fellow in science at Balliol College, Oxford, attending to matters of global import such as climate change. In the city of dreaming spires he is currently working towards 'a homogeneous Fischer-Tropsch process, which will enable the reduction of CO_2 to liquid hydrocarbons…. This would provide an alternative to the use of crude oils for fuels whilst being overall carbon neutral.' Not that I know much about the Fischer-Tropsch but I guess this is planet saving stuff. He's one of the legion of scientists we're all hoping will be able to save our bacon, or stop our own skins from turning into crackling under a fierce sun.

There were only two other Poles in Llanelli when Halina arrived, both of them women of about the same age. There was no Polish community, no Polish clubs, no Polish social life whatsoever. 'But that's what we wanted when we left Manchester. A big city has its advantages but it also has its pitfalls. We wanted to escape the ratrace, basically.'

Halina well remembers the first big influx of Poles into Llanelli. It was three weeks into May 2004. Europe had opened its borders to Poland and Poland, with its population of well over thirty million, was emptying. She recalls how swiftly they arrived and in such numbers.

> They came here from the first of May and we started to notice the Polish language and Polish cars but three weeks down the road I was shopping in a garden centre, on a lovely Sunday and Jeff Hopkins, the chief executive of Saveasy phoned me and said excitedly that lots of Polish migrants had been brought here by an agency and they had extreme difficulties with housing, employment and contracts. So Jeff and I met to see how we could help. It was a lucky coincidence for these Polish migrants, very lucky that there was a community organization which supported the local community, and looked after them as a credit union. But they also found access to the local M.P., to local councillors and so on. Access to health service, local authorities: we were able to provide such services or signpost them.

Llanelli was peculiar, in fact unique. An employment agency

emptied one town in central Poland, namely Zyclin, near the city of Lodz, and brought them all over to Llanelli. They recruited in the Polish town and had an office there. After six months the first wave of migrants brought their children and then the rest of their families over. Once the children entered our education system they proved very adaptable.

Having a credit union already set up was a Godsend. Jeff Hopkins is the chief executive of the Saveasy credit union. The former political agent for Denzil Davies, and a man keenly attuned to all the workings and machinations of Llanelli, he says that Saveasy builds on the long tradition of co-operatives in the area, when villages such as Trimsaran had their own co-operatives. Halina, seeking parallels, cites the crucial role they played in her native country where 'if the Government failed the co-ops filled the gap.' In Llanelli they've lent £8.5 million over a period of ten years. Currently, some eighty per cent of lending is small loans of under a thousand pounds, but crucially they are the sort of loans that the banks wouldn't be disposed to give. Poles and locals benefit equally from the existence of Saveasy.

Nobody knows exactly how many Poles live in Llanelli. The new Workers' Registration Scheme can't be trusted in this respect because not many workers know that they're meant to register with the Home Office and receive a certificate (costing ninety pounds, which in itself is a disincentive). Many workers are falsely listed as clerical workers when they are, in fact, packing meat. When they arrived in Llanelli many of the contracts they were given were only borderline legal, with guarantees of work but with no more than zero hours actually promised.

Many Poles hold on to old customs in their new home, as Halina explains. 'They can't break the habit of eating Polish food, even though Poland is now very Westernized. More Westernized than the west. The shops there are full of stuff though the people don't have money to buy them. There is a rich class though, which became wealthy by buying government assets and using them more efficently, a bit like Abramovich in Russia. But the country's not doing well. With eleven per cent employment, many emigrate to Spain, Sweden and Germany and so on. There's no work in Poland and no real benefit system – you have to beg for it, be really destitute. People have to rely on their extended families and so someone has to go to work abroad. The sad fact is that despite this being the twenty-first century, in Poland there are many malnourished children, especially in villages in rural areas. There is squalor and poverty and many want to try their luck elsewhere.' In Llanelli they are able to find Polish food in a very success-ful delicatessen called Lolek, in Park Street, selling fresh Polish bread, yoghurt, cheese and a huge range of meats and sausages. A new Polish shop is opening in Station Road, replacing one which closed its doors some months ago.

Selling Tyskie lager and more of those fantastic sausages.

The Polish government has recently been offering inducements to encourage people to return and some have done so, but these are rapidly replaced by new immigrants. It will depend on the number of jobs they can find here. They need to work for a couple of years before they can access any public funds.

According to Halina, Llanelli people have been 'generally welcoming, they find Polish people are good neighbours and respect the fact that the Poles work hard, are conscientious workers. There are those people, of course – many of whom don't work themselves – who begrudge the Poles getting these jobs.' There have been isolated incidents of anti-Polish graffiti appearing on walls and the media have sometimes turned a selective spotlight on the immigra-tion but generally Llanelli has absorbed the new migrants as it has other nationalities in the past, in the heyday of heavy industry.

Language is a barrier for the Poles just as surely as it is for an English-speaker trying to twist his tongue into some Polish pronun-ciations. And, for some, there's no crying need to embrace a new language. Employers often have Polish supervisors so workers don't need to acquire English. They watch Polish TV courtesy of Polsat, can read Polish newspapers and use the internet, in Polish. Yet Halina, with her fluent and precise English is proof positive that it's not an insurmountable barrier. She tells me how there are courses held at the local library and some employers have offered English lessons but the take-up hasn't been that great. So they've helped devise a sort of survival English course which they've been deliver-ing for the past eighteen months, with funding from the Unite union.

'We help them with the very basics. How to spell their own name, and their address and how to open a bank account, which we show them with real forms. Local volunteers help with pronunciation, working one-to-one. They're the sort of people you would never see in a classroom, but we turn these lessons into social events with refreshments and a raffle to win a dictionary and so on. Sometimes we get forty people in a hall.' Even the Welsh pronunciations are relatively easy for the Polish speech organs as they have the same sort of sounds in Polish; they're just a different flavour of linguistic soup. Just as surely as we can all enjoy *bigos* and cawl.

Just as the Poles came to and took to Llanelli so too the Jews who came before them. One of the most famous is Michael Howard, about whom Anne Widecombe famously said that he had 'something of the night about him.' Here's a quick life sketch, from Michael Crick's biography.[26] He was regular at synagogue. Parents were drapers. He went to Stebonheath Infants. Then Park Street Junior. One of the teachers there, Jean Pugh, 'knew he was going somewhere from the very beginning.' Formed a skiffle band in Llanelli. Keen soccer player. Said he was going to Parliament even as a young boy. Shone at Grammar School. Eight O levels. Carried on doing well. Gained a place at Peterhouse, Cambridge to study Economics and prepare for that political life he'd seen for himself. Conservative wunderkind with family connections to Transylvania. Prince of darkness. To some.

Mall Cop is playing at the Llanelli Entertainment Centre. The former Odeon and latterly the Classic Cinema was bought by the council in 1976, paying £65,000 of which fifty thousand had been raised by the Civic Theatre Appeal Trust. Live theatre and cinema has been sustained in the town by the centre ever since.[27]

Theatres have played an active role in the town's cultural life, from places such as Warren's Prince of Wales in Murray Street, to the Marionette Shows, Noake's and Johnson's. The Hippodrome, formerly the Royalty in Park Street welcomed such stars as Charlie Chaplin in 1908, as well as Gracie Fields and Mary Lloyd.

They once had to post a £5 reward for information leading to the 'arrest' of a gang of snuff blowers, who expressed their disapproval of any act they didn't like by blowing clouds of snuff on stage, causing fits of coughing and sneezing among the artistes. In 1911, Leon Vint from Exmouth made an application to build a theatre which later became the Palace Cinema, but still referred to locally as Vint's. I watched some of the early Bond films there and would itch after sitting on the seats. But it was worth it to see Ursula Andress come out of the waves. I needed a rub down with a damp edition of the *Radio Times* after seeing her appear, I can tell you.

A lot of drinking goes on in Station Road. You can have a night at the Met, or Metropolitan. There's the Vine with banners outside. 'Pool.' 'Happy Hour.' 'For a Good Night Out.' At VX Max they're offering shots for a quid and Strongbow at £1.99 on Fridays, 7-12.30. Cocktails, too. Slippery Nipple, £1.99. Sambucca, same price. The Turnstyle Sports Bar. Nice louvre doors, touch of class. The Rolling Mill, an old style drinking clinic. Two motability scooters parked outside. You've got to laugh.

We also pass Barnums, which used to be called the Whitehall Vaults. First topless pub in Wales. The popular barmaid was called Tinkerbell. Sadly she died in a recent house fire. Her presence was enough for one Baptist minister to dub the town the new Sodom and Gomorrah. The UK media flocked here to check it out. Now they're doing karaoke at Barnums, Wednesday and Sunday. First prize three hundred pounds. That's a hundred and fifty slippery nipples, keep the change.

There's a new Filipino food store just along from there called Pinoy & Oriental. And Heaven Nails. Then there are the tanning

salons, that modern craze. Burnish the flesh. Fitness Factory. Cocoa Beach. And the takeaways. New Golden Pool. Chinese and English. Marmaris kebabs and pizza. Bahn Mai Thai. And an Indian restaurant called Moods that offers chocolate curry. God in Heaven! And ironically positioned in the middle of all this cholestrol and alcohol is Llesol, the Holistic Therapy Centre. For all your macrobiotic needs. Deriges, for all your vacuum cleaner needs.

At night this street lights up with neon and globules of fat hang in the air. There's a linguistic shift as the hours wear on and the international language of drunks becomes the lingua franca, that slur of mismashed vowels and drowned consonants. They sound as if they're speaking Serbo-Croat. With gusto.

Maybe the topers and roisterers of Station Road should pay heed to what happened to one poor soul in the town who proved that too much boozing could end not just in the dock, but in the docks. One unfortunate drunk, Thomas Hanbury Powell, took his own life by diving into Llanelli Dock and left a cautionary note:

'I did this rash thing because of drink. It forced me to do, and I must make an end to myself this way. The snares of death compressed me round about, and the pains of hell got hold upon me... I hope all the young men of Llanelli will give up the evil drinking, and take a warning from me, dear friends.'

It's troubling stuff. Make mine a shandy.

We walk along past the site of Wherle's pawnbrokers and then pass between the sites of two tinplate works, both given plaques – Marshfield and Old Lodge.[28] In one set of flats built on the site Dyfed-Powys Police are sending sniffer dogs in through the front door. Llanelli has a huge drug problem. My brother, who works in probation in town, used to tell scary tales of people shooting ketamine, a horse tranquiliser, between their toes. Drug workers in the town tell me it's still a problem, exacerbated by people being able to source it on the internet.

Huw and I pause outside what used to be a public house called the Marshfield Tap. 'It didn't actually have a name; steelworkers would apparently say they were going off to get some water, were going to the tap. So the pub got that name much later.'

Just beyond is my old school. Ysgol Dewi Sant, where I received my primary education, even though there was a perfectly good school in Pwll. However my parents wanted me to have a Welsh language education. Dewi Sant School was the product of an almighty struggle to ensure there was such a thing in the town. It all stemmed from a local H.M.I. realizing that the Butler Act said that parents should have a voice in their children's education. There was advantage in this for Welsh speakers. He mentioned the fact in passing to Olwen Williams who set up a parents' association, even though she wasn't a parent herself. It raised a petition which was sent to the Ministry of Education in London and to the Director of Education in Carmarthen. Though the petition was sent in 1945 the parents had to wait until St. David's Day, 1947 for the doors of Zion vestry to open its doors to the thirty-four children who formed the first intake. This was the first Welsh school to be set up by a local authority and it paved the way for many many more throughout Wales during the years that followed.

Huw and I pass the old Hactos factory, which used to make a cough mixture we all had as kids. Apparently they've started to make it again on a different site. For hypochondriacal nostalgia, perhaps. We progress past the old copperworks. Huw tells me about the chimney, 'Stack Fawr was built by a husband-wife team, both steeplejacks – Mrs Zammit was every bit as good as her husband. The stack involved three quarter of a million bricks and was built high enough to ensure the fumes would clear the top of Bigyn Hill. In Llanelli the prevailing south westerly winds would push the fumes in that direction.

Nearby is the factory where the last copper was worked in Llanelli, at the Draka plant. Copper had been worked on the site for 207 years but then the company moved its operations to Derbyshire. To read the *Llanelli Star* is to realize that much of the industry in the town has an axe swinging over it. Especially as chill winds blow though the whole economy. Winds so chill they seem to blow in straight in from the Urals, biting the skin, threatening to tear it clean off. This town is being flayed. As it has been many times before.

As we swing back towards town from the North Dock end of Queen Victoria Road we pause to examine the plaque of the Cambrian Bridge. It commemorates the 1911 Railway Strike. As often happens with such things heat played its part. The weather was hot that summer, with Greenwich recording a temperature of 100 degrees Fahrenheit. There was industrial unrest to match the rising mercury, with a one-day strike called for Thursday 13 August by the

railway unions which was observed by all 500 railwaymen in Llanelli, their numbers bolstered by thousands of other demonstrators from the town and outlying villages, who thronged the station approaches, there to show solidarity and express their disgust at the low wages of as little as a pound a week for the poorest paid railway workers. The town's police force had mainly been deployed elsewhere, sent to Cardiff and Tonypandy, where unrest had been fomenting and trouble was expected. This is how Llanelli's very own historian John Edwards captured the events:

> Relations between the police and strikers in Llanelli was congenial enough and two trains were held up while two were allowed to progress onwards for London. But in the morning a railway shareholder and a J.P., Thomas Jones turned up at the station, having more than likely sent for troops. A contingent of 127 soldiers from the North Lancashire Regiment arrived from Cardiff, led by Captain Burrows. Scuffles ensued but the two trains held up overnight were allowed to leave. The police came back and to full strength, but the strikers still held the crossing gates. Jones and Frank Nevill sent a telegram to the Home Office asking for troop reinforcements and 250 men from the Devon Regiment and the Worcester Regiment arrived that afternoon, under Major Brownlow Stuart. The Riot Act was read out and troops moved into the crossing. Now tensions ran high and stones were thrown at passing trains.
>
> On the Saturday afternoon, while a meeting was held at Copperworks School a train started on its journey. As the guard went to open the gate the railwaymen's leader John Bevan, put his head symbolically on the track. The strikers put out the fire in the engine before eighty soldiers arrived on the scene. The crowd retreated and many sat on the embankments behind High Street and Bryn Road. Stones were thrown. Bugles sounded. The Riot Act was again read out. Then soldiers fired at a gang of young men. Two were shot dead. Another was shot in the neck. Another in the hand. The soldiers marched back to the station, in double quick time.

> A public meeting in town dispersed, marching to the station where they smashed all the windows, and smashing all the points, so that Llanelli was stranded. A train nearby was found to contain army uniforms and was duly smashed and ransacked. General looting ensued in the town, much of it right next to the police station. Soldiers stayed in the station while the sidings erupted and it wasn't until 350 men of the Sussex Regiment arrived that the streets were brought under control. But an explosion in one of the trucks killed a further four people.

This was described by the local newspapers as Llanelli's darkest day. There is no doubt that the blood spilled on that day has seeped deep into the annals and the town's collective psyche.

On a lighter note, my favourite Llanelli stories of all time concern railway station announcements. There was a time when a man called Eddie Lip supplied them. One day the train that was due to come in on Platform One instead came in on Platform Two and vice versa, so much to everyone consternation Eddie's voice came over the public address system saying, 'you over there come over here: you over here go over there.' One can imagine the passengers paralysed by these impossible options.

Now that might well be apocryphal but I can attest personally to the veracity of another announcement he made as I was there, as Max Boyce might put it. Trains used to leave at the same time on the hour throughout the day and stop at the same stations along the way. So the five past nine, say, would call at 'Gowerton, Swansea, Neath, Port Talbot, Bridgend, Cardiff, Newport, Bristol Parkway, Swindon, Reading and London Paddington.' Someone had clearly written out the instructions for all subsequent trains for Eddie to read, so when I went to catch the five past ten the announcement was read out with gusto and clarity and went 'the next train will be calling at Gowerton, Swansea, Neath, Port Talbot, ditto, ditto, ditto, ditto, ditto, ditto, ditto and London Paddington.'

I still don't know why he was called Eddie Lip, though.

The railway station is half way to being unmanned nowadays, though I remember when there would be all manner of staff on its two platforms. It's unprepossessing but mainly clean, and much cleaner than it used to be…

> Llanelly is one of the most uninviting towns on the Great Western line of railway for strangers to visit; and it is the general complaint of

travellers of its dirty and sombre appearance. In the first place, the railway station is a disgrace to a town of its size and importance, and nothing like adequate to meet its commercial demands. On entering the town, there is nothing to be seen but chimneys, stacks, smoke, black and dirty roads and blacker walls...[29]

Things improved when the indefatigable M.P. W.H. Smith opened a bookstall on the station which led to the *Llanelly and County Guardian* of 30 September 1875 describing how 'Station Road is now becoming quite a hive of industry. Shops of every description are springing up – grocers, bakers, tailors, shoemakers, saddlers, painters, public houses and pawnbrokers, and all except the latter are thriving well.'

Huw and I move away from the station and turn up Railway Terrace to Nevill Street, named after Charles Nevill, a former Mayor of Birmingham who had run a copper works there. He teamed up with fellow industrialist John Guest and a London copper merchant called William Nevill to build a copperworks in Llanelli, which in due course would also smelt silver and lead. It was built at Penros at Seaside in 1805 in which year production also started. As we've heard the stack at the works was a real giant, made up of no fewer than 700,000 bricks and standing over 320 feet tall.

A short tempered man, Nevill was also socially minded and in 1846 he built Copperworks School to educate the offspring of his workers. Previously they had been taught in a storeroom in the works. At Copperworks you could learn the three Rs, reading, writing and arithmetic, but also navigation, with a compass set into the floor of one of the classrooms.

Nevill was also a big man, over six feet tall and a cultivated one too, who acted as the French consul in the town and became High Sheriff for Carmarthenshire in 1836. He lies buried in Llangennech churchyard.

GLANYMOR

To wander around Glanymor and Tyisha nowadays is to see an area once pulsing with industry now fallen quiet. There are still endless terraces of small houses, built to house workers and their families and there is still a pronounced sense of community, even if it's one that is economically disadvantaged.

All that remains of the Glanmor Foundry, established in 1873 by blacksmith John Powell from Penygaer to produce heavy castings for the tinplate industry, is the laboratory block which sports a blue plaque. Powell had originally run a business known as Bryndrodin Foundry as a general ship's smith for the many ships that hoved into Llanelli's harbour. His foundry grew to a substantial size, covering an area of several acres and at its peak it employed 400 people. It was an important part of the industrial scene for 130 years until its closure in 1979, when it still employed 170 people. Powell, an important philanthropist and civic figure, died in Brynrodin House, Myrtle Terrace in July 1889, leaving a widow but no children. Nowadays it's a laboratory of the spirit, as the late R.S. Thomas might have put it, a centre for Christian care and enlightenment.

But the reason I want to pause at Glanmor is because of one of the workers, one of the most evocative chroniclers of Llanelli life, the writer William Glynne-Jones. He was born in 1907, the son of a carpenter. He had a physical handicap, with a cleft palate and harelip, which attracted cruel mockery throughout his life. You can just imagine the schoolyard nicknames, laced with acid, tinged with lye.

His connection with the Glanmor Foundry started at the age of fifteen as an apprentice moulder. He remembered his first day vividly: 'The new world I entered was strange and frightening. The factory yard was covered with a thick layer of red soot which seeped into our clothes, food and into the pores of our skin. The air we breathed was full of the tang of sulphuric and nitric acid. It bit into the men's lungs and made them cough and retch.'

His writing conjures up images of him riding to the foundry on a drop-handled bike, coming home with his face blackened and his clothes sodden with sweat. He would bathe, as did so many other people in the town, in a tin bath. No matter how drained he was by his physical labour he would retire to his typewriter, feeding his dreams of becoming a writer with the fiery heat of a furnace. He also read voraciously and he would yo-yo back and forth to the Public Library to stoke

the flames of his imagination. While literature was his abiding passion he also loved opera and music, painting and angling.

His devotion to writing would pay off. Later in his life Glynne-Jones would win the Rockefeller Foundation Atlantic Award for Literature in 1946. He penned several novels, created over a hundred short stories as well as a dozen books for children, including historical yarns such as *The Trail of the Frozen Gold*, about the Yukon Gold Rush, and *Pennants on the Main*, which chronicled the buccaneering life and times of the Welsh pirate Harry Morgan, later Governor of Jamaica.

He lived at No. 24 Andrew Street, near Zion chapel. His grandmother, a monoglot Welsh speaker, introduced him to storytelling, the young lad enjoying their homespun quality in the physical warmth of her woollen shawl. She told him about the women of Fishguard who masqueraded as soldiers to ward off a French landing force, and of H.M. Stanley and his explorer's adventures in Africa. Above the parlour door there was a picture of the Denbigh-born explorer, up to his waist in jungle ooze, firing at hippopotami. In mud, mud, glorious mud. His grandfather, meanwhile, shared with him a passion for poetry and later, at Bigyn Elementary School, a tobacco-chewing teacher called Mr. Jackson inculcated a love of literature by reading aloud books such as R.M. Ballantyne's *Coral Island* and tales of Jason and the Argonauts hunting for the Golden Fleece. Later, T.V. Shaw, an English master and latterly headmaster at Llanelli County, which became the Boys' Grammar School, was to continue that nurturing. And William Glynne-Jones' first cousin, William John Hughes, later to become the Hollywood actor Gareth Hughes, also lent him books from his own personal library.

Following his apprenticeship as a moulder at Glanymor, Glynne-Jones worked there for nineteen years until he left on grounds of ill health, marrying Doris Passmore, the daughter of a postman, and starting a family. He then decamped to Hornsey in London where he was to earn a living as a writer, realizing the far off dream of childhood. He took various jobs, from sub-editing magazines, work for *Argosy* magazine and as a reader for Metro-Goldwyn-Mayer. He also did stints as a film correspondent for a South African magazine and as a tutor in a Writers' Correspondence School. Writers such as Doris Lessing – future winner of the Nobel Prize for Literature – would drop in for tea. He then settled into the relative comfort zone of the Civil Service. All the time he was writing, writing.

Summer Long Ago and *The Childhood Land* received critical acclaim with the *Times* suggesting that he had a 'firm grasp of the boundless energy, the diabolical inventiveness and the short-sighted selfishness of children,' while Somerset Maugham said that his little boys are exactly like little boys, and the dialogue he had given them 'sounds to me extremely lifelike while the picture of life in a small seaside town was very engaging.' The *Western Mail* said he allowed the reader to see Llanelli, cast as Abermor in a 'radiant clarity as in the light of a spring morning.'

One by one his stories found a home – in *Strand* magazine, in the *Welsh Review*. By the late Fifties he was being published in *Esquire* magazine in the U.S., using the slightly cumbersome name William Glynne-Jones to distinguish him from other Welsh writers such as Glyn Jones and Gwyn Jones. Some, like Glyn Jones and George Ewart Evans, became lifelong friends.

I've read some of his books and while they have more than the occasional purple patch and saccharine streak they're sweet accounts of life as it was lived. In particular, *This Childhood Land* is full of a marmalade of names – Sunshy, Eleazar, Sarannie, Mostyn and Johnny Clampitt. Much as Laurie Lee evoked his Gloucestershire childhoood in *Cider With Rosie*, Glynne-Jones renders vividly a world of cinder picking and condensed milk sandwiches, Tenby rock, *potsh a menyn* and pigs' bladder footballs. They are books warmed by the quiet sun of happy memory, prose reminding one of the sentiment of Dylan Thomas' 'Fern Hill,' writing of days when the 'sun always shone on our lives. They were boyhood days. Days when life held no reponsibilities. When, seen through the eyes of my youth, everything was carefree and gay in my old home town.'

MACHYNYS

Old Llanelli and new Llanelli live cheek by jowl here. Here is South Llanelli. Traditional industry sits on the opposite side of the road to upscale housing. And when I say upscale, I mean it. The first time you visit Pentre Nicklaus you might blink and genuinely think you were in Cape Cod. That Provincetown feeling. Clapperboard on the houses. Yucca trees everywhere and near obligatory driftwood as decoration. Subdued pastel hues for all the houses. Smart cars parked in serried ranks. BMWs. Mercs. Audis. Like an open air salesroom. Walk from your home straight onto the golf course. Monks Health

Spa for all the pampering you can take. Upmarket food at the bar and brasserie. Here are some gastronomic edited highlights. Goats cheese strudel. Duck and pistachio terrine. Garlic and lime butter. White chocolate and passion fruit posset with shortbread. There are plans for a Hilton hotel in the next couple of years. It's an area on the up and up, with views across to Cefn Bryn and brackeny north Gower. Greylag geese honking overhead as they make for Machynys Lakes. Turner sunsets. A new community in the making. A bright shiny face for the town, seemingly airlifted across the Atlantic.

I've been inside some of the bigger houses and they are essays in light and space – commodious living with lots of optional extras. Such as a plasma TV to watch in the bath. Plumbed-in sounds. But I can't help feeling it's like a gated community without the gates. On the other hand you simply can't beat the views. Think Malibu if it overlooked Penclawdd.

Across the way from the entrance to Pentre Nicklaus on Embankment Road in Machynys you'll find old-style, heavy-duty Llanelli in the shape of 3Ks Engineering, which employs fifty people on two shop floors, each with high capacity overhead cranes. The firm's work is a mixture of heavy fabrication and machining, and has one of the largest capacities in south Wales. They recently built the new retractable roof for the Wimbledon tennis arena, a £1 million contract which involved them making twenty-eight panels weighing 16 tonnes, a project which involved all the staff working round the clock in shifts to finish on time. As you park here you can smell the hard graft mixed with the schoolboy scent of opening a jar of iron filings.

Ron Hanbury is chairman of the business, while his sons Kevin

 and Karl are its directors: 'I started in 1969, myself repairing machines. The firm grew accidentally. I used to buy old machines, make them up and sell them. I used to sell a lot to Malaysia. I employed a couple of people in the meantime.'

Rob Griffiths, a tool maker by training, is the sales and marketing manager. He explains to me the range of what they do here, and the sheer scale of things. They

make a lot of stuff for the offshore industries now, whereas in the past ninety per cent of their work was for British Steel. In his office he takes me through an array of photographs on the wall – back-deck equipment for marine vessels such as carousels, winches, davits, fibre-optic spools, ploughs and cable engines. There is offshore and sub-sea equipment, a frame for the back deck of a

ship for lifting remote operated vehicles, robust enough to operate in areas of polar ice. They've made davits for the American navy to lift lifeboats and another for the Dutch navy. I nod sagely as he gets all metallurgical on me and leaves me behind.

'We're very diverse and work in a range of metals, from specialized carbon steels through special nickel alloys to stainless steel and duplex. 3Ks is a little company in Llanelli making huge inroads, thinking outside of the box and we're bloody good at what we do. We're happy to take on big jobs, 100 tonne jobs. A recent project was a 2.6 metre diameter gas main for the new blast furnace in Port Talbot. But we'll do small stuff, too. If a little boy walks in here and he's snapped the frame of his bicycle then we've got boys out there who'd be only too happy to put a little weld on it and he'll be on his way. The work is very varied – a footbridge for a railway one week, a diving bell for a sub sea vessel the next.'

Machynys was once known as Monk's Island. There's a local legend they built a tunnel under the estuary. To check it out I spoke to Winston Thomas, who lived at Machynys Farm, suggesting that it was basically a big cellar. He corrects me straightaway. 'Not only a cellar, it's a tunnel. I've been down there. Even today I can take you there and show you where it is. Not many people can do that. I was born and raised there. I only went down so far, it went down quite a way, with every craftsmanship. The actual entrance to the tunnel was behind the front door of the farm, the stairway was about eight steps to the main floor. There was a small opening – five foot by three foot – so you had to go on your hands and knees to go in there, but when you got in there you could stand up, but that was one of the ways the

monks camouflaged the tunnel. It went down to the sea coast.' Smuggler's shaft or escape route, the tunnel has excavated a place for itself in the local imagination.

Nowadays subsumed into what is known as South Llanelli, its original name is perpetuated in the name of the Machynys Peninsula Golf Club, designed by Jack Nicklaus. There have been various explanations of the name Machynys – the name of a person perhaps, or a little island, but it first makes an appearance in a Charter in the *Book of Llandaff* from 735 AD where it describes 'An estate named Machinis with six modii of land (about 250 acres) given to Berthwyn, the Bishop of Teilo (namely Llandaff).' The wonderfully named Gwgan ap Gwynon had been excommunicated and in order to receive a pardon, and receive communion again, he had to cede this patch of land to the church. A farm existed there in 1375 when 'Makeneys in the hundred of Lanethly' had a tenant who paid eight pounds to the Exchequer of Kidwelly each Easter and Michaelmas.

On early maps the area is shown as an island and there is persistent reference to a monastery in the area, established by Saint Pyr or Piro, the founder of the monastery at Caldy Island off Tenby. In the 1600s it was the site of a fair.

Nearby Morfa, or saltmarsh, got its name in 1938, until then part of New Dock. You can walk along Ropewalk Road, after the rope works, where they would measure the rope by walking its length, or along Tregoning Road, named after Cornishman Tregoning's Morfa Tinplate Works.

The coastline hereabouts has been dramatically changed over the years leading to the disappearance of 'Y Morfa Mawr,' the great marsh which lay to the east of Machynys. The scheme to create the Great Embankment was started in 1808, stretching from Penrhyngwyn Point to Maesarddafen, diverting, in the process, the river Dafen from its southward course to a westward progress into Machynys Pool. Maps of the 1830s show a point of land known as a sker reaching out into the estuary. In the western part there was a narrow coastal strip referred to as the Warren, which suggests that rabbits were bred here. In the 1890s wreckers used the coast and there is a story about an unfortunate servant girl who was sent to lure ships with her lantern which set her clothes on fire, serving as an alarm for the crew. Legend has it that she was later found with her throat cut, and that her ghost still patrols the shore.

In the physical world massive change was being wrought on this stretch of coast. Industry came and lots of it: from the brickpits and brickfields of the 1840s through the 50s, which saw a new sawmill and another brickworks, to the 60s, with their chemical works and arsenic plant, through the leasing of land in the 1870s to build a tinplate works, an ironworks, rolling mills, reservoirs and cottages. Build, shape, alter, all the human instincts at work and doing overtime.

Photographs of the area show how industry transformed the landscape hereabouts, with foundries and stacks in busy huddles. Burry Works. Thomas and Clement Foundry, the New Machynys Foundry next to Eddie John's Burry Gospel Hall and the Burry Box Works, the Richard Thomas Mills, the Richard Thomas Ambulance Room, the Great Western Engine Shed, the Rail Wagon Repair Sheds.

It can be a wind-bitten place, as evidenced in the name Bwlch y Gwynt, a name which also has a resonance if you like martial arts. A local judo expert came from here. Steadman Davies, MBE was born in Springfield Terrace. He trained generations of youngsters, producing many champions in judo and aikido and his Saschirokwai Judo Club was held in high regard throughout the UK. He even built his own dojo near the Leisure Centre in Llanelli.

So, Machynys: a new community to replace an old one. Cape Cod a straight swap for the huddled terraces of old, which used to be illuminated by the infernal flames of the foundries as they pounded out the heavy metal music of the past.

In bright shards of memory local lady Eira McKibbin evokes the sound of Saturday nights when sleep was hard to come by:

> We missed our lullaby, the gnawing, roaring sounds of the gantry, clanging day and night. We missed the sound of the engines, laden with coal from the tip, steaming and shunting back and forth. Normally we could hear the trucks being coupled up, the steel pouring from the furnaces into moulds, the same furnaces that sent their orange glowing flames dancing on to my bedroom ceiling at night. It completely locked out the dark sky outside. Unless you

wanted to read, the candles stayed unlit and the furnaces gave us adequate light for "magic lanterns" on the walls.'[30]

Instead of those magic lanterns there is now a new chimera, 158 houses which look as if they have to belong somewhere else really. Go look at the place. Tell me its not Provincetown.

Standing on the shore at Machynys you'll often see Land Rovers and other vehicles out on the sands at high tide. Cockling has a long tradition in Llanelli. But times are hard. Cockles have been dying in huge numbers.

Rob Griffiths is a cockler, a man with one of the strongest grips I've ever encountered. Next time I struggle with opening a jar of beetroot I'll ring him up. He's been working the sands for years, having been on the waiting list for a licence for a long time, but he thinks the last decade or so has been challenging to say the least. During the last five years he's only managed to work for about one year.

'I blame water quality. The development of Llanelli has seen the sewage system go haywire and there's too much organic matter going out into the water, affecting the sands.'

Nowadays Rob's lucky to work for six to eight weeks a year. He's gone from earning forty thousand pounds a year to three thousand pounds a year. It angers him that he's paying for a licence he can't use and suggests it's like paying the South Wales Sea Fisheries Committee for the privilege of being out of work.

But when he is out in the estuary he's a man in his element. 'It's the best job in the world. I get to work with the tides, say I start at three in the morning I finish at seven and that's me done for the day. You live with the pros and cons. In the winter it's dark at teatime – you can't work in the dark so you lose the work. In the summer, though, it's fabulous.'

Rob gives me a quick lesson about the cockle's life story. 'It's spawned into the sea. It lives in the upper layers of the sea until it's heavy enough to sink. It sinks down, lands on the seabed and that's where it spends most of its adult life. It's supposed to live until three or four years old, maybe five years old but the problem we've got here is the cockles can't live past a year. It spawns and dies, spawns and dies. We don't know why. They get killed by something. They're healthy animals, which don't die, so these are killed.'

Rob blames Welsh Water and is actively seeking to prove it. If he does then he'll claim compensation, along with many others. 'I believe the cockles have been killed and I've served notice on Welsh Water that they're responsible. Once I've proved it, once the scientists prove it, I'll be suing them, so it's as simple as that.'

He reckons that to date 'there's fifty million pounds worth of cockles died. All the gatherers, the Penclawdd gatherers and us, are in the same boat, we're all skint. It's a shambles. When you look out there the whole of the estuary's affected, north and south, from Loughor Bridge all the way to Whitford and Burry Holms, everything's dead.' Rob trots out statistics with both passion and spleen. The sewage system in Llanelli is capable of treating 600 litres a second. It actually receives, he reckons, 1600 litres a second so there's an excess. 'Currently there are 5000 litres a second passing through the system and it has to go somewhere or the town would flood so consequently that 5000 litres a second, or roughly 345,000 tons of sewage is going into the Burry every day, an amount equivalent to the largest oil tanker in the world and more going into the estuary every day. The organic material that's contained in that liquid is having an effect on the estuary. That's what I believe is killing the cockles. The sewage itself isn't killing the cockles, the cockles are feeding well on it but it's the excess that's doing the damage.'

He cites huge growths of algal bloom in the estuary as further evidence of such changes and maintains that this is an industry that's being killed rather than closing down because of economics.

Rob is so fed up with not getting answers he's taken the matter to the European Commission, which is currently investigating Welsh Water, the Environment Agency and the Welsh Assembly Government for breaches of the Urban Waste Water Directive, the Habitats Directive, the Shellfish Directive, the Bathing Waters Directive and the Natura 2000 Directive. Rob is a man arming himself with knowledge.

'The coast here is one of the most heavily protected sites in the UK – it's a Site of Special Scientific Interest, a Special Protection Area and so on and yet the whole ecosystem is going tits up here. I've spent four and a half years fighting and I'm not sure if I'm getting anywhere. Who's going to pay the compensation if it's man-

made and who's going to fix it if it's man-made? The polluter should pay. Who's going to pay then? If the Environment Agency can find a dead salmon in the river and find out when it died, how it died and what it died of surely they can find out with cockles?'

It's a dispiriting tale, these disappearing cockles. Especially for a man such as myself who likes his stomach. Who likes nothing better than a baguette filled with bacon, laverbread and cockles. And a cup of tea strong enough to stand your spoon in.

notes

1. David Williams gave 'magnetic massage privately and free of charge, but as time passed his treatment and its effect became widely known and finally he gave up his employment and devoted the whole of his time to the work of healing, and as a result has had the great pleasure through his treatment of knowing the blind to see, the deaf to hear, the paralysed to walk and the insane to be restored to normal condition.'
2. Jim Griffiths, the first Secretary of State for Wales, was the town's M.P. and among many other things created the modern state benefit system. Tory politician Michael Howard can also be added to the list.
3. The Old Castle Works closed in 1957.
4. The Regal had a luxurious cinema where people could drink tea in a Palm Court lounge. It was built in 1929 at a cost of £ 50,000, the same as the Odeon cost almost a decade later. Other cinemas in the town included the Hippodrome (Haggar's), the Palace (Vint's) and the Llanelly Cinema and the Astoria.
5. This isn't the full extent of civic administration here. The Llanelli Town Council Offices are housed in the Old Vicarage just along from the Parish Hall which was built in 1887. Outside the hall there's a plaque noting that the suffragette Emily Pankhurst addressed the people of Llanelli here in January 1912.
6. The arms were presented to the town by Lady Howard when it became a borough in 1913.
7. The Ritz was glitz in Llanelli. Over the years bands such as Johnny Kidd and the Pirates, Gerry and the Pacemakers, The Undertakers, Nero and the Gladiators, Screaming Lord Sutch and the Savages, Freddie and the Dreamers and even Gene Vincent played here. Other local bands such as the Fireflies, the Blackjacks, the Meteorites and the Fleetwoods also took the stage.
8 This was to be the first of many great battles between the two who had both made their debuts the previous year. It was cat and mouse, tit for tat. In the 1980/81 season they met again in the UK semi-final with Steve again the winner. That season he was runner up in the Masters and retained the Irish Masters, also winning the Pontins Professional title. The following season Davis again beat him in the UK final but he won the Lada Classic as well as a third Irish Masters. He finally won the UK title in 1982, beating Alex Higgins in the deciding frame, and the next few seasons saw him reach the world quarter finals each year from 1984 to 1987. He did win the Welsh professional championship in 1985, 1986 and 1988, as well as the 1986 Belgian Classic and the Pontins professional title in '85 and '86, but success in ranking events eluded him. In 1988, however, he reached his second world final only to come up against Davis again only to lose again. Three Scottish Masters finals and one European Open final were the best Terry could manage during the seasons that followed, and he began a slow slide down the rankings from a peak of third, to finally drop out of the top 16 at the end of the 1994/5 season. He only played one more full season, but did enter the 1997 world

championships when, although qualifying for the final stages at the Crucible, he lost his first round match to Mark Williams – but only after taking his fellow Welshman to a deciding frame. Thanks to http://www.terrygriffithsmatchroom.co.uk/terry_profile.html for the detail of this history.

9. Backing me up is rock musician Deke Leonard. In his memoirs he writes about '…the Law Courts – a drab, grey concrete eyesore that looks like an upside-down beer crate – are particularly offensive because they stand on the site of what was once the Bullring, where we used to meet after school.' See the bibliography for details of the book which is warmly recommended. Leonard is a very funny writer.

10. An excerpt from this haunting song might serve to show just how evocative the names of these stations and halts were.

> No more will I go to Blandford Forum and Moretehoe?
> On the slow train from Midsomer Norton and Mumby Road?
> No churns, no porter, no cat on a seat?
> At Chorlton-cum-Hardy or Chester-le-Street?
> We won't be meeting again?
> On the slow train.?
> I'll travel no more from Littleton Badsey to Openshaw?
> At Long Stanton I'll stand well clear of the doors no more?
> No whitewashed pebbles, no Up and no Down?
> From Formby Four Crosses to Dunstable Town.
> I won't be going again?
> On the slow train…

11. Hugh Morgan Lewis kindly lent me a copy of a talk given by Alwyn Bowen Hurren, the Vicar's warden in June 1991 which was the source of much of the detail in this chapter. My thanks to both of them.

12. Jenkins, Simon, *Wales: Churches, Houses, Castles*, Allen Lane, 2008.

13. Lloyd, Thomas, Julian Orbach and Robert Scourfield, *The Buildings of Wales: Carmarthenshire and Ceredigion*, Yale, 2006.

14. Llanelli became a regular post town in 1828, as trade grew.

15. Stead, Peter & Williams, Gareth, *Wales and its Boxers: the Fighting Tradition*, University of Wales Press, 2008.

16. For a town with today's significant Polish population the polka seems prescient.

17. For more see http://www.bbcwhodoyouthinkyouare.com/stories.php?cid=39449

18. The editor of the *Llanelli Star* from 1991 to 2008.

19. The fairs were held bi-annually and could attract many animals and people. Some 300 horses were offered for sale here in 1932. By this decade the presence of the fair in a residential area was seen as offensive and the Llanelli Corporation exerted its powers under a 1929 Act of Parliament to discontinue the fair, despite protestations by the Earl of Cawdor that he was losing his 'feudal rights.'

20. David Rees was a wriggling mess of contradictions. He wanted the Welsh to be nationalistic and independent, yet he extolled the virtues of the British Empire. He also loved the United States and when 80 people left Llanelli for the States in 1854, fifty-five of them were members of his chapel. He was also famously frugal, maintaining that 'you can boil a bone ten times and still get something out of it.' After he wrote this piece bones started to appear on the lawn in front of his house and it became known locally as Plas yr Esgyrn, Bone Mansion.

21. Augustus John described him as 'born and bred in Wales to which country he felt himself bound by every tier of sentiment and predilection. He had nevertheless practised eating

black ants at school to establish his French ancestry.'Their first meeting when Innes was living in Fitzroy Street was an encounter of Bohemian minds and dress sense. Innes was wearing 'A Quaker hat, coloured silk scarf and long black overcoat which set off features of a slightly cadaverous mouth, prominent nose, and a large bony forehead invaded by streaks of thin black hair. He carried a Malacca cane with a gold top and spoke with a heavy English accent which now and then betrayed an agreeable Welsh sub-stratum.'

22. He fell in love with the light of southern France on a trip with John Fothergill in 1908, following a route taken by painters such as Derain and Matisse some years previously. He would have made for a testing travel companion. Innes neglected to bathe or wash that often and presumed that the spots that formed on his skin were to do with being unsalubrious, when in fact they were the first signs of tuberculosis.

23. Stead, Peter: *Acting Wales: Stars of Stage and Screen,* University of Wales Press, 2002.

24. The wheel was a smokeless wheel rim, mounted on which was a tyre of slightly larger than usual diameter. Both could be attached to a wheel with a punctured tyre by adjustable clamps.

25. Old castle, site of a Norman motte and bailey castle, where a round island of willows rises from the pond, known locally as Pownd Twym, literally hot pond, which used to be the tinworks reservoir. The area was peppered with references to a castle here, from Old Castle Works to Old Castle tinplate works and farms called Hen Gastell Fawr and Hen Gastell Fach.

26. Crick, Michael, *In Search of Michael Howard*, Simon & Schuster, 2005.

27. I had enormous pleasure appearing in some of the productions of the Phoenix theatre company under the guidance of the irrepressible Noel Rees. His love of theatre is infectious and probably accounts for my being on the board of National Theatre Wales today.

28. The Old Lodge Works and Nevill's Foundry were cleared up in 1952 with the nearby Marshfield giving way to the Maesgors housing development.

29. 2nd April 1874, *Llanelly and County Guardian*.

30. McKibbin, Eira, Machynys – *Yours Truly, Llanelli Town Council*, 2007.

EAST

TROSTRE BOXING

It's business as usual in the nondescript building on the edge of a car park within the grounds of Trostre Tinplate Works, just a lot of people trying to knock seven bells out of each other. This is the Trostre Amateur Boxing Club, run by one of the most remarkable men you're likely to meet. Gareth Howells. M.B.E. Member of the British Empire. Or Master of Boxing Excellence. Who worked underground and at the tinplate works. An eighty three year old who has trained generations of fighting men. And trains them still, three nights a week.

He's the gentle old man in the corner, his fingers in cut-off woollen gloves like the ones Harold Steptoe used to wear, seated near a small portable Calor Gas stove to ward off the cold. Gareth is the man they all respect – bruisers and bashers and bouncers alike. He really is The Master, puffing thoughtfully on his pipe as if he knows that no-one would dare point out there's a National Assembly smoking ban, not with these brawny disciples all around him. Puffing as if there's a truth in the poetic saying 'If God hadn't wanted us to smoke he wouldn't have given us lungs.'[1]

You can pretty much smell the testosterone as young men spar in the ring, others carefully wrap lengths of bandage around their fists, do frenetic skipping on the spot, or put in the hours on the bag work, pounding it with rhythm and vigour, as if they're working on a rib cage. It's a great soundtrack, too, the bee wing whirr of the ropes turning, the close contact work, all thumps and body blows, the dull percussive thuds as the rib cage turns to paste. It makes me feel effeminate and I look down at my poet's hands with shame.

They've been fighting in Llanelli for a long time. Saturday night is a contact sport around here. In the nineteenth century women, albeit 'masculine looking members of the fair sex' would fight on open ground near the Box Cemetery. Maybe that's why they call it boxing. And the town has created real champions, too. Like Gypsy Daniels who started life as William Daniels, the son of a rugby full back, David John Daniels. It was an American promoter who decided to exaggerate William's tan skin by dressing him up in bracelets, cheap and gaudy gypsy earrings and bandanas. As a twenty year old Gypsy won five of his six bouts in America. Despite the success his father was annoyed by the new moniker. In Britain he went on to knock a good few men out and in 1927 he became the Light Heavyweight Champion. He went on to claim some substantial German scalps and in his whole career, spanning 150 fights, he was only knocked out once.

As we speak a bright run of blood erupts from the nose of a young man called Emlyn, in the ring, but Gareth nods reassuringly at him and he carries on jabbing and weaving. Medical attention for hard men. Gareth tells me about his own life. His Welsh is beautiful. It's the language of boxing, too.

'Between the ages of fourteen to sixteen I used to lift weights with my uncle in his garden shed in Allt, Llangennech. He was a world champion at the deadlift, John Arthur Jenkins, who broke the record back in 1929, lifting over four times his own weight. I had another uncle who broke the world record but couldn't match that. When I was sixteen I wanted to put the gloves on, I was dying to do it. It was in me. It takes a lot to make me lose my temper but when I do go I really go. There was a twelve by fifteen zinc shed in Pemberton, right next to where the Scarlets have their new home. I had a word with Cliff Hall who was looking after the place. Went there and all my partners came and I trained them too and they allowed me to put the gloves on. I've always had lots of energy. That's how I started to smoke the pipe when I was thirty-two coz I couldn't stand still.'

He had an offer to go professional when he was eighteen but he didn't want to as he wanted to concentrate on his coaching. During the war years many boys were called up to the Army, leaving Gareth behind. He spent those years reading textbooks and asking himself how he could teach this better.

One of his sparring partners in this period was the father of boxer Colin Jones,[2] born about two fields from the gym: Gareth was born just one field away. They were blood brothers thereafter, bonded by respect for each other's fists.

Gareth talks to me in sprightly, fluid Welsh, the sort they can't teach you on an WLPAN course. His eyes twinkle, impishly, and he doesn't look like a man well into his eighties. Has his own teeth, too: itself a testament to his pugilist's gifts, the effective parry, the deft duck.

He started the club, originally known as the Bynea ABC, in 1942 in a garden shed in Llanelli, eventually finding a permanent home in Trostre. He has worked tirelessly in a voluntary capacity to train local youngsters for over sixty years and now has thirty boxers on the club roster. He's seen other clubs come and go in the town, delights in the permanence, the sense of tradition instilled in Trostre's members. They have their own style, a guarded secret. It's a technique the octogenarian hands on to all. 'I teach them stance. This club is different. I'm different. We go from one stage to the next. Parry. Come in with the left. I teach them footwork and bobbing and weaving, that's a bit of a secret with us.'

The other secrets include what's known as the Trostre slap. He points out one of the meatier boxers, a guy called John, who works as a doorman. As he spars he puffs like a warthog, sweat gushing out of him. But for God's sake don't tell him I compared him with a warthog. Those fists could turn me into fishpaste. I've heard a story. One night two guys set about him. He gave them some slaps. They didn't get up. Probably stayed down because they liked the pavement. Comfortable there.

Gareth is as dedicated now as he was in 1942, spending his evenings working at the gym to develop and inspire young boxers to become good athletes and well rounded citizens. His boys aren't vandals. He is invincibly convinced boxing is good for character. It teaches men to respect themselves and each other and, by extension, everyone around them.

'They can take a blow and land one. If called to defend themselves they can so, and have done. I don't want the sort of people who go looking for fights.' He won't take anyone under ten as he doesn't believe they are meant to box. Which means eleven year olds are.[3] Gareth often gets kids who have been bullied at school. After two or three months they don't get bullied any more. It's a simple as that.

He trains novices and champions and all the sluggers in between. To date the club has racked up two silver medals in the Commonwealth Games and two bronzes. Ruefully he reflects on the fact that they'd have had another silver had it not been for one of his boys having a cut above the eye before the end of the fight.

'In Llanelli they need to be able to defend themselves – there are more drugs and so on. There was no kicking back in the old days. Then, you'd go out the back to settle things. If you kicked someone in those days no one would speak to you.'

Many of the boxers speak Welsh, young men such as Jamie Rees, a twenty-four year old from Hendy who comes over to speak with us. He's been fighting for three years. Going to be a medic. He's a science graduate so he can do an accelerated medicine degree. Instead of five years do it in four. He's just come back from Bolivia. Worked in a hospital in Cochabamba where the staff spoke a dialect of Quechua. Boxing, for Jamie, is a sport that requires a lot of discipline which you can apply to life as well as the ring. 'We don't just get a boxing lesson, we get a lesson in life. Gareth teaches us to respect, to behave with respect for ourselves, our friends, our opponents but also to compete with all our hearts, all our effort, one hundred per cent and fight Trostre style which is famous all over the world. There are secrets to the way we fight and I took an oath not to reveal them. But everyone knows about the left hand and right hand but here you learn how to *cwtsh* up, how to move around the ring, how to hit at an angle so it's not just about throwing punches. There's a lot of thinking in the ring. To box you have to train, you have to have discipline. You have to have that not just when you come through the doors but also in the rest of your life and the discipline I've had here with Gareth I'll keep for the rest of my days.'

He's been sparring with a man who's compelled to fight for slightly different reasons. Nicky Thomas, a sixteen year old from Pontardulais, says his style is mainly defence. He tells me that it's not wise to go mad in the attack all the time, that I should wait for the opponent to come to you. Which is wise. And flattering. As if he thinks I'm going to step in there! He explains that he can take a battering, especially sparring with Jamie. He only started boxing six months ago and faced stiff parental opposition but he kept on nagging. He was playing rugby and wanted something with more contact. 'I enjoy it, it's fun, getting to batter people and getting battered and staying fit. I didn't expect boxing to be so hard. My mother still doesn't want to watch me but my father says go for it. Dad's proud now, he likes it now.'

Meanwhile Gareth Howells is looking for more champions such as Jonathan Rees, who trains here. Gareth desperately wants a medal in the Olympics. For Wales of course. When I ask him the obvious, crass question he says he doesn't plan to retire. 'I'm not meant to leave people', he says, lighting his pipe, looking at the fists hammering flesh.

When his fighters shake Gareth's hand, as they leave, they hold onto it, caressingly almost, like men in love, marks of absolute respect. And there is a stillness to Gareth, a Zen quality, like someone who knows something special, who understands. You have heard the sound of one hand slapping....

TROSTRE

Mae bys Mari Ann wedi brifo,
A Dafydd y gwas ddim yn iach;
Mae'r baban yn y crud yn crio,
A'r gath wedi crafu Johnny bach.
Sospan fach yn berwi ar y tân,
Sospan fawr yn berwi ar y llawr,
A'r gath wedi crafu Johnny bach.

(Mary Ann's finger is hurt/ And David the servant isn't well/The baby in its crib is crying/And the cat is scratching little Johnny/The little saucepan is boiling on the fire/ The big saucepan is boiling on the floor/And the cat is scratching little Johnny.)

The anthemic Llanelli song, '*Sosban Fach*', ensures that the name of the town is inextricably linked with the making of tin. It may sound like nonsense verse but when sung collectively, with unbridled passion and all the air in your lungs it can be a rousing number indeed. Tin had been manufactured in the Llanelli area as far back as the early eighteenth century, when production started in Cydweli and Llanelli. The area had all the requisites for making tin in the form of ample running water supplied by a triad of rivers, namely the Dafen, Lliedi and Cille, along with a coalfield. The coal industry which preceded it, along with the manufacture of copper, had demanded good port facilities and the tinmen could consequently benefit from these. The railways had arrived and sulphuric acid, necessary for the

manufacture of tinplate in those days, was conveniently a by-product of making copper. So tin was produced on a grand scale. And saucepans, too.

Llanelli was often known as Tre'r Sosban. Still is by many Welsh speakers. The Welsh Tin Plate and Metal Stamping Company in the Cambrian Works near the North Dock produced saucepans dipped in enamel which were exported across the world under the 'Goat' brand. Established in 1891, the business was employing 1000 people by the 1920s and was the biggest works of its kind in Britain. It even made its way into the poetry of Robert Graves, who conjures up an image of the Welsh Fusiliers singing it as they marched to what would be the massacre at Mametz Wood in a poem which refers to Llanelli:

> Rough pit boys, from the coaly South,
> They sang, even in the cannon's mouth,
> Like Sunday Chapel, Monday's Inn.
> The death trap sounded with their din.
> Who knows a tune so soft, so strong,
> So pitiful as that saucepan song;
> For exiled hope, despaired desire
> Of lost souls for their cotttage fire?
> The low at first, with gathering sound
> Rose their four voices smooth and round,
> Till back went Time; once more I stood
> With Fusiliers in Mametz Wood.
> Fierce burned the sun, yet cheeks were pale,
> For ice hail they had leaden hail;
> In that fine forest green and big
> There stayed unbroken not one twig.
> They sang, they swore, they plunged in haste
> Stumbling and shouting through the waste;
> The little 'Saucepan' flamed on high,
> Emblem of home and ease gone by.... [4]

Inn. Din. In. Tin. Sounds like the making of tinplate. This is the process in a nutshell. Take bars of iron and roll them to end up with eight thin sheets measuring about 5 feet by 2-1/2 feet. During the finishing process these were cut in half, coated with a thin layer of tin and packed into boxes with 112 sheets to the box.

The building of Trostre on the site of two farms, Heol Hen and Maes-ar-Ddafen Fach, completely changed the architectural landscape of the eastern part of Llanelli. In his book *Crwydro Sir Gâr*, the inveterate Welsh traveller Aneirin Talfan Davies had enthusiastic things to say about the new development. [5]

> Trostre. This is a new name that will claim a prominence in the future life of Wales. There they raised a new tinworks which has already revolutionized life in Llanelli. It has changed the pattern of the society

that grew as a consequence of the legion of steel mills in the Llanelli area. Instead of noisy, dark mills and burning furnaces came a new factory – Trostre – and with it a sort of severe beauty which belongs to the place. Without a doubt this is the most beautiful modern building, standing on flat levels to the left of the main road from Bynea to Llanelli, and running parallel to the railway. I must admit I like the minimal lines of the new factories.

And the building even inspired an englyn by W. Rhys Nicholas which describes the way the building claimed the fields, replacing silence with yet more din.

Adeilad lle bu'r dolydd – a dadwrdd
Didaw lle bu'r ffermydd,
Darfu bro y rhodio rhydd,
I'n tir ni daeth tre newydd.6

Work on building Trostre started in 1947 at a time when many of the old hand mills were closing, with the spectre of unemployment looming over some 12,000 people. Their skills would have been lost were it not for Trostre, which started production in 1951 with an output of 400,000 tonnes each year. This has grown to some 500,000 tonnes. Over this time, Trostre Works has remained a leading supplier of high quality light gauge steels supplying over fifty countries worldwide. Substantial investment in new plant and technology, people, training and research and development, keeps Trostre at the forefront of European tinplate production, though layoffs punctuate much of its recent history.

One of the most intriguing and often unheralded parts of the site is the Trostre Works Cottage and Industrial Museum. This is mainly housed in the former Maes-ar-Ddafen Fach farmhouse and was restored by Walter Hodges, the Head of the Estates Department of The Steel Company of Wales. He recovered timber for the joists and roof supports from the South Wales Tinplate Works when that was demolished in the early 1940s. The roof was thatched and the outer walls painted pink to echo the practise of adding pig or ox-blood to lime-wash when painting the outside of a dwelling. Finally, a search was made for antique Welsh furniture, china, paintings and other household commodities of bygone days to furnish the cottage. By August 1957, the work was completed. What had once been a derelict farmhouse had been transformed into the Trostre Works Cottage and

Industrial Museum as we more or less see it today.

In the cottage garden, heavier items of equipment have been erected to preserve them for posterity. These include a complete old-type two-high pack-mill, a 'Millbrook' rotary pickling machine, a small wrought iron annealing cover and stand, a hand annealing charger and a single sweep 'Abercarn' type tinpot. There are also a number

of items on display such as trolleys, tin moulds and boshes.

It's many years since I visited Trostre to do some filming for BBC Wales' *Homeland* series, but I was struck by how unindustrial the main factory seemed, with computers driving the production process and people working in white collars as well as blue ones. I suppose I had images in mind of the old style tinplaters, the punishing process, with workers drenched in salty perspiration and permanently working in danger. But the scale of the cottage, and the quaintness of its contents, compared with the enormous bulk of today's Corus plant suggests how far and completely times have changed, and Llanelli with it.

DAFEN

This village is named after the river which runs through it. In this case the river was named after an animal, specifically 'a tamed or domesticated animal.' There might be links with Daventry and Davenport in England. Dafen was a quiet little hamlet in the early 1840s. That was, until Richard Nevill decided to site a tinplate works there. Once built, the village grew around it like topsy.

Housing sprung up for workers drawn from Baglan, Maesteg and Margam. Gors coal pit started in 1850. The Tinworks School opened in 1852, with leave of absence for many pupils during the potato picking season. Maescanner Baptist Chapel threw open its doors in 1863. A works reservoir was dug in 1865. Busy, busy, busy. An Anglican church was built in 1870. And of course there were nine pubs as well as other entertainment – the village had the first brass band in Llanelli. To build more and serve the industry they opened a brickworks. The Gors Galvanizing Works came to keep company with the tinplate works. One of its most interesting employees was a Zulu warrior called Gebuza Nungu,[7] whose father came to England with King Cetawayo as a prisoner after the Zulu War and whose great-grandfather was an eminent witchdoctor and chief named in one of Rider Haggard's novels.

Dafen is still an industrial area today. There are success stories such as Daniels Fans, which make bloody huge industrial fans. Sold the world over. I've seen them. Axial and centrifugal. For all your fan needs. And Avon Inflatables down the road, too. For all your rafting needs.

But for me the village is forever linked with one person – Dorothy, or Dot Squires. As someone once said, if Ethel Merman and Edith Piaf had mated, then Dorothy Squires might have been the result. What a concept! Squires was one of the most popular singing stars of the 1940s and through her partnership with bandleader and composer Billy Reid was a top of the bill theatre act and a successful recording artist on both sides of the Atlantic. She was born Edna May Squires on 25 March 1915 at the Travelling Van, Bridge Shop Field, Pontyberem, the daughter of a steelworker, Archibald James Squires and his wife Emily. Dorothy's first job was as a sales assistant at Woolworths and later she worked in a tinplate factory. An early experience – watching Al Jolson in *The Jazz Singer* – was to have an abiding influence as the young Edna May made up her mind that she, too, was going to be a singer. I met her when she was in the autumn of her days, teetering on heels, a tad confused by the day of the week. It was hard to imagine the glamour puss and party gal who bought flowers to present to herself. But she still let a genuine trail of stardust trail in her wake as she walked away.

The early Dot performances were in Llanelli, with bands such as the Denza Players, who appeared at places such as the Ritz ballroom, but when she turned eighteen she decided to head for London to carve out a career. Not knowing anyone, she ended up in Croydon working as a nurse, but fate prevailed in her favour when she had an audition in a variety agent's which led, via a terrible opening night in cabaret when she forgot her words, to a contract to sing at the Burlington club. American pianist Charlie Kunz was in the audience one night and gave her the opportunity to make her first radio broadcast. A few months later she worked with Billy Reid for the first time. It was the start of a fruitful and later stormy relationship.

She cut her first disc in 1936 with the song 'When the Poppies Bloom Again', followed by a good many other songs. But war brought a temporary lull to recordings, that is until 'Coming Home' recorded on 1 May 1945 and released just before VE Day. It went on to be a success on record and on the radio, capturing the emotions of the soldiers, both bloodied and battered, weary and shell-shocked as they came home to a changed world. Dorothy and Billy were now involved personally as well as musically, even though Reid was married.

Squires' star was most certainly in the ascendant in the late 1940s, with millions listening to her on BBC Radio's Variety Bandbox. She also started appearing at the London Palladium.

The 1950s were quiet on the professional front but turbulent on the emotional one, with Billy and Dorothy splitting up. He kept the Astoria Theatre in Llanelli's New Dock Road area while she kept their home in Kent, which would see some wild celebrity parties as was Dorothy's wont. Champagne occasions. Starry, starry nights.

In 1952 she met a young actor called Roger Moore and a year later she was married to this man who would be both Saint and James Bond. She was now getting hit singles and the move to New York and latterly Hollywood gave her a new audience, and she appeared at places such as the Moulin Rouge. Elvis Presley was often in the audience, putting in requests. He was a fan. Now, that's someone you'd like as a fan.

By the early 1960s Dot had teamed up with tinkling pianist Russ Conway to record hits such as 'Say It With Flowers.' This led to engagements at the Talk of the Town, following in the patent leather footsteps of such luminaries as Sammy Davis Jr, Tony Bennett and Eartha Kitt. Unfortunately this was also the time when her marriage began to flounder and this was to cast a shadow over much of the decade. She did manage to record a semi autobiographical live album in the Regal in Llanelli, which was released on the Decca label. By the 1970s she was racking up hit after hit though she felt that she was being ignored by TV and radio. She decided to take the bull by the horns and booked the Palladium with her own money. Many people questioned the wisdom of this, but the tickets sold out. Further Palladium gigs followed and buoyed up by this success she booked New York's Carnegie Hall and the Dorothy Chandler Pavilion in Los Angeles. Soon she was being booked by impresarios right, left and centre and hits such as 'My Way' were catapulting her further into the limelight.

The seventies saw her involved in a great deal of litigation – taking on papers such as the *Daily Express* over allegations that she had bribed a BBC producer to play her songs. She had by now gained a formidable reputation as a demanding monster with a politician's hide. Tragedy struck when her underinsured Bexley home burned to the ground, her pet poodle dying in the conflagration. She then moved to a seventeen-bedroom home in Bray on Thames, which was flooded. Court costs left her bankrupt in 1986 when bailiffs turfed her our of her Bray home. Now very much on the slide she lived in bed and breakfast accommodation.

Her last stage performance was in the Brighton Pavilion, but she returned to Wales to live a reclusive life in a house loaned to her by Edna Coles. Life continued to hurl challenges at her. Cancer was diagnosed. She was admitted to Llwynypia Hospital in March and died on 14 April 1977.

R.I.P Dot. A great and tragic entertainer. Check out her songs. She can belt them out. Good as Minnelli at times. And Streisand. Truly.

THE COLLECTIVE NOUNS OF THE NATIONAL WETLANDS CENTRE

This is the place then, to witness
a congregation of birds
a dissimulation of them
a flight of them,
a veritable volery.

Survey, on bright areas of standing water,
Or airborne, or on rushy banks
Secretive in their skulking,
A plump of waterfowl, a plump of wildfowl,
A bunch, a company, a coil,
A knob of widgeon:
A descent of woodpeckers
(From the school of hard knocks)
And, amassed, a herd of wrens.

On the lagoony reaches, picking at weeds

A cover of coots, a covert of coots
A whole black raft of them, while overhead,
Like so many flying reptiles,
A pterodactyl flight of cormorants,
Ugly necks outstretched to snapping point.

But beware, then, a hover of crows
a murder of crows
a storytelling of crows.

Run the names like ticker tape – a battling, a brace,
A flush, a paddling, a plump, a raft of ducks
Working the wet margins, looking for crowfoot.

And, eruptingly, from an edge of reeds, a spring of teal, like feathered
missiles!
And cast to four winds, a leash of plovers,
A fling of dunlin, over a desert of lapwings, a deceit of them, too.

Theatrically, a cast of falcons,
Enchantingly, a charm of goldfinches,

Perched twitchingly on stands of teasel and teasing seeds from purslane,
Shepherd's purse,
Alongside a trimming and a trembling of linnets,
Like a Motown song about spring and its demeanour,
Yes, that happy.

So cue up the disc, with, on backing vocals,
A tremolo of larks, an exultation of them!

Huntingly, a hedge of herons, out to spear eels
Showily, a band of jays, scouting for acorns
Prettily, a bouquet of pheasants in a flowering of feathers
And then, white as stars, elegant as ladybreath
 A bank of swans
A bevy of swans
A drift of swans
A game of swans
A herd of swans
A squadron of swans

A wedge of swans
A whiteness of swans

And let me suggest a new one

A serenity of swans.
Add that one to your list.

THE NATIONAL WETLANDS CENTRE

We are walking through an area of reeds and standing water, creeks and lagoons, a place where continents meet, an international, cross-roads, a place with no boundaries. It is also water vole heaven. Hyperbole? Overblown prose. Hit a purple patch? Most certainly not, sure as eggs is eggs.

In the summer the National Wetlands Centre at Penclacwydd is alive with birds, many of which have winged in from Africa, such as the swifts, or Devil birds, which scythe over the lagoons on still June evenings, screeching like banshees. The reed beds will be alive with small birds, such as reed warblers which will have spent the winter in the savannah and scrub country stretching in a great horseshoe around the forests of Congo. The male birds return first to seek out territories. When the females arrive a little later they're greeted by unified singing, a male voice chorus, excited in the reeds.

In the autumn and winter there'll be even more birds that have flown south to avoid the ice plates and punishing snow flurries of winter, so there'll be birds that have flown in from Greenland and the Far North, such immigrants as redwings, fresh arrivals from the taiga region of Russia, which guzzle berries as if there's no tomorrow. These travellers to the National Wetlands Centre for Wales are truly cross-border migrants, many, such as the black tailed godwits, brought here by the exigencies of migration and the quest for longer days. Altogether some two hundred species have been seen here, including more than a smattering of rarities, such as long-billed dowitcher, green-winged teal, Richard's pipit, and red-footed falcon. Such birds can make some birdwatchers twitch as if they've been rigged up to the National Grid.

Unlike the legions of birds that visit Penclacwydd from all points, from Greenland to Ghana, Central African Republic to Canada, Nigel Williams, the Centre Manager, and my willing guide, is a more sedentary species: he's lived within two miles of the place all his life. Born in Glasfryn in Felinfoel, then Pemberton, he then moved to Brynawelon, Dafen which, as the crow flies is just a short hop away. His roots are as firmly planted in Llanelli as the uncommon black poplar trees we walk past as we saunter out through the reeds. You can hear Llanelli as he speaks, in his accent. To my ear it's as pleasant as the sound

of wind soughing through reeds. Accents are comforting, the sound of the clan. And I've lived away a long time.

Nature has been Nigel's lifelong passion, starting with the boyish pleasures of fishing for minnows and collecting frogspawn. It was an interest that kept him going when he worked in industry, at Avon Inflatables, making rubber boats. 'When this centre opened seventeen years ago I wouldn't have dreamed that I would be running the place today.' There are thirteen staff, sixteen part-timers, and sixty volunteers.

He started off volunteering himself. Then, in 1994, a vacancy occurred and he was lucky enough to get in. His predecessors in the job, Tony Richardson and Geoff Proffitt, used to be called curators. Which may have too much museum dust about it as a title. It's too vital a place for that.

It was Sir Peter Scott, the urbane naturalist who first had the idea of creating a centre at Penclacwydd, buoyed up by the success of others he had established, not least that at Slimbridge on the Gloucestershire side of the Severn, where captive birds with clipped wings showed off their finery alongside Bewick's swans, which flew in to winter.

Industry was in a parlous state of decline in Llanelli and the council was desperate for something to replace the jobs. Why could-n't it be tourism? Scott's vision was timely: the council wanted to turn the salt marshes here into a landfill site and there was a proposal to build a chemical plant where the visitor centre now stands. The councillors went to Slimbridge for a day out and saw how Peter Scott's vision could apply. At the same time the borough's planning officer, Clive Davies, whilst on holiday, chanced upon Abbotsbury, a Dorset swannery and thought he's like something similar in his patch. So Penclacwydd was part of the first phase of the area's touristification before being linked to the Millennium Coastal Park. This was a gargantuan undertaking, with Llanelli Borough Council, the Welsh Development Agency and Welsh Water involved in a £27.5 million project to regenerate miles of coastline and no fewer than two thousand acres of land.

The Centre opened in 1991 on formerly low grade agricultural land and the creation of a variety of habitats such as brackish and freshwater scrapes, wet meadows, a six acre lagoon, a network of ditches, landscaped grounds and reed beds provide habitats for a wide variety of birds.

In 1999 the reserve expanded with the creation of the two hundred acre Millennium Wetland, which is part of the overall coastal development, stretching for twelve miles from Loughor Bridge to Pembrey Country Park along the coast of the north shore of the Burry Inlet. It's proved a hit with tourists. Carmarthenshire's the new Pembrokeshire, as Nigel puts it.

Nigel gives me a history lesson as we pause to admire those poplars, pointing out that twigs may snap off for no reason, then float away and grow as new saplings. 'The farming had declined here over the years so we bought some land. The council owns adjoining acres and then Welsh Water purchased a parcel to the east so they donated the land they didn't need to us, so all of a sudden our acreage grew but we didn't have money to do anything. But then we dovetailed with plans for the Millennium Coastal Park and sparked the potential of a fantastic wetland. One ingredient we didn't have was water, other than what came out the sky and we worked out that we could easily create a wetland by blocking off drains and building up the water levels. Wetlands are easy to destroy – simply drain them and you've got dry land and you've got land to build on which is one of their downfalls of wetlands. So, they're easy to destroy but we've proved here

that they're equally easy to create.'

In total the site now covers five hundred acres, with two hundred acres of saltmarsh, the Millennium Wetlands and a plot of land where they graze some animals in the winter. To date, 197 bird species have been recorded here, fifty-eight of which have bred. Over forty species can be expected throughout the year.

One of the most totemic birds for the Centre is the bittern, a normally skulking bird, which can look like a large domestic hen, hunched up with its long neck drawn in. But if the bird suspects danger it may 'freeze' with neck and break stretched vertically, when the streaked plumage provides perfect camouflage among the dried reeds.

These past three winters he's had up to three birds overwintering. In the spring Nigel waits in vain for that heart-stopping moment when he'd hear a bittern booming, a curious mix of foghorn and lowing cow which announces that the male bird is looking for a mate. Nigel wistfully admits they probably don't have the necessary acreage for them to breed, but cheerfully points out that there is a network of suitable places nearby – the huge reed bed at Llangennech, the fenland near the old Morlais colliery – segments of reed over at Oxwich on Gower and other areas at Witchett Pool near Pendine. They bred at Oxwich up until the 1970s so there's no reason they shouldn't come back.

Nigel and I are now so deep in the reeds that we can no longer see the huge mass of the Trostre tinplate works. Until the trees planted matured the bulk of the factory was one of the most striking features of the place. But here among the Phragmites reeds, we seem a long way away from the mean and vulgar works of man, even though much of the waterscape here is, ironically, man-made, shaped by digger and 'dozer. As nearby mallards splash in the shallows Nigel is waxing lyrical about mammalian life hereabouts: 'It's one of the two most important sites for water voles in Wales. The presence of these animals persuaded us to change our plans for the design of the reserve. We were surveying all of the plants and all of the other species to see what we had, a sort of stocktaking exercise if you like, and in just a few days we realised that the reserve was one of the largest vole sites in Wales – you have to travel to Anglesey to find anything comparable. They're widespread throughout the site – the fantastic thing here is that they can disappear from one location and then be found at another. There's that much space for them to come and go.'

And so much coming and going. The water vole, a frenetically busy creature that can consume nearly eighty per cent of its body weight each day, kicking up clouds of mud when it's threatened.[8] It can give birth up to five litters a year, with an average litter of six little volelets. It is often mistakenly called a water rat, not least by Kenneth Grahame, the author of the 1908 children's classic *The Wind in the Willows*.

But Grahame's water rat, Rattie, is really a vole, and the largest vole in Britain at that. Unlike a rat it has a blunt face, rounded ears and a furry tail – it's altogether cuter. Or as Grahame puts it, 'a brown little face with whiskers. A grave round face, with the same twinkle in its eye... Small neat ears and thick silky hair....' Cute as Christmas.

Cute but condemned: the water vole is the fastest declining mammal in Britain and has disappeared from ninety-four per cent of its historic sites. Its loss would be more than just aesthetic, a list of animals reduced by one. It's part of the food chain, so predators, such as bitterns, who like nothing more than torn carpaccio of vole, would be denied. Sadly, the future of of nature's unequivocally cuddly creatures still hangs on a spider's thread.

One of the most appealing ways of sighting voles is by going out in a canoe, which vistors are allowed to do during the summer months, when most of the birds are at their northern breeding grounds.

Being out on the water brings you into a different relationship with the aqueous, watery world, as Nigel explains. 'When we take on the paddle it looks like a different limb or a different shape, so our shapes change – we're low on the water and we're not so upright and tall and we're in a canoe – so birds don't see that as a threat. You can go up to a flock of ducks which might have flown away in other circumstances. It's a grand way of bringing people and wildlife together.'

The reserve seamlessly connects with the estuary. The National Wetlands Centre for Wales is situated on the northern shore of the Burry Inlet, which is regarded as the most important estuary for wildfowl and waders wholly within the country. Bird numbers on the whole of the Burry Inlet are at their highest in the winter when over 50,000 birds can be present.[9] A cold snap can bring huge influxes of birds from further east.

By now we've reached the British Steel hide, a comfortable, substantial shelter and viewing post, away from the whip of the wind, where you can sit on wooden seats and scan the mud of the so called 'scrape' in front of us, so-called because a bulldozer scraped it into shape. There are hundreds and hundreds of birds out there – the higher the tide the more birds are pushed up from the estuary. Nigel points out dunlin on the shore, a flock of wigeon and remarks that something's flushed the birds out because everything's in a tight flock.

Such a concentration of birds acts as a magnet for avian predators. Hen harriers, in shape like stretched buzzards are familiar sights, quartering the reeds. So too are peregrines, super-fast falcons, which can drop like a stone to decapitate a bird below.

Some of Nigel's best moments have been here, overlooking the scrape, at times of the year when there's a huge turnover of birds. He revels in the fact that he has this as his back garden so to speak: he lives in a house on the reserve. He loves to be here first thing in the morning; with a spring tide there's a huge mass of water and the landscape is flooded and he has thousands of birds in front of him. It looks like he's having a Damascene two minutes. His eyes burn brightly. A man in love with a place.

Nigel breaks off from his rhapsody to chat with one of his colleagues, who is repairing a broken bund, the retaining wall which keeps the sea out. A sort of adult version of the boy putting his finger in the dyke.

Some of the most noteworthy birds on the scrape look like dabs of titanium white, fresh squiggled from the artist's paint tube. These are little egrets, which only a few years ago used to set twitcher's pulses racing but which are now commonplace. Nigel explains: 'One turned up in the early 1990s – birdwatchers from all over the country came to see it. There were three the following year. In 1994 seven turned up, stayed the summer, then overwintered. Our peak was no fewer than 392 birds. Why? Well, weather – milder winters. Nobody would have predicted that fifteen years ago. We have summer plants flowering in October. All indicators that something is happening in the climate.

'This year we also have a spoonbill overwintering – that's unusually rare – that bird should be in North Africa. For more casual visitors the bird they all want to see is the kingfisher. That's the one they always remember seeing for the first time.' And that flash of electric blue, or even better, a bird on a perch trying to still a wriggling stickleback is certainly the vivid stuff of memory.

For Nigel, all the avian comings and goings here are nothing short of miraculous. There's a tiny little bird called the chiff chaff which he catches at their summer ringing site, where they tag them with tiny aluminium rings. 'When they arrive they're less than six or

seven grammes – ten or eleven when they're leaving in the autumn. That will give them enough energy to get to Africa but without carrying any excess which might weigh them down to the extent they never arrive at all.'

As we walk back to the visitors' centre we enjoy looking at the captive collection, birds with their wings clipped. Our conversation naturally drifts to foxes and he describes the measures they've taken to prevent them getting in – the fences buried three foot into the ground and twelve foot high not to mention the three strands of electrified wire on the outside which give them a bit of a kick and discourage them. Not forgetting the birds themselves: the Romans used geese as burglar alarms.

We conclude our visit with a conservation success story, as we get up close and personal with the two gangs of Ne-nes or Hawaiian geese, the national emblem of Hawaii, and a species which is naturally tame, like the animals of the Galapagos. Nigel explains that when Captain Cook first inhabited the island, man settled and accidentally introduced rats to the islands. The rats' staple diet consisted of Ne-Ne chicks and Ne-Ne eggs. To deal with the rats they introduced mongeese which also liked noting better than a good slap up of Ne-ne chicks and eggs. Many years later the geese were reduced to thirty or forty pairs. So, Sir Peter Scott went over and brought back a couple of pairs. They now breed in Llanelli and birds from the U.K. have been reintroduced to Hawaii. Don't ever say there's nothing exotic about Llanelli.

Nigel shares a valedictory story before I head for the car. One day he met a visitor who, untypically, was very upset, stamping his feet and cursing. It turned it out the man was a psychiatrist, who said that for years he'd been prescribing drugs to people for depression when 'this is what I should have been prescribing, this place.'

And the man has a point. As the sun glints on the estuary, and the wheeling flights of wigeon turn overhead, and the wind sussurates through the standing reeds, a visit here is somehow medicinal, a balm of sorts for the battered twenty first century soul.

Window Shopping at Trostre Retail Park
(in the style of Peter Finch)

Make the most of now,
Fresh and pretty cotton for summer
Hot brands, cool prices, O2,
Health beauty gofal harddu
Funtastically famous toys
Please ask staff for help
Accessorize, two years interest free
Credit, beauty club reward club
JJB, HMV, TK MAXX, BHS, M & S, KFC, W H Smith,
While stocks last, Tesco Extra
Holiday hypermarket, new collection
Apply now, win a pair of tickets
Apply now, get closer
Dive in for great deals, Dorothy Perkins, Wallis,
Longhaul Florida, Blu-Ray from £10
We sell iPods
Missselfridge.com
Big deals
Big deal
Cotton pique polos
All this and more
Save 50% all sat nav, wide fit shoes,
P&O new ship,
X Box 360.
Zip Wax Wonder, we can change,
Apply now, oils and additives,
Hydro active, 100 styles
Vat is down, Quiksilver,
And so are our prices
Keep your number
Keep your phone
Made to last
Sized to fit
Red Herring Floral Top
Removable Air Inserts
Buy a Bottom
Get a Top Free
London Paris New York

Customize your drinks
Mango passion fruit frappuccino
Drive thru, *gyrru trwodd*,
Apply now
Neu Look, Next, B&Q,
Buy one get one free
Listen to the beat and your eyebrows will follow
UK's favourite footwear retailer,
Boots, we fit kids' shoes
Half price, half price,
Apply now.
Clinton Cards, Clarks, First Choice Holidays
As seen in *Glamour*
Win a VIP screening, Vodafone
Sizes 8 to 22 available
Hugmeez now in stock
(We just want to be hugged)
Mid season sale
Subject to availability
Win a surfboard
Monsoon, Samsung, Tocco, Ultra free
No current vacancies
Unlimited free music
For one month
Peacocks
Next resort,
The HTU magic with Google is coming
River Island, two room design consultation
Brantano Footwear
La Senza, Starbucks,
£18 maxi dress
Receive ten pounds in vouchers
Lovingly detailed top
35 days to return or exchange
New cake shop
To protect the quality of our coffee
We ask you not to smoke.

THE RETAIL PARKS

This could be anywhere whatsoever in the UK. Nowheresville. Latte city. It's where the big names, the multiples have parked up now that they've deserted the old town centre. It's a sort of retail vampirism, sucking the life-blood out of Llanelli's shopping streets. That's why they call it out of town. W.H.Smith. Marks & Spencer. The retail chains. All inextricably linked. But they've pulled in some new attractions. Subway sandwiches. Starbucks for caffeine. HMV. Lots and lots of new roundabouts linking Trostre Retail Park with South Trostre Retail Park and Pemberton Retail Park. You need a car to get here, mind, and not everyone in the town has one. It certainly suggests that walking is a dead art.

Robert Lloyd, the former editor of the *Llanelli Star*, thinks that the out of town development has to be seen both in terms of its deleterious effect on the old town centre and its rejuvenating effect for the wider local economy.

'It's a net gain for Llanelli as the out of town development is probably better because the overall effect is more people in employment, more people coming into the retail parks because we get people drifting in from the Gorseinon and Loughor end. You walk around Morrisons and you'll find people from Carmarthen and so on. It's the classic doughnut effect because effectively we've taken out the bit in the middle – Marks and Spencer and Woolworths. The middle of the town has to reinvent itself as the high street names aren't likely to come back. The likes of Boots stayed but Top Shop is going. But I can see there's a net gain.'

Rising behind the various temples to Mammon – the Morrisons, the Tesco Megasuperextra or whatever it's called – and the looping and interlocking roads that link the retail parks is the new home for Llanelli rugby, Parc y Scarlets. For some of the players such as Dafydd James it's had to replace a magical arena.[10]

'Magic is the right word. When you ran out on to the pitch at Stradey there was an aura about the place. It just felt special. But with the new stadium we have the best of everything, and it is all here. We have the best training facilities in Wales, probably in Britain. Everything is on the spot.

'Even the pitch is tremendous. They have kept the terraces so I'm sure that the magic will transfer. Of course it is hugely in our favour that we have such a loyal and determined support. That isn't going to change. It's not just a great place to play the game. It's a great place to watch the game.'

Fittingly, the first match at the place featured two of Wales' most traditional sporting rivals – Llanelli RFC and Cardiff RFC – who went head-to-head with the home side proudly topping the Principality Welsh Premiership on November 15, 2008.

Scarlets managing director Gareth Davies looks to ecclesiastical architecture for a good metaphor for the place, another cathedral of rugby taking shape: 'The stadium is for our rugby region and supporters to enjoy and to take pride in. Our identity as Scarlets is so crucial to our success. It celebrates our independence and our passion. It's fundamental to our aim to create a cathedral of regional rugby. With sosbans on the posts, this stadium is distinctly Scarlets in heart and soul.'[11]

But attendances haven't been good. Local historian Huw Lewis, who guided me through a lot of this book, says that many people now watch the games on TV. 'The move to Pemberton has broken the tradition of people meeting up in town and deciding there and then to walk to Stradey Park to watch a game. There's no way to walk to the new stadium. No pavement even. Then the price of the tickets shot up and this broke the old habit. There are now so many handicaps to going there.'

I've also met people who stay away as a protest against the current management. There have certainly been a lot of empty seats when I've seen games on TV. Even when the Barbarians came to play here, when a young Llanelli team put on a sterling display.

But the stadium will work or be made to. They've already reduced ticket prices. Management heads are rolling. It will work. Because there's a tenacity which lies at the heart of so much of Llanelli life and it's that gutsy instinct that will win through, or muddle through or just stubbornly somehow bloody well get through. Just as one day a Phoenix will rise somewhere on Stepney Street and float on shimmering wings over the pound shops, its irridescent sheen catching the light as it banks above Machynys. And jobs will return, as if the cold economic winds, no, the freezing economic gales, never did gust through and threaten to blow the whole damn town down. Because such global matters as the complete collapse of the banking system will never quite extinguish local pride and a simple love of home. Remember then: Llanelli. A tough place built of grit and spunk, founded on debt and deliberation, on industrialists' vision and workers' sweat which flowed as freely as the rivers Dafen or Lliedi, a town which put down thick radical roots of tradition and rose with a flair for hard graft. Where the old folk still speak a dialect of Welsh that falls like beautiful leaves from their desiccated lips. From the *colfen*, the local word for tree. And where the rugby has to make do as other religions seem to decline. Llanelli. It's like any other town, only different.

Notes

1. Taken from Peter Finch, *Selected Later Poems*. 'Ex Smokes Man Writes Epic.'
2. Gareth uses the word *pantner*, which is Llanelli Welsh for partner and he's not on about emotional partners. He means it in the sense that Kirk Douglas or John Wayne use when they ride into Deadwood or out into Indian territory in the movies, rounding up mavericks, shadowing Apaches, howdy pardner. This is the Wild West, after all.
3. This is what one pleased blogger had to say about the effect of Gareth's gym: I have always liked watching boxing but I never really appreciated it properly until my 11 year old started training. Initially it was to bolster his fitness for rugby in the off season but he likes it so much he will carry on and we have even turned the garage into a gym complete with weights, bench and punch bag.

   The guy running the gym is Gareth Howells MBE an 82 year old who has been training fighters for over 60 years. Over the last few months he has shown my boy how to block & jab, hook, cross etc etc and taught him footwork exercises aptly named like 'ring-a-rosies' and 'gee-gees'. He teaches everyone the same way and the progress my boy has made in 2 months has been fantastic. He has just had his first bag sparring session but he is a few steps away from his first ring sparring (although he has gone through his moves in the ring). He trains 3 times a week alongside Welsh champions and the effort they all put in is tremendous; it gives me a whole new outlook on what it takes to be a boxer.
4. This is an excerpt from a poem which appeared in the Guardian on the 3rd April 1919, written by Graves at Kinmel Park Camp, Rhyl. It continues....
5. *Crwydro Sir Gâr*, Llyfrau'r Dryw, Llandybie, 1955.
6. My prosaic rendering of it goes 'A building where once where fields/And incessant noise where once was open country/The age of walking freely has ended/To our land has come a new town.'
7. Gebuza Nungu appeared in a command performance in front of King Edward VII when he was still Prince of Wales, giving an exhibition of dancing and spear throwing.
8. 'Law aims to get water vole out of a hole', *The Times*, Wednesday 27 Feb, 2008. Water voles are joining angel sharks, roman snails, spiny seahorses and short-snouted seahorses on the protected list.
9. The Burry Inlet is the most important estuary wholly within Wales (as the Severn and the Dee share shores and birds with England). The 50,000 birds which overwinter explain its string of designations – Special Protection Area, Ramsar site, Site of Special Scientific Interest.
10. *Llanelli Life*, December 2008.
11. The capacity in the stadium, including the terrace area, is 14,870. The stadium can extend to a full capacity of 15,180 with the placement of tiered temporary seating in front of the Link Telecom East Stand when required for bigger matches. Rare for new stadia, there is a terrace area in front of the Gravells North Stand for those who specifically want to stand, as requested by the Scarlets Supporters Trust. This area can hold 1,780. The stadium is a joint venture partnership between Carmarthenshire Council and The Scarlets.

THE PHOTOGRAPHS

BIBLIOGRAPHY

Berry, Dave: *Wales and Cinema: the First Hundred Years*, University of Wales Press, 1994

Bevan, Alun Wyn: *Straeon o'r Strade*, Gomer, 2004

Bowen, D.Q.: *The Llanelli Landscape*, Llanelli Borough Council, 1980

Craig, R.S., Protheroe Jones, R and Symons, M.V.: *The Industrial and Maritime History of Llanelli and Burry Port, 1750 to 2000*, Carmarthenshire County Council, 2002

Crick, Michael: *In Search of Michael Howard*, Simon & Schuster, 2005

Crocker, Glenys (ed): *Alexander Raby, Ironmaster*, Surrey Industrial Group, 2000

Davies, Byron, *Dafen Recollections*, Llanelli Borough Council, 1996

Davies, Byron, *The Glanmorfa Foundry and Engineering Co. Ltd*, Carmarthenshire County Council, 1999

Davies, John, Jenkins, Nigel, Baines, Menna and Lynch, Peredur: *The Welsh Academy Encyclopaedia of Wales*, University of Wales Press, 2008

Davies, Keith: *Cofio Grav*, Y Lolfa, 2008

Davies, Russell: *Secret Sins: Sex, Violence & Society in Carmarthenshire 1870-1920*, University of Wales Press, 1996

Denton, Tony and Leash, Nicholas: *Lighthouses of England and Wales: A Complete Guide*, Landmark Books, 2007

Ebenezer, Lyn: *Cwrw Cymru*, Gwasg Carreg Gwalch, 2006

Edwards, John: *Llanelli: Story of a Town*, Breedon Books, 2007

Edwards, John, ed.: *Tinopolis: Aspects of Llanelli's Tinplate Trade*, Llanelli Borough Council, 1995

Ferris, Paul, ed.: *Dylan Thomas: The Collected Letters*, J.M. Dent, 2000

Glanmor and Tyisha History Group: *A People's History: Glanymor and Tyisha, No.3*, 2006

Glynne-Jones, William: *This Childhood Land*, Batsford, 1960

Gower, Jon: *A Long Mile*, Carmarthenshire County Council, 2004

Holroyd, Michael: *Augustus John*, Vintage, 1997

Hornsey, Brian: *Ninety Years of Cinema in Llanelli*, Stamford, n.d.

Hughes, Gareth, ed: *A Llanelli Chronicle*, Llanelli Borough Council, 1984

Hughes, Eric: *Kidwelly: Memories of Yesteryear*, 2003, self published

Hurford, Vernon: *Memories*, Llanellli Borough Council, 2006

Innes, John: *Old Llanelly*, Llanelli and District Civic Society, 2005

Jenkins, J. Geraint: *Welsh Ships and Sailing Men*, Gwasg Carreg Gwlach, 2006

Jenkins, Nigel: *Acts of Union*, Gomer, 1990.

Jenkins, Simon: *Wales: Churches, Houses, Castles*, Allen Lane, 2008

John, Augustus: *J.D. Innes*, Sheffield, 1961

Jones, Edgar Dennis and Jones, Lucy Doreen: *William Glynne-Jones*, Llanelli Borough Council, 1995

Jones, Ivor: *Airfields and Landing Grounds of Wales: West*, Tempus, 2007

Leonard, Deke: *Maybe I Should Have Stayed in Bed: The Flip Side of the Rock 'n' Roll Dream*, Northdown, 2000

Llanelli Community Heritage: *Felinfoel Heritage Guide*, n.d.

Llanelli Community Heritage: *The Blue Plaques of Llanelli, Vol 1*, 2008

Lloyd Hughes, D.G.: *Y Clwb Bach, Porth Tywyn: the Burry Port Reading Room and Club*, 1981

Lloyd, Thomas, Orbach, Julian and Scourfield, Robert: *The Buildings of Wales: Carmarthenshire and Ceredigion*, Yale, 2006

Lovegrove, Roger, Williams, Graham and Williams, Iolo: *The Birds of Wales*, T. & A.D. Poyser, 1994

Mair, Bethan, ed.: *Cerddi Sir Gâr*, Gomer, 2004

McKibbin, Eira: *Machynys – Yours Truly*, Llanelli Town Council, 2007

Morgan, Kenneth: *Rebirth of a Nation, Wales 1880-1980*, Oxford University Press, 2001

Nicholson, John A.: *A Historical Miscellany: Book Two*, Llanelli Borough Councill 1994

Nicholson, John A.: *Pembrey and Burry Port: Further Historical Glimpses*, Carmarthenshire County Council, 1996

Nicholson, John A.: *Pembrey and Burry Port, Their Harbours, Shipwrecks and Looters*, Llanelli Borough Council

Ogilvie. M.A.: *Ducks of Britain and Europe*, T. & A.D. Poyser, 1975

Rees, Dylan: *Carmarthenshire*, University of Wales Press, 2006

Rhys, Ann Gruffudd; *Cwm Gwendraeth a Llanelli*, Gwasg Carreg Gwalch, 2000

Robertson, David: *Llanelli Memories*, Llanelli Borough Council, 1994

Thomas, Richard: *Llanelli and District Heritage*, Llanelli Rural Council, 2000.

Stead, Peter: *Acting Wales*, University of Wales, 2002.

Stead, Peter & Williams, Gareth: *Wales and its Boxers: the Fighting Tradition*, University of Wales Press, 2008

Symons, Malcolm: *Coal Mining in the Llanelli Area: Vol 1, 16th century to 1829*, Llanelli Borough Council, 1979

Swann, Donald, *Swann's Way: A Life in Song*, Arthur James, 1993

Various

Ordnance Survey, Explorer 178, Llanelli & Ammanford

Llanelli Rural Council, Heritage leaflets, 1 – 4

INDEX

ACKNOWLEDGEMENTS

Many, many people have helped with this book. Huge thanks to series editor Peter Finch for the chance to explore my own roots and contribute to the 'Real' series. and for sterling guidance along the way. His own books are outstanding templates for making it and keeping it Real. I've very much enjoyed reading all the books in the series but hope this one makes Llanelli sound more interesting than Swansea, which was chronicled by another friend of mine, Nigel Jenkins. Only kidding. Ah! the old rivalries. Grateful thanks also to Mick Felton and his colleagues at Seren for steering the volume through the press.

Thanks to all of the writers listed in the bibliography but especially to John Edwards, whose works about Llanelli gave mine a bedrock. Many people gave generously of their time and helped in a multitude of ways so thanks to erstwhile cocklefisherman Rob Griffiths, to my best mucker Emyr Jenkins who took some of the better photographs (pages 12, 13, 14, 96, 101, 190), to former political agent Geoff Hopkins, who has been a source of Llanelli insight for many a long year, to Tracey Jones at Machynys Homes for showing me around their spanking new houses and Halina Ashley at the Polish-Welsh Mutual Association. Grateful thanks also to Nigel Williams at the National Wetlands Centre at Penclacwydd, to Phil Davies and John Reed at Felinfoel Brewery, Howell Morgan, Gareth Howells at Trostre Boxing Club, Adrian Davies at BBC Wales, local business-man Barrie Davies, Stefan Chrinowsky, Ron Jones at Tinopolis, walking companions Hugh Lewis and Lyn John, former Llanelli Star editors Cathryn Ings and Robert Lloyd, Captain Winston Thomas of Pembrey Airport, all the courteous and helpful staff at Llanelli Public Library, Jon Williams and Nick Rolfe at Ffos Las racecourse, Owain and Spencer Davies at Spencer Davies Engineering at Burry Port, to 3Ks Engineering, Geraint Hopkins of Ghost Watch Wales, historian and good chum Peter Stead (from Swansea), Neil Perry and Dave Hughes at Pembrey Country Park and last but certainly not least to town centre manager Andrew Shufflebotham.

Thanks also to my darling wife Sarah, who did lots of proof reading and generally helped sift out mistakes and general wrongness, though

I readily assume the burden of guilt if there are any mistakes or omissions. Importantly Sarah made me happy as I wrote this, as she does at all other times. Diolch cariad.

The book is dedicated to my two daughters, Elena Dôn and Onwy Siân, in the hope that my past helps shape their future.

ABOUT THE AUTHOR

Jon Gower comes from Pwll and was educated at Llanelli Boys' Grammar School and Girton College, Cambridge where he read English. He has written or edited nine previous books, including *An Island Called Smith*, which won the John Morgan travel writing prize. Other works include *A Long Mile*, the history of his home village and a collection of short stories called *Big Fish*, while he has also penned poetry and plays both for radio and stage. His first Welsh language novel, *Dala'r Llanw*, was published to great acclaim in 2009. Over the years he has worked for the BBC, HTV and the RSPB and was BBC Wales' arts and media correspondent between 2000 and 2006. He is married to Sarah and they live in Cardiff with their two daughters. Jon won a major Creative Wales award for 2009-10 which he is using to explore Y Wladfa, the Welsh settlement in Patagonia.